www.wadsworth.com

wadsworth.com is the World Wide Web site for Wadsworth and is your direct source to dozens of online resources.

At *wadsworth.com* you can find out about supplements, demonstration software, and student resources. You can also send email to many of our authors and preview new publications and exciting new technologies.

wadsworth.com
Changing the way the world learns®

Clinical Ethics Casebook

Second Edition

PETER HORN
Capital University and
The Ohio State University College of Medicine

WADSWORTH

THOMSON LEARNING ™

Australia • Canada • Mexico • Singapore • Spain • United Kingdom • United States

Publisher: Holly J. Allen
Philosophy Editor: Steve Wainwright
Development Editor: Eric Carlson
Assistant Editor: Kara Kindstrom
Editorial Assistant: Anna Lustig
Technology Project Manager: Susan DeVanna
Marketing Manager: Worth Hawes
Advertising Project Manager: Bryan Vann

Print/Media Buyer: Doreen Suruki
Permissions Editor: Stephanie Keough-Hedges
Production Service: Shepherd, Inc.
Copy Editor: Colleen Yanda
Cover Designer: Ross Carron
Cover Images: PhotoDisc
Compositor: Shepherd, Inc.
Printer: Webcom, Limited

For more information about our products,
contact us at:
Thomson Learning Academic Resource Center
1-800-423-0563
For permission to use material from this text,
contact us by: **Phone: 1-800-730-2214**
Fax: 1-800-730-2215
Web: http:/www.thomsonrights.com

Wadsworth/Thomson Learning
10 Davis Drive
Belmont, CA 94002-3098
USA

Asia
Thomson Learning
60 Albert Street, #15-01
Albert Complex
Singapore 189969

Australia
Nelson Thomson Learning
102 Dodds Street
South Melbourne, Victoria 3205
Australia

Canada
Nelson Thomson Learning
1120 Birchmount Road
Toronto, Ontario M1K 5G4
Canada

Europe/Middle East/Africa
Thomson Learning
Berkshire House
168-173 High Holborn
London WC1V 7AA
United Kingdom

Latin America
Thomson Learning
Seneca, 53
Colonia Polanco
11560 Mexico D.F.
Mexico

Spain
Paraninfo Thomson Learning
Calle/Magallanes, 25
28015 Madrid, Spain

Library of Congress Cataloging-in-Publication Data

Peter, Horn.
  Clinical ethics casebook / Peter Horn.—2nd ed.
  p. cm.
  ISBN 0-534-56092-X
  1. Medical ethics. 2. Medical ethics—
  Case studies. I. Title.

R724 .H63 2001
174'.2—dc21   2001055939

Contents

Preface

This casebook consists of a number of cases drawn from a variety of areas of clinical practice. It samples a range of topics and issues, especially in medical and nursing ethics. It presents a variety of brief, concrete examples of situations that raise challenging ethical questions and problems. Discussion questions follow each case.

The book aims to include the following:

+ clear writing,
+ cases that can be understood and appreciated independently of other parts of the book,
+ concise cases, one or two paragraphs in length, and
+ a few discussion questions for each case.

These questions are designed to (1) guide the reader to appreciate the moral complexity of the situations, (2) suggest challenges to various popular answers to the situations, and (3) provide guidance for structuring possible answers. In being caused to think critically about these cases, one is prompted to think as well about many of the other controversies in clinical ethics.

I have taught introductory and clinical ethics for twenty years to undergraduates as well as to graduate and specialized audiences. These have included some classes comprised of nursing students, others of medical residents, and also large groups of hospital personnel from all areas of health care and allied health professions. From having worked in all these settings, I found sufficient similarities that could be addressed in the present work.

This book is designed to fill a gap. Presently, bioethics books (including those in medical and nursing ethics) tend to be either anthologies of articles drawn from philosophical and clinical journals, and so quite technical and complex, or casebooks that present lengthy cases followed by pages of fine-grained analysis. Both of these formats are valuable; however, many teachers, students, practitioners, and other readers find it useful to supplement these other resources with case vignettes. They also find their thinking about the cases facilitated and stimulated by the inclusion of discussion questions. This book asks questions and explores possible answers rather than giving decisions or procedures. In that sense, it attempts to emulate Socrates' method of inquiry and teaching.

The content should prove challenging and interesting to readers of all backgrounds, ranging from college freshmen up to and including practicing physicians and nurses. Both beginners and professionals benefit from discussing the subject together, whereas more technical expositions can exclude some readers.

I am a philosopher, and so my work partly reflects awareness of literature in that discipline as well as its characteristic methods. As an applied ethicist, I let relevant news developments provide content for some of the cases. As is true of most teachers, students force me to present materials clearly and vividly.

The general topics included can be found in the table of contents. The main headings include standard categories, such as informed consent, confidentiality, and life-and-death decision making, as well as more specialized topics, such as HIV/AIDS, pediatric, and mental health contexts. The book includes cases addressing some of the most current controversies, such as problems about people with Alzheimer's disease, difficulties with advance directives such as living wills, managed care, tobacco use, and complexities of assisted suicide. The topics range from standard, traditional issues and situations to the more unusual and new.

Readers will notice connections and overlaps among the issues. Some cases' classifications are semi-arbitrary: they might equally well have been placed within other chapters. For example, some transplantation issues concern both allocation and life-and-death decisions.

The book keeps use of technical philosophical and clinical terminology to a minimum, although discipline-specific concepts, when they would enhance clarity and authenticity, do appear. A number of technical terms are explained, either when first mentioned or in the ethics glossaries at the back of the book.

Some of the book's cases are actual, some are hypothetical, and some are a combination. Many of the cases include alternative suppositions among the discussion questions. This is a standard method in teaching by means of cases.

Readers should appreciate what the book is intended to be and what it is not, and how to make the best use of the book. For courses, teachers can use the book productively with another book (although this book's very brief introductions and glossaries provide some background to the area). This does not purport to be an exhaustive, all-purpose, stand-alone introduction to clinical ethics. Thus, it does not present in depth a variety of ethical theories or methodologies. These important tasks are left to teachers and other books. The book is, however, designed to be a resource that students, teachers, and other readers will find useful for understanding and discussing the field of clinical ethics.

Teachers and other ethics books also present analyses of the issues raised as questions in this book. To repeat, the book is not presented as a substitute for other sorts of bioethics books or to take the place of the teacher.

There are a number of possible audiences for the book. It can be read with some benefit by almost anyone, since everyone is affected by the health care system. College and university students might read this in any of a variety of courses, including ethics and pre-profession classes. Students in graduate and professional programs could also use the book. Finally, health care practitioners (physicians, nurses, pharmacists, and others) will find themselves challenged by the book. Those who have read the cases as they evolved often commented that they sounded like real clinical situations. This is no coincidence, since the cases were designed in consultation with clinicians in a number of areas.

Occasional mention appears of laws, but laws change, and, ethically, we want to decide which laws are justified and which are not. Also, many laws differ from state to state or from country to country, so the specification of what "the" law says would need to be limited to the current state of the law in a particular jurisdiction. In clinical practice, people need to know the laws that apply to them; yet such knowledge does not provide the key that will solve or eliminate all their ethical problems.

I have not usually provided outcomes for the cases. The book aims to provoke thinking. Of course, the need to provide an outcome seems especially puzzling for cases that are partly or completely hypothetical. To understand more about my reluctance to describe outcomes, it helps to recognize that: first, the use of a bad decision-method (in any domain) may turn out well; and, secondly, the use of the best method does not guarantee a favorable outcome—much less a morally justified one.

The formulations of the cases present a variety of situations and issues. Some situations may be problematic because they are somewhat dilemma-like, with good reasons pulling in different directions; others can be challenging because of people's seemingly inadequate recognition of the actual or potential moral wrongness of some behaviors.

I have some observations and some hopes. Sometimes, when presented with a difficult or challenging case or issue, people will naturally try to escape from the seeming difficulty or negative aura associated with a behavior. This is usually done in one of several ways.

+ question whether a factual claim is true
+ inquire whether a factual account is complete
+ challenge whether the claimed value-ordering is plausible
+ deny that even the most apparent problem exists.

These responses sometimes work. Attempts to avoid unnecessary concern about non-problems and about unfounded accusations can help. But people also have a responsibility to themselves, to their professions, to their co-workers, their patients, and others affected by behavior to work at realistically assessing and solving moral problems. While I do not think that every *claimed* moral problem actually is a problem, I hope that this book will excite readers and encourage them to decide what should and what should not occasion further inquiry. I also hope that the book will inculcate some ability and willingness to ask difficult and important questions about health care.

In this edition, dozens of new cases have been added. New topics include conflicts of interest, patenting of life forms, the role of culture and religion, stem cell research, futility, cost analysis, placebos, and theories of personal identity. The code of ethics appendix has the most recent version of the International Council of Nurses' Code of Ethics, as well as the 2001 versions of two important codes: the American Nurses Association's Code for Nurses and the American Medical Association's Principles of Medical Ethics.

Acknowledgments

The book's clinical dimensions have been enhanced by several further sources. A few deserve special mention. For some two dozen of the cases, I have adapted materials developed by Tony Hope and Bill Fulford for the Oxford Practice Skills Course. More than two dozen of the cases in the present work build on cases used in their program. Their cases appear in the course's manual written by Hope, Fulford, and Anne Yates (Oxford University Press, 1996). The practice skills course has now become part of Ethox: The Oxford Institute for Ethics and Communication in Health Care Practice.

A number of the pediatric cases arose from contributions of hundreds of people who have worked with me to plan and present the Ethical Problems Conferences since 1981 at Columbus' Children's Hospital. Other philosophers, as well as the hospital's nurses, attending physicians, housestaff, social workers, psychologists, pastoral care people, the Education Department, and Ohio State's Department of Pediatrics assisted in the process. Colleagues in the Department of Psychiatry at The Ohio State University contributed to the shaping of the mental health cases and other cases.

People deserving special thanks for having read and commented on substantial portions of the book or the new cases include Bema Bonsu, Angela Button, Tom Christenson, Doris Edwards, Louis Flancbaum, John Mahan, Rick McClead, Susan Nash, Shary Ratliff, Bernard Rosen, and Donald Smeltzer. Colleagues in Philosophy and Religion at Capital University also provided constructive thoughts.

For nursing perspectives, thanks are due to nursing students and colleagues at the School of Nursing at the University of Northern Colorado, Mount Carmel College of Nursing, and the School of Nursing at Capital University. Early on, I found guidance and encouragement from Art and Nancy Bartlett, Brendan Minogue, and Robert Ginsberg.

At Wadsworth, Peter Adams, the Philosophy Editor until recently, provided reliable ideas and advice. Also at Wadsworth, Kerri Abdinoor, Kara Kindstrom, Laura Larson, Howard Severson, Steve Wainwright, and many others have been very helpful in enabling the book to become a reality.

LIST OF REVIEWERS

Reviewers for the new edition were:

Jill Winland-Brown, Florida Atlantic University

Janet Lewis, Juniata College

David Newell, Washington College

Alan R. Whitman, Carnegie Mellon University

Reviewers for the previous edition were:

Robert Baker, Union College

Donald Beker, University of Texas-Austin

Lynn Pasquerella, University of Rhode Island

Michael Potts, Methodist College

Brian Phillip Wetstein, University of Guelph

CHAPTER I

Professionalism, Part I

Professional Codes, Roles, and Boundaries

ROLES

Some professional roles are moral; some exist as a society's or a profession's conventions or rules of etiquette; others arise from statutes, court decisions, or organizational decisions. Patients, families, and providers need to know the behavior standards expected of health workers. The health workers themselves equally can benefit from guidance in terms of publicly promulgated statements, rules, and guidelines for good practice.

RULES

What are rules of conduct in professional practice and what are they not? In a sense, these rules are not different from the rules we use in every other area of life. Everyone, not only physicians, should "first of all do no harm." Keeping private matters that are properly private is important whether one is a nurse, a teacher, or a bartender. On the other hand, under special sorts of circumstances the consequences can be especially profound and the assumed trust especially strong, so that the rules should be adhered to even more rigorously than in other contexts. Nevertheless, it should be kept in mind that all rules can have reasonable exceptions, so people must avoid assuming that citing a rule applicable to a situation will conclusively establish what ought to be done in that situation.

CODES

Although professions have codes, members of those professions seldom question or reflect on their own code. Here, for example, are a few significant questions. What functions does a code of professional ethics have? Are all such codes on a par? In other words, do some have greater force or authority than others? Might the codes conflict, either internally or with each other? Documents and rules require interpretation for understanding and application to real situations. How, then, should a code (such as those for physicians, nurses, and researchers) be interpreted? How strictly should a code be followed? Will it have omissions, or does it cover every conceivable situation? Does a code make dubious or unclear claims? What revisions would improve a code of ethics? How practical is a given code?

TRADITIONS

Most of the preceding observations and questions about rules and codes apply to traditions as well. In general, questions need to be asked about the justifying force of traditions and the sort of authority they provide.

SPECIAL RESPONSIBILITIES

These are obligations that arise from the practice of an occupation or, more generally, from standing in certain relationships to people (such as having made a promise or being a child's parent).

BOUNDARIES

Professionals need to think about the proper limits of relationships involving them. What sorts of relationships—whether with patients/clients or with other health workers—should be prohibited? What sorts are questionable but ought to be tolerated? What sorts may even be praiseworthy? Given the number, variability, and complexity of possible sorts of relationships, these questions can become very difficult to answer.

In some cases, professionals must recognize special risks, perhaps those involving increased likelihood of exploitation of power differences or vulnerabilities. The professional should know these in order to protect patients and to avoid awkward and improper-appearing situations as well as morally prohibited ones.

1.1   INTERPRETING THE HIPPOCRATIC OATH

Dr. O, a physician, refers to the Hippocratic Oath when in discussions about ethical matters. (See the appendix, page 177, for a copy of the oath.) He has always kept a copy of the oath on the wall of his office and believes that it states the essence of what it is to be an ethical member of his profession. In particular, he focuses on several parts of the translation of the oath including the following:

+ "I will never give a patient a lethal dose of medicine, even if asked for it. . . ."
+ "I will protect the sick from harm and injustice. . . ."
+ "Whatever I hear in the course of my practice, which ought not to be spread about, I will keep secret."

a. To what extent and how literally should Dr. O adhere to the oath? For example, in its first words, one swears by Apollo, Asclepius, Hygeia, and all the gods and goddesses of the ancient Greeks. Also, in its first half, the oath requires one to repay debts to one's teachers and to provide free teaching to their male descendants.

b. What are the oath's functions now, 2,500 years after its formulation by Hippocrates? Is it largely ceremonial and symbolic (as some have maintained), or does it state concisely many of the basics of what ethical physicians should keep in mind?

c. It says that one will not practice surgery. Does it follow that Dr. O ought never to do so? Surgeons are now trained in medicine, and so people no longer consider this prohibition applicable. How should one decide which parts to take seriously and which not?

d. What should one do if two parts of the oath conflict? For example, suppose protecting a patient from harm would support providing a lethal drug to reduce a patient's suffering and indignity.

e. In what ways might the oath be used as a guidance for doing or not doing some action even if one does not subscribe to everything the oath says?

1.2   *INTERPRETING A NURSING CODE OF ETHICS*

The latest version of the American Nurses Association's *Code for Nurses with Interpretive Statements* was approved in 2001. Its provisions (without the interpretive statements) appear in this book's appendix, page 188.

N has been a nurse for twenty years. She is distressed because, in her judgment, the hospital where she works frequently provides sub-standard care, has lapses in staffing coverage, and discharges some patients partly for financial reasons. N works hard and devotes herself to her patients. She feels that, in so doing, she earns her pay and discharges her responsibilities to the patients and her employer.

a. Interpretive statement 6.3 states: "Acquiescing and accepting unsafe or inappropriate practices, even if the individual does not participate in the specific practice, is equivalent to condoning unsafe practice. Nurses should not remain employed in facilities that routinely violate patient rights or require nurses to severely and repeatedly compromise standards of practice or personal morality." In light of this, should N consider quitting, protesting to the hospital, speaking to her nursing organization, contacting the media, or some other option?

b. Provisions 7 through 9 address responsibilities beyond those of the nurse's individual patients. Interpretive statement 8.1 affirms "The nurse has a responsibility to be aware not only of specific health needs of individual patients but also of broader health concerns such as world hunger, environmental pollution, lack of access to health care, violation of human rights, and inequitable distribution of nursing and health care resources." Statement 8.2 says that ". . . the nurse supports initiatives to address barriers to health, such as poverty, homelessness, unsafe living conditions, abuse and violence, and lack of access to health services." Based on statements 8.1 and 8.2, to what extent and in what ways is N obligated to decrease poverty, homelessness, violence, and other societal problems? As a nurse, does she have a stronger obligation to address these problems than other health care workers do? A stronger obligation than other citizens do? If so, then why? Do the code's interpretive statements impose significant new responsibilities upon nurses, or do they merely call nurses' attention to obligations they already have?

1.3   INTERPRETING THE AMA'S CODE OF ETHICS

The Council on Ethical and Judicial Affairs of the American Medical Association issued, in 1990, a statement on "Fundamental Elements of the Patient-Physician Relationship." It begins by pointing out responsibilities of patients for their own health care and then lists six main areas of rights of patients. These, very briefly summarized, include rights (a) to information needed for informed decision-making, (b) to accept or refuse recommended treatment, (c) to courtesy and dignity, (d) to confidentiality (with exceptions specified), (e) to continuity of health care, and (f) to have available adequate health care.

As part of the sixth right, it states, "Physicians, along with the rest of society, should continue to work toward this goal. Fulfillment of this right is dependent on society providing resources so that no patient is deprived of necessary care because of an inability to pay for the care." (See the appendix, page 186, for this document.)

a. What obligations does this seem to impose on physicians in terms of political activity?

b. How should one understand the notion of "necessary care?" Does it mean care that is necessary to prevent premature death, or care that is necessary to cure all curable pathologies and to comfort whenever possible? Does it entail increasing preventive measures?

c. How does the AMA statement compare with the interpretive statements for part 11 of the American Nurses Association code? There, it states that "nurses have an obligation to promote equitable access to nursing and health care for all people." It also states, "Nurses should actively promote the collaborative planning required to ensure the availability and accessibility of high-quality health services to all persons whose health needs are unmet."

d. Do the six categories of rights listed earlier capture the main sorts of ethical priorities physicians ought to keep in mind? What, if anything, has been omitted? Does the document provide practical decision-making guidance? Should it? Can it do so? (The AMA, ANA, and other professional associations have issued supplemental statements, sometimes characterized as "interpretations," of the main list of provisions referred to earlier.)

1.4   CONSCIENTIOUS REFUSAL TO PARTICIPATE IN A PROCEDURE

Nurse Y has many strong, religiously-based beliefs. One of these is that sterilization is morally heinous. Sterilization, she thinks, precludes many possible human lives from coming into existence and developing themselves. Therefore, she feels especially upset when a physician, Dr. Z, tells her that she will assist in the sterilizing of an institutionalized, severely mentally retarded fifteen-year-old girl, W. She finds the sterilization doubly objectionable because W has not consented to the sterilization. Nurse Y announces to the doctor that she cannot, in conscience, have anything to do with the sterilization. Dr. Z understands that Nurse Y has strong beliefs about sterilization, but would otherwise have to hire, temporarily, a nurse to assist. She thinks that Nurse Y should be reprimanded for a sort of behavior verging on patient abandonment.

   a. Is this a situation in which there is a clear morally right or wrong behavior? If so, what is it and why?
   b. To what extent ought professionals, including health workers, follow their consciences when the dictates of their consciences seem to conflict with their work responsibilities?
   c. What might be the most effective ways of avoiding such conflicts? If someone can reasonably foresee having to refuse to do something because of conscience, perhaps one should notify one's supervisor and anyone else who would be involved in such situations. What if one could not reasonably anticipate such a situation, though?

1.5   WAITING ROOM WAITS

Dr. X keeps almost all of his patients waiting in his outer office an average of an hour and a half after their scheduled appointment time. They are then shown to a smaller room where they wait an average of another twenty minutes before the doctor arrives. When asked about this practice, Dr. X defends himself by saying that many patients cancel or miss their appointments, so he has to overbook. Furthermore, he states, he often has to take care of urgent or emergency situations, and these must take priority.

   a. Would Dr. X's area of specialization be relevant to deciding about the acceptability of this practice?
   b. Would knowing the number of cancellations and missed appointments be pertinent? The number of urgent and emergent situations?
   c. Is there a morally relevant difference between occasionally having to wait an extra fifteen minutes and always having to wait an hour and a half or more?

d. Should the patients be entitled to compensation for their inconvenience? Many professionals charge for missed appointments. Might patients be entitled to charge, or at least receive a discount, for delayed appointments?

e. Suppose the doctor claims that he is not blameworthy since the receptionist does the scheduling. Is this excuse persuasive?

1.6   THE STAFF DISAGREES

Mrs. C is dying of brain cancer. Her wishes cannot be determined because she has become incoherent. Her family is willing to go along with the health care team's judgment, and most of them have accepted her impending death, but one physician on the unit insists on doing everything possible to keep her alive as long as possible.

a. Suppose the staff were more evenly divided. Would that influence your judgment about how to proceed?

b. Suppose the facts were such that only one person was willing to let Mrs. C die, and everyone else wanted to go all out to keep her alive. Could a decision to let her die be justified?

c. Suppose a nurse is the lone dissenter. What should the nurse do?

d. Suppose the one dissenter is the attending physician. Should her wishes prevail?

e. Suppose the person who disagrees is a resident. What are his options?

f. What responsibilities does a person have when unable to change the opinions of others?

1.7   RELATIONSHIPS WITH PATIENTS: SOME BOUNDARY ISSUES

Nurse B, who is twenty-five, has spoken many times briefly with a clinic patient, Mr. C, who is thirty. She feels comfortable with him and would like to invite him to have coffee to talk further.

a. Suppose that, instead of Nurse B's patient, Nurse B would like to talk more with a family member of the patient.

b. Suppose that Mr. C is a former patient. Would it matter how long ago he had been a patient?

c. Suppose the nurse would like to invite the person to have a drink.

d. Suppose she would like to invite the person to have dinner.

e. Suppose there is no possibility of an accusation of attempting to use the coffee, drink, or dinner to pursue an amorous relationship. Would that be relevant?

f. Would the nature of the nurse-patient relationship matter? In other words, are some of these professional relationships such that they would not be compromised by having coffee, a drink, or dinner?

g. What are the reasons for prohibiting relationships between health workers and patients? How rigid is each prohibition? Are these reasonable rules of conduct?

h. One way of thinking asserts that prohibitions should be based on something like an increased likelihood of exploitation of the professional-patient relationship. Given this view, how much of such an increased likelihood of exploitation must exist for it to become unethical? Any increase at all? A slight increase? A significant increase?

i. Should nurses have different guidelines than physicians about boundaries and relationships? Why?

1.8   RELIGIOUS CONVICTIONS EXPRESSED IN A PUBLIC SETTING

Nurse R has deep religious convictions. She thinks of these as providing ultimate meaning for her life and structure for her behavior. Since they are so central for her, she expresses them readily in her communications with people. She is an excellent nurse in terms of providing highly skilled, experienced, empathic care for the patients at the public hospital where she works. Indeed, she describes her work as a religious calling, her way of living out her religious beliefs.

While her belief system provides a source of motivation for Nurse R, it also sometimes causes discomfort in people. Some of her coworkers grumble about it. Others accuse her of being unprofessional in disclosing to them and to patients something they believe should be private. Sometimes, patients mention to other nurses on her unit that they both admire her work and also wish that she would refrain from mentioning God so often in her conversations with them. Finally, the hospital's administration, through her supervisor, tells her that, since she works at a public institution, she must refrain—unless asked to do so—from saying anything religious.

a. Is the administration's decision, passed along through the supervisor, justified? Are they respecting the public nature of the institution or violating Nurse R's freedom?

b. Is Nurse R's behavior justified? Is it more accurate to think that she is praiseworthy for working at a vocation that is an expression of her deepest beliefs, or that she is unprofessional for imposing on others, including patients who cannot choose to leave the room, a world view that might add to their discomfort?

c. In a public institution such as the hospital where Nurse R works, how might a policy strike the right balance of allowing people freedom of religion while avoiding an environment that exposes patients and employees to unwanted expressions of religion? How is this case similar to and different from the desire of some people to be in smoke-free environments?

d. Suppose Nurse R worked at a private hospital, although one not affiliated with any religion. Would that affect any of the prior points?

e. Suppose that, instead of her religious views, Nurse R communicated her strong political beliefs.

1.9 PHYSICIAN-ASSISTED EXECUTION

Dr. G is a general practitioner who believes in the use of the death penalty for certain crimes. His state uses execution by lethal injection, which requires that a physician be involved to assure the proper dosage and route of administration of the lethal drugs, and to pronounce the person dead. Dr. G has volunteered to help in this process. Some of his colleagues believe that he is acting unprofessionally and lobby for legislation discouraging physician participation in executions.

a. Would Dr. G's participation be more or less moral if he were against the death penalty? Is he "only doing his job," as he claims?

b. In defense of his actions, Dr. G argues that, if he didn't do it, someone else would anyway. How effective is this as a justifying reason?

c. Suppose Dr. G did not participate in the execution but only pronounced the prisoner dead. Would that affect the morality or immorality of his action?

d. If one is opposed to the death penalty, does it follow necessarily that one oppose physicians' and nurses' participation in its implementation? If one is for the death penalty, then must one also believe in the acceptability of health workers' implementation of it?

e. Is the fact that the death penalty is a legal punishment a good reason—perhaps sufficient—to justify physician or nurse participation in its implementation?

f. Suppose a condemned prisoner had a cardiac arrest the day before execution. Should Dr. G revive the person to execute him the following day? (Situations of this general sort have happened.)

g. Suppose the prisoner suffered from a mental illness so severe that he did not understand his situation. Should Dr. G provide antipsychotic medication to restore the prisoner to mental competence in order to execute him? (This situation actually occurred.)

1.10 ACCEPTING GIFTS

Mrs. I was a patient for a month on a medical unit in a hospital. The former patient greatly appreciates the help and encouragement of those who provided her care, so she brings to the unit generous checks for all those she remembers. The staff inform Mrs. I, to her great disappointment, that they are forbidden, by institutional policy, to accept individual gifts of substantial value. She demands to speak to the person in charge of the policy and is directed to an administrator who tells Mrs. I that this is a long-standing policy of this and almost every other hospital. The administrator suggests that Mrs. I might wish to make a donation to the hospital, which is conducting a fund-raising drive. Mrs. I feels hurt and angry that she is unable to demonstrate her appreciation to the individuals who came to mean so much to her.

a. Some people claim that, although accepting inexpensive gifts is permissible, accepting gifts of moderate value is not. Are they right?

b. The gift is offered after only the patient has been discharged. Because the appearance of attempting to buy special treatment would no longer arise, is gift giving under these circumstances permissible?

c. Are gifts likely to corrupt one's professional judgment? If so, then how and why?

d. Should both physicians and nurses be prohibited from accepting gifts? If a different standard applies, what is its justification?

e. Suppose the patient were from a background or culture that found it customary or even obligatory to give gifts. Would that affect the practice's moral acceptability?

1.11   A HATEFUL PATIENT

Mr. O is a patient who requires frequent attention, makes many unreasonable demands, insults the staff, and generally makes life miserable for them. They try to provide a high level of professional care for him but increasingly find themselves tempted to do the minimum necessary. They are, after all, humans who have finite patience.

a. Is there anything morally questionable about providing less than enthusiastic care for a patient, as long as the quality of care meets necessary minimum standards?

b. Should health workers be entitled to courteous behavior by patients?

c. Should patients who create discomfort for health workers be informed of this point?

d. What steps should be taken to ensure that this patient receives good care?

e. Should a referral be made to a psychologist for either the patient or the staff?

f. If the patient behaves abusively toward the staff, can that patient be required to have counseling or face being transferred to another institution?

g. Suppose that a family member of Mr. O, rather than Mr. O himself, is obnoxious or abusive toward the staff. Would that significantly affect the ethical judgments in any or all of the applicable preceding questions?

1.12   A DOCTOR TREATS HER FAMILY

Dr. W's daughter has broken her arm. Dr. W sets the arm. She understands that treating one's own family is frowned upon, but Dr. W feels no remorse. She believes she has simply made effective use of her knowledge and skills to alleviate suffering.

a. Are there problems with Dr. W's reasoning? What are the reasons for discouraging or prohibiting, in most circumstances, physicians' treatment of their own families?

b. Would Dr. W's specialization and the nature of the illness or injury be relevant to deciding? Is another physician readily available? Are the injury and treatment at home? Suppose it is not an emergency situation.

c. Suppose, instead, the daughter had a mental disorder, and the mother is a psychiatrist. If the mother were to provide care in this case, would the daughter be more likely to receive substandard care? How would the daughter be able to confide matters that she might not wish to share with her mother? How would the mother be able to view her own relationship with her daughter with any professional distance?

d. Suppose the daughter had a urinary tract infection or a symptom of a sexually transmitted disease. Would these kinds of treatment be more troubling, assuming the parent is a suitably qualified physician, if the parent is the opposite sex of the child? Should there be an absolute prohibition on family care of this sort?

1.13   THE DOCTOR WHO TREATS HIMSELF

An adage states that a lawyer who represents himself has a fool for a client. Many would apply a similar notion to physicians who treat themselves. Dr. B has insomnia. He prescribes a sleeping pill for himself. He knows that many of his colleagues do likewise. He has high blood pressure, but he monitors it and adjusts his blood pressure medication accordingly.

a. Are all, most, or some instances of health workers treating themselves unwise? How is an unwise decision different from an immoral one?

b. Which seems more risky—self-prescribing sleeping medication or self-prescribing blood pressure medication? If medication should be taken "as needed," should it require an independent person to judge that, or is the doctor/patient able to evaluate that for himself or herself?

c. Since it is often difficult to be objective in one's own case, does it make sense to say that Dr. B is violating his duties to himself?

d. Are there any professional standards that Dr. B is violating? If not, should there be guidelines for such cases?

CHAPTER 2

Professionalism, Part II
Protecting Patients and Judging Professional Competence

Basic to much of the meaning of professionalism in health care is patient-centeredness. The patient's good must be considered in any situation. This involves a presumption in favor of patient good, and it is very strong. As we shall see later, however, when we consider questions about consent and refusal of treatment, the good of the patient may not always trump all other ethical considerations.

People live in a complex web of relationships, roles, and responsibilities. Because of this, difficult conflicts of loyalties and obligations develop. Navigating a sequence of decisions while recognizing these loyalties and commitments can be very difficult, personally and professionally. Health workers need to think more about how to acknowledge and constructively resolve disagreements about patient care.

Protection of patient interests ties in with professional competence to provide good health care. Arguments abound about who is sufficiently qualified and who is most qualified to provide various sorts of health care. Some confounding factors—such as people's egos, loyalties to one's profession and worldview, and prospect of financial gain or loss—interfere with people's efforts to decide who should (and who may) provide health care.

Sometimes, different beliefs about how much pain ought to be relieved, and how it should be relieved, stand in the way of optimal patient care. At other times, uncertainty and different risk-benefit judgments produce different decisions about pain management.

All of these topics are addressed in this chapter's cases.

2.1   A DOSAGE ERROR
AND AN INCIDENT REPORT

A patient, Mrs. D, receives the wrong amount of a medication yet is not harmed. The hospital is experiencing financial pressures, and people's jobs are in jeopardy. A coworker who discovers the error considers several alternative courses of action: (a) speak with the nurse who gave the wrong medicine/dose, (b) insist that she write an incident report, or (c) report the person, but only if she does not voluntarily write an incident report.

a. What would you have done? What *should* you have done? If they are not the same in this case, why aren't they?

b. If the consequences are minimal for the patient, then is it as important to consider reporting the incident? What if there were no pattern of errors by the nurse in question?

c. Would it be sufficient to speak with the person who administered the medication, or should something further be done?

d. How strongly must you urge the person to write an incident report? Should you threaten to report the person if she does not write the report? Might one write a report without including it in the chart, or vice versa?

e. If the person still refuses to write the report, should you then blow the whistle on her?

f. Can it be morally permissible for the employment concern of the individual or the financial security of the hospital to enter into the decision? For example, suppose the person admits making the mistake, but is afraid of being fired if she discloses the error. Should you report the person anyway?

2.2   OOPS

Mrs. A, seventy-four, had been hospitalized for repair of an aortic aneurysm; however, she developed a fever and other symptoms of infection. Her health care team gave her conscientious attention, but she wound up hospitalized five days instead of two. The prolonged infection had, in all likelihood, resulted from less than scrupulous hand-washing by one of her many caregivers. A wound infection had turned into a drug-resistant septicemia, which required expensive intravenous antibiotics. To compound Mrs. A's problems, she was given an antibiotic to which she was allergic. Fortunately, Mrs. A escaped being one of those who die each year from medical errors.

a. Does the fact that almost no errors are reported mean that caregivers are seriously negligent in accepting responsibility? Is it better understood as reticence to report due to a normal avoidance of risk to themselves? How often do people volunteer unflattering information about themselves? What are the consequences of fear of malpractice suits?

b. Can medical decision-making be done accurately by consumers and health care providers without sufficiently thorough information about risks?

c. If staff are required to work long shifts and double shifts, would that not lead to more errors? If someone is harmed after a worker has been on duty for

eighteen hours, how should the blame be apportioned? Might those who design and approve such schedules be considered responsible?

  d. Is a missed diagnosis a mistake in the same way that giving the wrong amount
  of a drug is a mistake?

  e. Hospitals are now phasing in computerized systems for tracking records and
  prescriptions, including software to check for and flag what seem to be errors
  or excessive risks. Would use of computers to decide on diagnoses and treatments also be a good idea, or does that sound questionable?

  f. How should conflicts between service needs and staffing shortages be resolved?

2.3   *A PATIENT IN PAIN*

When physicians and nurses studied the management of pain some years ago, they
learned that the strongest pain medications, narcotic analgesics such as morphine,
were dangerous and likely to cause addiction and so should be prescribed minimally,
preferably when the patient had made it clear that he or she was in pain. Now, pain
specialists view the subject very differently. Especially for short-term (for example,
postoperatively) and end-of-life situations, pain medications are prescribed and administered preventively, to be administered in smaller amounts but more frequently.

After Miss B, age fifty-eight, had a malignancy surgically removed, her surgeon
prescribed a narcotic analgesic to be given by intramuscular injection (IM) every four
to six hours (symbolized "q 4–6 h"), as needed (abbreviated "prn"). The medication
is only sufficiently effective for three hours, and the woman has to request more of
the medication, which she then receives when the (understaffed) nurses are able to
provide it, but not sooner than four hours after the previous injection. The drug then
takes a while to be effective. As a result, the woman suffers moderate to severe pain
much of the time.

  a. If *causing* someone to suffer unnecessarily would be morally wrong, is *allowing* someone to suffer unnecessarily (and avoidably) also wrong?

  b. How might one explain the phenomenon that many patients fail to indicate
  when they are in pain?

  c. How might the nurses help minimize Miss B's pain?

  d. Is it necessary for the woman to experience any pain at all? Is it morally permissible? If so, why?

  e. Might an IV (intravenous) drip, or PCA (patient-controlled analgesia) provide
  a satisfactory alternative method?

2.4   *GOOD SAMARITAN AFTER A BEER?*

Dr. E, a physician on vacation, witnesses a traffic accident in which several people
appear to be hurt.

  a. Should she intervene? If so, then how strong is the moral obligation to do so?
  Would intervention be morally wrong, obligatory, or supererogatory (praiseworthy but not morally required)?

b. Suppose she has had one or two beers. Apart from prudential (self-interested) considerations, to what extent should the physician's slightly inebriated state be considered relevant to her decision?

c. If the law does not require intervention, should that be considered important, morally? If the law does not legally protect such interventions, should that be considered, morally?

d. Suppose that Dr. E has had enough beer so that she is aware of feeling inebriated and finds that she would not be required to use fine-motor skills or complex diagnostic thought processes in any way that would jeopardize the accident victims.

2.5   PATIENT CARE DURING A STRIKE

The nurses at a large hospital, after months of discussion and debate, have decided to strike for better pay, improved working conditions, elimination of mandatory overtime, and—they argue—thereby improved patient care. Nurses have begun to form picket lines outside the main hospital entrances. Tensions have increased, and accusations of irresponsibility and injustice have begun flying from and toward the strikers.

a. Would such a strike only be acceptable if the nurses were part of a union? If so, why? If not, why not?

b. To what extent do the nurses have moral responsibilities to the current patients? To potential patients? To themselves and their families?

c. To what extent does their responsibility to maintain levels of patient care limit their collective bargaining power?

2.6   UNLICENSED ASSISTIVE PERSONNEL

City Hospital has been experiencing financial pressures. One way to address these pressures is to hire minimally skilled unlicensed assistive personnel (UAPs) to perform some of the tasks previously assigned to nurses. These tasks range from changing bed linen to monitoring intravenous lines.

a. Should this use of UAPs be disclosed to the hospital's patients, or would such information merely risk unnecessarily alarming them?

b. Some claim that this measure compromises patient care. Others assert that, done properly, it instead frees up nurses to coordinate and evaluate care and to perform work requiring more skill. How should one decide the force of each of these views?

c. Can one run a hospital without, at some points, having to make decisions involving trade-offs of quality of patient care to enable containment of costs? If so, how should one begin to rank-order areas for making such cutbacks?

2.7 TURF OR EXPERTISE, PART I: PODIATRISTS OR ORTHOPEDIC SURGEONS?

Dr. O, an orthopedic surgeon, claims to be the most qualified to treat a man's recurrent foot injuries, whereas a podiatrist, Dr. P, maintains that he would be a better choice. The patient wonders whom to choose. In this area, members of both professions are legally permitted to perform the procedure. He is reminded of a few years before when his mother's family practitioner, a chiropractor, and an osteopath each suggested that she or he would be the best choice for the mother's back pain.

a. To what extent can a health care consumer make an informed choice when presented with such options?

b. What criteria should one use to decide among such claims?

c. How should we think of such conflicts—as members of different professions competing for money, as an expansion of consumer choice, or as concern for protection of the patient?

d. When controversies arise between obstetricians and family practitioners about abortions, between optometrists and ophthalmologists over minor eye surgery, between gastroenterologists and general surgeons about endoscopy, how should one decide?

e. American physicians are under a restraining order, from the Supreme Court, enjoining them from making any negative statements about chiropractors. The Court ruled that such statements would be a "restraint of trade." If a chiropractor claims the power to cure arthritis or cancer, is there any reason to think that it would be unethical (apart from the *legal* force of the court's ruling within its jurisdiction) for a person to advise patients not to believe those claims?

2.8 TURF OR EXPERTISE, PART II: NURSES OR DOCTORS?

In many areas, laws have recognized advanced practice nurses as permitted to perform responsibilities previously reserved exclusively for physicians. Typically, the nurses have a master's degree in that area or considerable experience and have passed certification tests (such as certified nurse midwives) in that specialization. Some physicians argue that they have more education and training, and so they would be preferable for provision of care.

Ms. A, a pregnant twenty-two-year-old, considers having her baby with the help of a nurse-midwife rather than an obstetrician. She feels more comfortable with the nurse, and believes it to be more "natural" and just as safe for her and her baby.

a. How should health care consumers such as Ms. A decide among different professionals, each of whom asserts competence (or even claims to be the preferred choice) in an area?

b. In what sense and to what extent is this a matter of the individual consumer's responsibility, and to what extent is it a matter for health care researchers, professional organizations, practitioners, or legislators?

c. How should one use relevant statistical information about deaths and complications of women and babies, in addition to value judgments, to determine whether women should be allowed (or even encouraged) to use a particular method of childbirth? Thus, suppose that one method was slightly (say, 1 percent) more likely to result in deaths or serious complications. Would that suffice to preclude it?

2.9   TURF OR EXPERTISE, PART III: PSYCHIATRISTS OR PSYCHOLOGISTS?

Mr. Z, forty-eight years old, has recently experienced fears, work problems, and worries greater than he has ever felt before. He considers asking his family physician about it but decides instead to consult a mental health practitioner. One friend recommends a psychiatrist, and another suggests a clinical psychologist. He does not know which, if either, to contact.

a. Assuming Mr. Z is not experiencing hallucinations or delusions, would it be equally acceptable for him to consult either a psychologist or a psychiatrist? Is one profession probably or definitely the better choice for him at this point?

b. Should health care coverage be a decisive factor in the man's choice?

c. Suppose Mr. Z has a religious affiliation. Are clergy—pastoral counselors—as effective as (or perhaps more so than) mental health practitioners such as psychologists, psychiatrists, or psychiatric social workers? What facts might help people make this choice?

CHAPTER 3

Ethical Issues
in Health Care Education

In settings dedicated to both education and patient care, goals of those two activities may conflict. Some people deny that those conflicts do actually occur or assert that the two goals always reinforce each other—that teaching hospitals actually provide better patient care, for several reasons. But it is not at all obvious that this is universally true. Both values—health care education and health care itself—are, however, essential. This chapter presents attempts to specify situations in which one value may be compromised by the other. Consider the following factors as you read the cases:

Informed consent: Patients may feel pressured into consenting to be examined or even treated by medical and nursing students. At some institutions, it is viewed as not a choice at all, because if you have chosen to come to a teaching hospital, you have, as such, consented to be examined and practiced on by students/housestaff.

Privacy compromises: If five or ten students (again including residents/registrars) need to observe or learn a procedure, then the patient's privacy seems to take a back seat.

Risk to patients: Because those who are learning procedures, by definition, are less experienced, and competency arises from experience, then the learners are less competent. Further, to the extent that likelihood of a procedure being completed safely and efficiently is a function of level of competence, it seems to follow that patients in educational settings are at somewhat greater risk.

Relationships: Many sorts of relationships might exist between those who teach and their students. At least some relationships may, however, present ethical problems. The most clear sort is a romantic relationship and the tensions, suspicions, and potential for conflict of interest it involves.

Overwork: Traditionally, housestaff have been assigned very long stretches of time on duty and on call. These could extend to twenty-four or even thirty-six hours. Again, although some people deny that such schedules compromise judgment or coordination, they at least *seem* to create a situation in which optimal patient care could be sacrificed to a notion of optimal educational exposure.

Objections to assignments: A student may, for reasons of conscience, object to performing an educational exercise or procedure (such as the vivisection of a living dog). Should the student be given a different task or exercise, or should the student be told that the exercise is required?

3.1   EDUCATION AND (IN)EXPERIENCE: TWO VIGNETTES

Scenario 1: A resident, Dr. M, performs a procedure—a lumbar puncture—for only the second time. It requires some skill and is always painful to the person undergoing it. Her first time, although more gradual than for more experienced practitioners, had gone satisfactorily.

Scenario 2: An experienced surgeon, Dr. C, performs a complex coronary bypass procedure for the second time, although performing it twenty-five times is judged necessary for full competency. The apparent problem with the situation—perhaps a sort of Catch-25 in this case—is that someone can *become* sufficiently competent only by doing something in a *less* competent way.

a. Are the situations of the resident and the surgeon substantially different? If so, then how?

b. To what extent should the resident or the surgeon inform the patient of his or her level of (in)experience? Is it morally necessary to inform the patient of the level usually considered necessary for optimal treatment?

c. If a patient is unaware of his or her physician's *comparative* inexperience, does it follow that the patient has not given valid informed consent?

d. How should we best balance the various value considerations here?

3.2   EDUCATION AND RISK

A medical student, Mr. W, is learning to do various invasive procedures (such as lumbar puncture, blood drawing, intubation, catheterization, and cardiopulmonary resuscitation). These are the first few times the student has attempted these procedures or has attempted them without supervision present.

a. Is the patient at any greater risk of injury or pain than if a more experienced person were performing the procedure?

b. Suppose the patient is at increased risk of injury or pain, and this matter has not been made known to him or her. Is there something objectionable about this omission?

c. Is the patient entitled to any such information? Why?

d. Does the fact that the patient is being treated in a teaching institution signal that she or he has tacitly consented to be exposed to any increased risks/discomforts?

e. Should the patient take for granted that receiving treatment at a teaching hospital produces a favorable benefit-to-risk ratio since the benefits of state-of-the-art care exceed the harms of being practiced on by those with less experience?

3.3 PRACTICING INVASIVE PROCEDURES ON THE NEWLY DEAD

Mrs. X, a hospital patient, suffered a cardiac arrest, could not be resuscitated, and so has just been pronounced dead. Medical students are immediately summoned to practice procedures, including intubation and (additional) CPR, on her. Neither the patient nor her family had been informed of this educational practice.

a. Since this seems to constitute an exception to the ordinary practice of obtaining informed consent for procedures, including autopsies, how might it be justified?

b. Some argue that it is perfectly acceptable to practice procedures on those who have just died, because (i) that practice is necessary for students' education, (ii) it does not harm the patient—who is dead—and, finally, (iii) it avoids informing people to protect the sensibilities of the families since they do not know of the practice. Do you agree with some or all of this reasoning?

c. Others maintain that they don't tell people because too few would give consent before their deaths. Is this a good reason?

d. Is educational necessity, or educational value, a sufficient reason to circumvent informed consent? Is the need for informed consent sufficiently important to jeopardize optimal medical education?

e. Is there an alternative that would enable one to obtain informed consent without impeding the acquisition of clinical skills?

f. Should these procedures have been done on animals instead, or would that practice have raised further serious ethical problems?

g. Should the state legally require autopsies to determine the causes of death? (Under such a policy, just as there is a presumption of entitlement to harvest organs in a "presumed consent" plan, individuals would have to specifically announce their wish of opting out to be excluded.)

3.4 HOW MUCH WORK IS EXCESSIVE FOR RESIDENTS?

Housestaff are told they must work long stretches of time and many hours a week as a customary learning method. They are also told that such a schedule provides optimal continuity of care for patients.

Nurse A observes residents she judges to be sleep deprived who are diagnosing and treating patients.

a. What sort of residency workload is excessive? How would you decide whether there is a problem, either for the residents' well-being or for the quality of patient care, arising from this housestaff scheduling practice?

b. What about the claim that the scheduling is necessary because the program simply cannot afford to hire more people to perform these responsibilities?

c. What about the claim that the scheduling is valuable because it provides the residents with a sample of the demanding schedules they will encounter later?

d. What of the argument that more hours of work mean more hours of educational experience?

e. Is someone who has been working for twenty-four hours more likely to be impaired? If so, then how does this differ from being alcohol or drug impaired?

f. Some people use what might be termed the "family test." What would you choose for a close family member's treatment? Suppose you knew your mother or child were being taken care of by someone who had not slept for thirty hours. Would you be uncomfortable?

3.5 STUDENTS AND RESIDENTS OBSERVE OB/GYN AND UROLOGY PATIENTS

Medical students and residents observe as women undergo obstetric and gynecological exams. To facilitate learning, they also help with the exams. On another rotation, the same students and other residents observe and practice as men are given urological examinations. A number of the patients are uncomfortable about the groups of people observing and probing them, but the patients assume that they must consent to the practice to receive care.

a. Do patients in teaching hospitals have an obligation to allow themselves to be observed and examined by students? By interns and residents/registrars?

b. Should the students, or their supervisors, obtain permission for each such observation/examination? Only for the first time? Should those who refuse some or all such examinations be discharged as soon as it is safe to do so?

c. Should the right to refuse to be observed or probed depend on the type of examination (for example, an innocuous ear examination versus an embarrassing pelvic examination)?

d. If patients were permitted to refuse students access, might it jeopardize the system of medical and nursing education? Suppose only 10 or 20 percent refuse, rather than 80 or 90 percent. Would that make a difference?

3.6 PRESSURES ON RESIDENTS TO OVERLOOK POSSIBLE WRONGDOING: TWO VIGNETTES

Scenario 1: Resident I is subtly encouraged by her supervising attending physician to overlook suspected instances of domestic violence, including child abuse and spousal abuse. This practice is allowed, it appears, to shield the attending physician from inconvenience as well as possible litigation associated with identifying people as possible abusers.

Scenario 2: Resident J is also told to avoid requesting an autopsy when inquiry about, or determination of, the cause of death might create discomfort in the next of kin.

Some of the central conflicts here seem to exist between protection of prudence (self-interest) and respect for various moral responsibilities.

    a. May either resident—to protect her career—disregard what she otherwise believes should be done?

    b. Is there a method for minimizing such conflicts?

    c. Should the residents be expected to jeopardize or sacrifice their careers by taking a moral stand in these cases? Or would that entail asking them to be almost saintly in their self-sacrifice?

3.7 RELATIONSHIPS BETWEEN STUDENTS AND TEACHERS: MORE BOUNDARY ISSUES

Dr. L is an attending physician at the hospital where Dr. M is a resident. Drs. L and M become friends and, after some months, more intimately involved. Dr. L tries to avoid demonstrating any special treatment toward Dr. M. Many of their colleagues are aware of the relationship. They have a variety of attitudes toward it.

    a. Are Drs. L and M doing something morally wrong? If so, then exactly why is it wrong?

    b. Would the moral justifiability of their relationship be different if they were married?

        i. Suppose they had already been married for several years when Dr. M entered the program.

        ii. Suppose they get married now.

        iii. Suppose they are, and remain, unmarried.

    c. Would it be preferable if they were open, possibly even on record, about their relationship? Thus, should Drs. L and M inform their respective supervisors about the relationship?

    d. To the extent that Dr. L has any authority over Dr. M, does the relationship create an actual, potential, or apparent conflict of interest? Does it create an appearance of impropriety? Would concerns or suspicions of preferential treatment be understandable on the part of Dr. M's peers?

    e. Should Dr. L formally exclude himself from any situations involving the evaluation of Dr. M? Suppose he is the only specialist in a specialty that is required of all interns.

    f. Would a rule prohibiting such relationships be a good idea or a bad idea?

    g. Suppose Dr. L were a senior resident or registrar rather than an attending physician. Suppose Dr. M were a medical student rather than an intern. Suppose that, instead of Dr. M, Dr. L were seeing Nurse N. Would some of the same questions indicated earlier arise?

h. Some argue that any attempt to judge the morality of relationships between consenting adults is unwarranted. Are they correct?

3.8   VIDEOTAPING PATIENTS

Many hospitals have as part of their mission the education of health care workers. At these thousands of institutions, a role reversal of sorts occurs: the patients, in an important sense, help the doctors and nurses by providing them with opportunities to learn. The "teaching" done by the patients is, obviously, not usually among the reasons the patients have in mind when they go to the hospitals' admitting offices, clinics and emergency departments.

Video has become an increasingly useful tool in some areas of education. To aid in teaching students to perform a new surgical procedure, a clinical faculty member, Dr. H, tapes several such procedures. He also videotapes, for purposes of critical evaluation, some of the residents' work. Dr. H removes a large cyst from Mrs. G's abdomen. She is not told that the entire procedure is being taped.

a. What ethical problems about privacy and informed consent might exist here? Or is there no moral problem about this sort of practice?

b. What are some possible explanations as to why Dr. H did not inform Mrs. G that she would be taped? Should he have told her? Why?

c. Suppose a resident, in obtaining the signature on the informed consent form, discloses that the procedure will be videotaped, and Mrs. G says that she would rather they not tape her. Would the teachers be justified in reminding her that she is a patient in a teaching institution?

CHAPTER 4

Managed Care and Health Care Business

This chapter's cases focus on several areas at the intersection of business ethics and clinical ethics, since they have to do with the responsibilities of business and financial dimensions of health care. The allocation chapter (Chapter 15) will also overlap these areas.

MANAGED CARE AND HMOS

Increasingly, over the past decade, the structure of much American health care delivery has come to be modeled on that of (other?) business. A lot of the decision making about provision of health, medical, nursing, psychological, social work, and other services is approached in terms of competitive organizational management principles as well as patient care priorities. In part, managed care arose as an attempt to find a middle path between two systems, each of which had insufficient political and public opinion support: a completely market-driven, fee-for-service system and a completely nationalized, socialized system. These are, of course, only two of many alternative possible systems.

The phenomenon of managed care has created uncertainty and alarm for both health care consumers and health care providers. With increasing frequency, hospitals, nursing homes, and medical partnerships consolidate or go out of business. More and more people are covered by managed care plans, especially HMOs— health maintenance organizations. Managed care, designed to save money, decrease paperwork and unnecessary treatment, and improve the level of health care provided to most people, has, in part succeeded. But it has also, in many cases, resulted in de-creased flexibility of choice and—with providers preimbursed—has given the health care providers an economic incentive not to treat people.

MARKETING AND SALES TECHNIQUES; RESEARCH AND DEVELOPMENT

The promotion and distribution of some products, such as pharmaceutical products, raises questions about possible improper methods. These are aimed at housestaff and students as well as at attendings and community practitioners. Some of these tech-niques include advertising in newspapers, magazines, and professional journals; the use of gifts to practitioners and students; lunches; and retreatlike meetings.

Many people have questioned the potential for problems occurring in connection with drug companies' sponsorship of research and educational programs. It would help if we could clarify whether clinicians' judgment *would* actually be influenced at all or whether they might appear to be in an improper relationship with the business. These concerns are not impossible to address by discussion and empirical investiga-tion, and they merit further discussion.

4.1   HMO-PHOBIA?

As people have grown more aware of the extensive effects of managed care, espe-cially HMOs, we hear increasing questions and worries about this new form of health care delivery.

Miss E, thirty-three years old, belongs to her employer's HMO, InProHealth. InProHealth has implemented *protocols,* a device used by HMOs to provide guid-ance about how health care is to be provided. Miss E's physician, Dr. F, thinks that she should perform some laboratory tests to determine what has caused Miss E's loss of energy and vertigo. Dr. F thinks the additional tests would enable her to rule out a brain tumor. The tests are not approved by the protocol, and so Dr. F tries to de-cide whether to go through the time-consuming, elaborate, uncertain appeals process to attempt to get an exception to the prescribed routine.

a. Is anything wrong with this situation? If so, how might it be remedied?

b. What factual information would be useful or even necessary to evaluate an HMO morally?

c. Assuming that managed care plans, including HMOs, help control costs, must all such measures involve trade-offs of important moral values? How can ex-cesses be curbed without setting limits? How much flexibility is compatible with having rules, guidelines, and procedures?

d. Do you agree with the critics who have contended that managed care plans in-volve, by their nature, a conflict of interest by working toward a financial goal—cost minimization—that is often incompatible with the goal of providing the best care for patients?

4.2 A MANAGED CARE FIRM REQUESTS A PSYCHOLOGIST'S REPORTS

Clinical psychologist Dr. R has, for the past two months, provided weekly psychotherapy for Ms. W's anxiety disorder and other personal problems. A representative of the managed care organization sends Dr. R forms that require the psychologist to spell out, over a number of pages, exactly what Ms. W suffers from and what they discuss. Dr. R understands that, for the therapy to be reimbursable, she must supply the detailed, specific information to the provider.

a. Is the managed care organization too intrusive, or is it merely trying to assure proper use of its reimbursements?

b. Is it unfair to require more detailed information about mental health conditions and treatment than for other sorts of health care?

c. If the information is kept in the organization's database, who should be permitted access to it? Potential or present employers? Government agencies? The courts? Other insurance companies?

d. Suppose the organization requires a second opinion in Ms. W's case before it will continue to pay for her psychotherapy. Does this requirement place too great a burden on Ms. W? Are psychological or psychiatric cases relevantly different from other conditions where second opinions are required?

4.3 MANAGING MANAGED CARE

CarePartners Incorporated numbers among its employees Mr. E, who designs its policies; Ms. G, who administers and monitors them; and Dr. O and Nurse P, who provide care. The R family is covered by CarePartners' HMO. Other than the annual fee, they usually only need to pay a small amount (copayment, or "copay") each time they visit a physician. The organization works by means of *capitation*: a fixed amount is set aside for each person enrolled, so there are incentives to keep people healthy and to provide minimal care, since cost containment is an important goal.

To curb perceived abuses, legislation has prohibited certain practices, including:

+ mandating twenty-four-hour discharges of mothers and children after birth,
+ requiring people to travel hundreds or thousands of miles to medical centers to receive some complicated treatments,
+ excluding physicians from participation for extraneous reasons,
+ providing obstacles to access to specialists,
+ prohibiting physicians from organizing their own systems, and
+ limiting the types of bonuses and other financial incentives that might tend to discourage doctors from making certain sorts of more costly clinical decisions.

a. Are these types of legislation unwarranted intrusion by the government, or are they proper use of governmental power to protect health care consumers?

b. Should the extent of regulation be a function of the range of choices consumers have?

c. Is capitation, insofar as it provides incentives to withhold or minimize care, an evil? Or is it something that may be necessary to discourage uncontrolled health care expenditures and to give more people access to higher-quality, more carefully monitored health care?

d. In what sense and to what extent does each of the persons mentioned above (E, G, O, P, and perhaps others, such as executives and shareholders in CarePartners) have moral responsibility for the health care received by the R family?

4.4   CHANGING HOSPITAL OWNERSHIP

Central General Hospital recently became part of one of the most significant changes in American health care delivery in recent years: the change in ownership of many hospitals. As a nonprofit, tax-exempt hospital, Central General had, for over a hundred years, provided care to people in the area, including a number who were unable to afford to pay. They had used cost shifting to make this possible. Under the ownership of a for-profit national corporation, Health Affirmations, they have made a number of changes. They have consolidated some departments, laid off some employees, and implemented other methods that would enable them to remain maximally efficient and competitive. Some of the employees (present and past) as well as some people in the community have objected to the changes as harmful.

a. Is something wrong with hospitals being run on a for-profit basis? Does it amount to profiting from people's illnesses and injuries, or does it rather earn its pay by providing a valuable service?

b. Should our moral assessment of the hospital's activity be a function of its mission statement? Would it be wrong if it changed its mission statement somewhat? Should its mission (that is, its most basic goals) be, at least partly, a function of values and priorities independent of those its board of trustees or owners choose to affirm?

c. To what extent may the hospital's operation be guided by considerations of the interests of the stakeholders, including the shareholders, of Health Affirmations?

d. Does a corporation have a moral responsibility to be part of society's "safety net," or is that supererogatory—praiseworthy, but not morally obligatory?

e. When a business, such as a factory, closes, it can have a significant impact on the community in which it is located. Suppose the management of Health Affirmations decides that Central General is just not sufficiently competitive in the marketplace to keep its doors open. Should the potential impact on the area's level of health care delivery be among the constraints governing the decision about whether to close the hospital? Is it plausible to compare such a decision to that of a chain of supermarkets closing one of their stores?

f. What, if anything, is the community's stake in the nonprofit hospital?

g. Is it economically realistic to expect health care organizations not to respond to financial constraints? Is it morally permissible to allow needed health care access to be limited or denied because of financial considerations?

4.5 ADVERTISEMENTS IN JOURNALS AND OTHER PERIODICALS

Pharmaceutical firm PQ purchases glossy ads, sometimes of several pages in length, in scientific clinical journals. PQ's critics claim that their products sell well because they are so heavily advertised, while the corporation's defenders maintain that they can afford to advertise because they sell good-quality products. PQ has now decided to extend their marketing, by means of advertising in national newsmagazines and local newspapers, a few of their products that are available by prescription only. These ads would include a phrase advising readers to ask their doctors about the advertised products.

a. What are the different plausible effects on prescribers' judgment/decision making?

b. If advertising were not believed to influence behavior, why would companies spend money on it?

c. Is an advertisement a scientifically reliable source of information? Will it attempt to provide a balanced, impartial, critical perspective on its subject, the product offered for sale?

d. Suppose your physician were being completely candid and said, "I'm prescribing this for your heart condition. It's the brand I see advertised everywhere." What would you think about his or her decision-making powers?

e. Is there a difference between advertising in professional journals and in periodicals, such as newspapers, that are read by those who are mostly not health care professionals?

4.6 PHARMACEUTICAL RESEARCH FUNDING

Administrators and researchers of a study of pheloxytine decanoate, a new drug intended as an antipsychotic, know that the source of funding for their drug research is the GHI company, the manufacturer of the drug they are testing. The researchers maintain that this situation poses no ethical problem, however, for the following three reasons:

+ They are trained scientists and thus virtually immune to bias.
+ The research subjects do not know whether they are in the treatment group or the control group.
+ The money was given to their institution, St. X's University, rather than to the researchers directly.

a. Concerning the first reason, in what sense does being a scientist ensure or make more likely that one will be free of intentional or unintentional bias? If scientists are *assumed* free of bias, why is there a standard methodology to use a double-blind study (in which those gathering data, as well as the subjects, do not know who is in the control group)?

b. About the second reason, does the fact that the *subjects* are "blind" to whether they are in the treatment or control group eliminate any possible bias on the part of the researchers?

c. Suppose the money were given directly to the research team. Would that then become morally unacceptable (or more unacceptable than otherwise)?

4.7   A SALESPERSON TREATS RESIDENTS TO LUNCH

A representative of L-Labs, a major pharmaceutical firm, offers to treat residents to lunch at an expensive restaurant. The meal is offered, the representative says, to provide a location and a comfortable environment to inform the residents about a new product, the drug Vasotril.

a. Should the meal be viewed as a bribe, and thus morally unacceptable, or is its purpose more benign?

b. Suppose it is a moderate-priced restaurant or an inexpensive one. Would either of these morally alter the situation?

c. Suppose the residents already know about Vasotril. Would there be any morally acceptable reason for the lunch in this case?

d. Suppose the residents could get the same product information by means of a two-page flier.

e. In what sense is the representative performing a valuable educational function, and in what sense is he "buying access," as people sometimes describe it?

f. Will all the residents remain just as likely to judge Vasotril accurately in comparison with its competitors? Will all of them remain no more disposed to prescribe Vasotril than they would have been otherwise?

g. All the residents insist that the lunch will not influence their future decisions about whether to prescribe Vasotril. Does this change the ethical implications of accepting the lunch?

h. Is there a sense in which the acceptance of the lunch offer creates an appearance of impropriety?

4.8   DRUG SAMPLES FOR PATIENTS

The dozen patients seated in Dr. Y's waiting room hardly notice as a well-dressed man with an oversized briefcase enters and walks past the receptionist. He is Mr. RX, a pharmaceutical representative. The nurses show him to a drug storage closet, which he scans. He begins removing from his sample case to the shelves handfuls of small packets of his company's pills, liquids, and ointments. Almost all of these are available only by prescription. Dr. Y will give these to more than a third of his patients, when he believes that those drugs will benefit the patients. Use of the samples will, he thinks, save those patients the cost of purchasing these drugs they need.

a. Is Mr. RX, Dr. Y, or Mr. RX's employer doing anything morally questionable? If so, then exactly what and why?

b. What impact will the free distribution of these promotional samples likely have on the price of the company's drugs? Suppose the use of the samples increases sales of the product.

c. What impact will the distribution of the samples likely have on the physicians' prescribing habits and on the patients' perceptions of the products? Might physicians and patients be subject to influence by brand recognition?

d. Is Dr. Y serving as part of a marketing program for Mr. RX's employer?

e. What about the argument that the arrangement is win-win, with everyone benefiting, patients and manufacturers alike? Is this fair to other pharmaceutical manufacturers who are competing with the sample distributors? Or should they just do their own distribution of samples?

4.9   CONFLICTS OF INTEREST

Internist Dr. I, who takes a particular interest in health care stocks, has a diversified stock portfolio. He owns shares of stock in:

+ a clinical laboratory,
+ an imaging partnership,
+ a pharmaceutical company,
+ an HMO, and
+ a food supplement manufacturer.

a. Might the existence of any of these potential financial benefits influence his professional judgment? If so, in what ways?

b. In *boundary violations* (see cases about relationships and gifts in Chapters 1 and 3), people's extraprofessional, personal relationships might affect their professional judgment. How are the ethics of boundary violations like and unlike those of conflicts of interest? Does the presence of *dual roles* as a source of bias count as a relevant similarity?

c. Consider similarities and differences with *blinding* in research. The use of that practice is designed to minimize the likelihood of bias, even among those who attempt to be scrupulous.

d. Some people perceive clinicians with investments in areas related to their practices as compromised by them. Is this based on the public's ignorance and excessive cynicism? Is it based on accurate observations and inferences?

e. How might institutions and society monitor for conflicts of interest? What policies would help?

4.10 PHARMACEUTICAL COMPANIES AND DEVELOPING NATIONS

Bayn Sellworth Ltd manufactures a broad range of pharmaceutical products. They have come under pressure to modify their prices so as to consider the needs and income levels of people in developing nations. Those urging them to re-think their prices argue that justice requires them to charge a fourth of their usual price for vaccines, a fifth for AIDS drugs, and half for antibiotics.

a. Should decisions about prices depend on the extent of the profits gained from that product in those nations? Upon whether they are a profit-making firm at all?

b. Some argue that it should not be considered an issue at all, since Bayn Sellworth is a private corporation, with prices and profits to be market-determined. Do you agree?

c. Do pharmaceutical companies have greater responsibilities than other businesses to people in developing nations? Do all businesses have greater responsibility than they acknowledge?

d. Which of these would make for an ethically desirable and appropriate pricing formula?
   i. Setting prices based on standards of living/ability to pay of countries?
   ii. Providing life-saving drugs for free to poor people?
   iii. Consulting with the firm's stockholders to see what they deem acceptable?
   iv. Some other pattern of pricing?

4.11 BIOPATENTING HUMAN GENOME SEQUENCES

Scientists at the University of Researchusetts, funded by GenomeTech Corporation, have discovered the sequence for an important part of the human genome, a sequence very likely to play an important role in the creation of an enzyme missing in people predisposed to develop Alzheimer's disease. The university and GenomeTech both have some claim to patent rights for the sequence. GenomeTech will, legally, have primary claim. The conflict could mean delayed and more costly development of treatments for the disease. On the other hand, the support from the university and the company facilitated the discovery of the sequence.

a. Are parts of the human genetic structure the sorts of things that should be able to be patented? Or should they be thought of as information within the public domain? What should the law say about these issues?

b. Should financial support of scientific work, such as the development of new drugs, justify claims to proprietary rights? If it should, then ought the withholding of the information—because of limited access—carry with it responsibility for the harms that befall those unable to make use of the findings?

c. Suppose conferring proprietary rights leads to a delay in the development of treatment for Alzheimer's disease because many researchers will not be given the gene sequence. Is it permissible to abridge property rights in these cases? What if the treatment is not delayed but instead proprietary rights lead to substantially increased costs for treatment? Is a greater financial burden on the patients grounds for denying proprietary rights for the human gene sequence? Should this be decided based on the numbers of people deprived of treatment? Of life-saving treatment?

d. Which of the following reasons has persuasive force in deciding about biopatents?

   i. It risks placing too much wealth and power in the hands of a few.

   ii. Living things are not the kinds of things that should be patented.

   iii. One's biological nature is, as such, owned exclusively by oneself.

   iv. Human beings are special and beyond being owned or captured by molecular descriptions.

   v. Just as no one should be allowed to own all of humanity's noses in perpetuity, no one should be permitted to own the genes that code for noses—or for any parts thereof.

CHAPTER *5*

Research

Biomedical and behavioral research, so vital for the continued growth of knowledge that underlies practice, must be done in ways recognized as morally acceptable.

Moral problems often occur when those involved in research neglect to follow basic guidelines. Many of the ethical oversights and lapses stem from the researchers' very commitment to their work. Often, the raising of moral questions and criticisms feels to them to be obstructionism from people willing to sacrifice good science due to overscrupulous moral piety.

OTHER SPECIES

Use of other species for research, at least since the mid-1970s, has brought with it a storm of controversy. People's reactions to it range from the abolitionists, who oppose all research on other species, to the permissivists, who would allow all animal research if it would help humans. Between those two polar opposites we find regulationists, who would allow selected research if carefully supervised and monitored. Probably most people, if asked, would place themselves in this category.

INFORMED CONSENT

Informed consent on the part of subjects of research is acknowledged by everyone as an essential precondition, both morally and legally, for research to be permitted. Although this point seems basic, straightforward, and something everyone agrees about, it turns out that many sorts of research can have, at best, only indirect or questionable consent. One way to put this is by means of an apparent paradox: in many cases, true, informed consent is, at the same time, both necessary and impossible. Here is why.

First, much research is performed on other species, and in animal research, obviously, informed consent cannot be obtained. It strains credulity to think that the animals experimented on would consent even if they could consent.

A second area of research in which true informed consent cannot be obtained is that which is performed on people incapable of consenting because of lack of mental capacity to consent: babies, profoundly retarded people, and people with severe neurological and mental disorders, to mention some. In those cases, a parent or legal guardian provides proxy consent. The person providing the consent should do so with the would-be subject's best interests in mind.

A third group of research subjects are those who, though possessing some ability to comprehend and participate in decision making, do not have full capacity to do so. These include many of the so-called special subjects: young children and some people with mental disorders or mental retardation that may result in increased vulnerability or compromised or diminished decision-making abilities.

A fourth category of subjects consists of those who, although fully mentally competent, might either lack full information or wind up consenting in questionable circumstances. Some examples are people undergoing great stress, those who are induced to consent by prospect of financial rewards, individuals who do not fully comprehend the description of the research, and those who consent because they want to cooperate with coworkers of those providing their care.

In the ethics of research, therapeutic research is contrasted with the nontherapeutic. The first of these is intended both to acquire new knowledge but also to benefit the subjects of the research. The second only aims to acquire new knowledge, knowledge that may well benefit *others*. Other things being equal, there is a heavier burden of justification placed on those who would do nontherapeutic rather than therapeutic research.

Similarly, a heavier burden of justification exists for those who would do research that poses greater than minimum risk to the subjects—especially for human subject research.

Other factors often mentioned in consideration of the ethics of research include avoidance of exploitation, proper scientific methodology, protection of subjects' privacy, and minimizing use of deception. See some of the relevant codes of ethics in the appendix for further research guidelines.

MINIMIZING RISK AND MINIMIZING BIAS

Most safeguards for research subjects are based on the level of risk to which the studies would expose the subjects. What is a sensible way to pair levels of risk (classified in ways such as "minimal risk," or "slightly greater than minimal risk") with types of protections? Are concepts such as "minimal risk"—typically interpreted as the level of risk ordinarily encountered in everyday life—sufficiently clear and applicable?

Although risks are estimated carefully for human subjects, animal subjects of research can be subjected to risks deemed intolerable for humans—including infliction of disease, pain, and death. The legal protection is greater for some species than for others. How much risk and harm are acceptable for various animals, and how should we balance the possible good for humans with harm to animals?

Whether due to increased vulnerability, inability to provide consent, or other reasons, to what extent should there be limits placed on the use of "special subjects" such as children, fetuses, and people with mental illness—each of whom is afforded special protection by regulatory guidelines—as subjects of research?

What about research that is not intended to benefit the subjects, although there is some chance that it might add to the body of generalizable knowledge? In some instances, drugs and procedures need to be tested on a range of groups if the suitability of these drugs or procedures for use in those groups is to be determined. How does the value of the possible (even if not probable) knowledge justify testing them on those unable or less able to consent?

Deciding what constitutes a *bias* can be controversial. One area of special interest is that of *conflict of interest*. The ethical significance comes from the possibility that people's decisions might be skewed by factors extraneous to the purely professional, evidence-based considerations. Conflicts of interest may exist in several areas of health care.

Investments, consultants, and speaker fees. Practitioners can have financial interests in firms related to areas of their practice. Others collect fees as consultants, given that they are knowledgeable about certain areas of medicine. Is there something questionable about their entering into such relationships? Drug manufacturers hire physicians to be on their speakers' bureaus. The doctors are highly paid for traveling extensively and doing presentations on the products. They are speaking as applied scientists. Some critics have raised questions about the propriety of such arrangements.

Conflict of interest in research. Researchers encounter circumstances in which it appears that their judgment might tend to be influenced by biasing factors due to the researchers' financial interests. What criteria will help in the formation of justified opinions about (a) when there is an *appearance* of impropriety; and (b) when people might be reasonably inferred to have their judgment improperly influenced by self-interest?

Science and experience. While not about conflict of interest, another issue arises from different standards of evidence. To what extent are one's own professional experiences a reliable resource for disciplines supposedly based on rigorous scientific studies? How should health care professionals mesh their own clinical experience with the findings of carefully controlled, statistically sound studies?

5.1 A RESEARCH SUBJECT'S COMPREHENSION CONFUSION

Researchers have presented in writing eight single-spaced pages of explanatory information to the subjects of a study. The subjects have signed the informed consent document, but it is not clear that they have read and understood it completely.

When asked about it afterward, they do not remember very clearly exactly what they volunteered for.

a. If someone cannot recall the specifics of what was in the document signed, does that provide some reason to question whether the original consent was valid?

b. One can be persuaded by adequate evidence at one time but then forget at a later time the specific nature of that evidence. What sorts of specifics *ought* to be recallable for the consent to have validity?

c. Should the health workers proceed as if informed consent has been given?

d. What assurance should be sought at the original time of signing that the subjects understand what it is that they are consenting to? Or is such a challenge unnecessary?

5.2 PARENTAL RESEARCH INCENTIVE

Researchers offer Mrs. and Mr. D several hundred dollars to enroll their four-year-old child, T, in a diabetes research protocol that will involve some inconvenience and discomfort to the child. T will have the equivalent of a few tablespoons of blood drawn each week.

a. Is the money offered best thought of as deserved compensation, permissible incentive, a gesture of gratitude, or questionable bribery?

b. What effects may the money reasonably be expected to have on the parents' decisions to participate? How much difference does the money make for the people's sense of their well-being? To what extent does the offer manipulate their choices or exploit poor people, rather than "sweetening" the offer? Or is it merely an opportunity to supplement their already modest income?

c. Some guidelines interpret incentives as "coercive" if the money will be likely to affect willingness to participate. Does this enable one to distinguish proper from improper incentives?

d. If the research were therapeutic—intended to benefit the child—would that contribute to its acceptability?

e. Because most drugs prescribed for children have not been tested specifically on children, and yet children often respond differently to drugs than do adults, does that add to the justification for finding additional ways of enrolling children in such studies?

5.3 COMPENSATING PARENTS
FOR RESEARCH ON THEIR CHILDREN

Dozens of children and adults at a large hospital participate in a study that entails some discomfort and inconvenience to them. The researchers are being paid, through grant funding, to conduct the study, but the participants are *not* offered any compensation. They assume that the satisfaction of knowing that they are participants in the growth of knowledge should be its own reward. Further, the notion of asking for money to help out a scientific inquiry sounds unseemly.

a. Would reimbursing the subjects be likely to affect the scientific validity of the study? How might it contaminate or compromise the study's scientific rigor?

b. Would reimbursing the subjects represent questionable behavior on the part of either the researchers or the subjects? Why?

c. Should the subjects be reimbursed only to the extent that they have to endure discomfort? Are the subjects relevantly different from any other employee?

d. Should the study participants—either the parents or the children—feel awkward about raising the topic of reimbursement for participation? Why? Should the people who are sharing in the funding feel likewise? What exactly *is* the morally relevant difference between the two groups?

5.4   HOW MUCH DISCLOSURE IS NEEDED FOR CONSENT?

Asthma researchers at six institutions participating in a collaborative study of a new drug and behavior regimen explain in some detail the tasks to be required of the subjects and the known risks and benefits, and they inform the subjects-to-be that they are free to withdraw at any time. All of the preceding have been included in virtually every code of research ethics since the Nuremberg Code (see the appendix, page 178) as necessary for obtaining informed consent. The researchers, however, do not make known to the subjects the exact reason for the study or whether any individual will be in the placebo control group or the treatment group.

a. Given the omissions, does this mean that the subjects have not given valid informed consent?

b. If good scientific research design requires that subjects not know if they are in the treatment group or the control group, does it follow that there is a significant number of people—those in the placebo group—who receive less than the best possible treatment?

c. Suppose the study is a "crossover," with the groups changing from treatment to control and vice versa. Would such a research design ensure that no patient is deprived of a treatment?

d. Most research regulations and guidelines require that patients not be deprived of existing safe, effective treatments to test a new drug or procedure. Does this mean that only those who suffer from presently untreatable conditions may be research subjects?

5.5   RELYING ON STUDIES AND EXPERIENCE

Dr. V and Nurse W work together in a community practice. They both keep informed of studies printed in their professional journals. These studies have been carefully designed and conducted by reputable researchers and the results reviewed by the journals' referees. They therefore have some claim to scientific validity. Some, in fact, have been replicated. Nurse W and Dr. V make some use of the journals' articles. They also fulfill their continuing education responsibilities by means of educational programs.

At the same time, V and W rely on their own clinical experience and sometimes reports from colleagues. They believe that sometimes scientific studies are mistaken and that their own experience provides a useful source of further information to guide their professional judgment.

a. Are Nurse W and Dr. V inconsistent in their thinking? In what way can they coherently claim that the journals and educational presentations provide the most reliable information in their areas and at the same time claim that their experiences should override such apparently reliable knowledge?

b. Given that personal experience is an important source of our practical knowledge and judgment, how should one reason from isolated experiences to general conclusions?

c. Should there be limits to the use of either personal experience or scientific claims when they conflict?

5.6 BALANCING HUMANS' AND MICE'S INTERESTS

A hundred mice are used as research subjects to study the therapeutic effects of a drug for some cancers. The mice are exposed to carcinogens until a considerable number develop cancer. Half of the mice with cancer are then given the new drug, whereas the remaining mice with cancer are given placebos as members of the control group. The drug induces hair loss, vomiting, and/or seizures in almost all. There is not a statistically significant difference between the groups' survival rates to indicate any therapeutic efficacy.

a. How would a lack of evidence for efficacy be considered a scientifically significant finding?

b. Would the logical possibility of an improvement in human health suffice to justify the use of the hundred—or even thousands—of mice to test this drug?

c. Might the amount of suffering imposed on the mice by the inducing of cancer and the side effects of the drugs be outweighed by the potential benefit for humans?

d. How would one begin to compare the infliction of suffering on animals with the benefits to humans? Should numbers be relevant?

e. What if the disease were very rare in humans? Would that matter?

f. Is the inability of mice to consent relevant to deciding whether it is morally justified to use them in research?

5.7 NONTHERAPEUTIC RESEARCH WITH ALZHEIMER'S PATIENTS

A research team has enrolled 120 people who have Alzheimer's disease. The subjects of the research, who have this progressive degenerative disease of the brain, are no longer competent to consent to their own care. Likewise, they cannot validly consent to be subjects of research, so their families or other legal guardians have provided the consent for their participation in the study, which involves some uncomfortable diagnostic procedures as well as being given frequent tests of their abilities.

In standard codes of behavior for research, nontherapeutic research (not done with the expectation that it will benefit the subject) requires a strong burden of moral proof. Further, proxy consent, though legal, lacks the clear authenticity of informed consent by an autonomous, mentally competent individual.

5.8   A PROXY'S "CONSENT" FOR RESEARCH

The W's enroll their children in a research study. The children themselves could not—because they are minors—volunteer to participate in the studies, although those who are deemed able to understand are asked to *assent,* a notion weaker than consent. The study's design requires twice-weekly drawings of blood samples.

a. Is there a sense in which people cannot "volunteer" anyone else for something?

b. Is the situation essentially similar, ethically, to that of mentally ill or mentally retarded adults who are enrolled in studies by their guardians, or are there some crucial relevant differences?

c. Would the value of the knowledge to be gained justify the study if those who would benefit would be children of the future? Or would it be exploitation of the children who are the subjects of the present study?

5.9   PHASE I CLINICAL TRIALS ON CHILDREN

Phase I clinical trials represent an essential part of clinical research. They are performed on human subjects to gather information about toxicity or maximum tolerable dosage of drugs. Their primary intent, then, is to obtain information that will benefit (or prevent harm to) future patients.

In this case, hematology/oncology researchers approach the parents of a four-year-old girl dying of a sarcoma, a form of cancer, and for whom extensive chemotherapy has not worked, with the request that they enroll the girl in a Phase I trial for a new drug. The parents feel torn. They want to help other children in similar situations, yet they also want to do what is best for their daughter.

a. If the research is nontherapeutic—that is, if it is not intended to benefit the person who is the subject of the research—may the parents ethically consent to it?

b. If, furthermore, the study will probably add to the child's suffering, is it acceptable to consent for the research to be performed?

c. At her age, is her assent—her verbal permission—to participate meaningful? Would it be permissible without her assent?

d. How might one construct a justification for providing proxy consent—that is, consent for others—that is not based on what that person would want or on what would benefit the person?

e. If the preceding seems to pose problems for allowing such studies, how then can most medical research proceed, since Phase I studies are necessary as a first step in determining the safety and effectiveness of *most* treatments and drugs? This seems especially important in light of the fact that most drugs prescribed for children were not tested on children.

5.10 EXPERIMENTAL TRANSPLANTATION FROM OTHER SPECIES

Transplantation of organs or tissues from other species to humans (xenotransplantation) elicits reactions from acceptance to squeamishness to disapproval. Baboon bone marrow has been experimentally transplanted into an AIDS patient. Some researchers advocate transplantation of organs from other species into humans. Agencies and commissions have worked at designing guidelines for such procedures.

Miss E has kidney disease and will soon need a transplant to stay alive. There are no donated kidneys available for her. Her physician knows of a researcher in a nearby university medical center, Dr. T, who could perform a xenotransplant. Dr. T has been practicing procedures with other primates and pigs. Miss E and her doctor are growing more desperate each day as her condition deteriorates. They begin exerting pressure on Dr. T to do the transplant.

   a. Is there something questionable about using animals as organ sources? If so, is it more questionable than using them in research or as food? If so, then how or why?

   b. Is the use of a primate, such as a baboon or chimpanzee, as an organ source more morally troubling than the use of a pig or sheep? If so, then why?

   c. Does the transplantation of organs from other species raise ethical concerns? If so, then why? If organ transplantation from other species seems wrong, then what about transplantation of tissue from members of other species? What about the use of vaccines made using eggs?

5.11 IS IT A BIRD? IS IT A PLANT?

GenOma Inc. specializes in engineering transgenic organisms. These include transfer of genes between closely related species (such as two kinds of flowers), remotely related species (insects and fish), and distantly related species (animals and plants). Some of their projects use the transfer of genes from other species into humans. They have found a gene in halibut that suppresses the accumulation of plaque in arteries, and they have discovered a gene in a beetle that lowers the likelihood of some types of tumors.

They have just rolled out their latest "beta version" organism—a parrot with an immunity to several diseases due to a begonia's antibiotic-producing gene. Now they want to begin the experimental transfer of the halibut, beetle, and parrot/begonia genes to the conception of humans, in the hope that doing so might benefit humanity's health.

   a. Is such experimentation too risky? Who should be able to make such decisions?

   b. Is the crossing of species lines especially troubling? If so, then exactly how or why is it ethically troubling?

c. Are any of these scenarios especially distressing? If so, then which one(s), and why?

d. Would it matter if the procedure were performed on adults rather than at the reproductive stage?

5.12   RANDOMIZED CLINICAL TRIALS AND ERRORS

Randomized clinical trials (RCTs) constitute an important part of biomedical research. To obtain scientifically valid results, they require that half of the subjects, the control group, receive placebo, existing standard treatment, or no treatment at all. Without the use of this sort of methodology, much reliable knowledge could not be generated.

Mrs. R, age fifty-nine with painful arthritis, has consented to participate in an RCT that is evaluating a new drug. She does not experience much relief from the drug she is given over four months and is unsure whether she is in the treatment or control group. The researchers assure her that she is performing a valuable public service to others in society and people in the future who stand to benefit from improved treatments—or who will be protected from ineffective "treatments." She finds less comfort from this knowledge, however, than she would experience from relief of the pain from her arthritis.

a. Research subjects understand that they can drop out of a study at any time. Could their awareness that they are part of a combined effort that requires sufficient participants, however, inhibit their willingness to leave a study?

b. For the study to be truly randomized, subjects must be kept uninformed about which group they are in. Does this mean that they are less than fully informed?

c. Do researchers sometimes have potentially conflicting loyalties, both to gather knowledge about effective and ineffective treatments and also to help the subject feel better? Which loyalty should be maintained if these commitments do not necessarily coincide?

d. Suppose you are the principal investigator (PI) of the study, and the preliminary data indicate that the experimental drug is not more effective than the placebo. At what point do you have a responsibility to inform the subjects of this or to consider discontinuation of the study?

e. Suppose the study involves the use of a harrowing experimental chemotherapy—one with many accompanying effects such as nausea, vomiting, and cramps—for patients with leukemia. Would your responses be the same as they were to the previous question?

5.13   CONTROVERSIAL FETAL RESEARCH: TWO VIGNETTES

Two groups of scientists propose research projects involving fetuses:

✦ A first group, affiliated with the public University of West Carolina, wishes to perform research on aborted first-trimester fetuses.

+ A second team, working at the privately funded Wilshire Institute, wants to perform research on early embryos formed by in vitro fertilization.

a. Would the likely significance of the knowledge gained by the proposed research affect the moral acceptability of the research?

b. Does the age of the embryo or fetus matter to the moral permissibility of the research? In what sense (if any) should decisions about the acceptability of research depend on whether the fetus is one day or nine months old?

c. Would the fact that a fetus was created by in vitro fertilization as part of an attempt to help an infertile couple have children be relevant to the moral rights or moral status of the fetus?

d. Does an aborted human fetus differ, in morally relevant ways, from an aborted fetus of another species, such as a dog? Suppose the fetus, at a given point (say, one month) does not appear much different than the fetuses of other mammals.

e. How does the proposed research compare or contrast, morally, with experiments that involve combining sperm and an egg in a petri dish?

f. Are any circumstances applicable to the first proposal that differ from the second proposal so significantly that only one should be permitted?

g. Should both, neither, or just one of the proposed research projects be allowed? Should either or both be supported with public funding?

5.14   CONFLICT OF INTEREST POLICIES

Western State University recently implemented policy guidelines to regulate conflicts of interest for researchers. They include the following:

+ Researchers may not own more than $10,000 worth of stock in a company for which they conduct research.

+ They may not receive more than $10,000 in fees from companies sponsoring their research.

+ They must disclose any financial interests in sponsors when they publish or announce their results.

+ They may not spend more than 25 percent of their time working outside the University.

At other institutions, researchers are only required to disclose if they own more than 1–10 percent (the percent varying among institutions) of a company for which they are doing research.

a. Is there reason to think that $10,000 represents a plausible minimum amount that might begin to bias a researcher's professional judgment? Could it depend on the wealth of the researcher or other factors? What empirical evidence or studies would help to clarify this?

b. How can the effects of financially caused bias be determined? Will a combination of intelligence, commitment to one's work, and an intention to be fair eliminate all but the most deliberate forms of bias? How reasonable is it to expect researchers to possess all of these qualities?

   c. How would one judge whether such guidelines are effective in assuring scientists' integrity?

   d. Does the fact that all financial interests must be disclosed in publications imply that people's judgments might be compromised by any extraneous interests? If so, why are they permitted up to $10,000 in stock or fees?

   e. Do conflict of interest policies cast an unwarranted cloud of suspicion over researchers? Do researchers have an incentive to deny conflicts of interest?

5.15   A MARKETPLACE OF IDEAS?

Professor H works at an academic medical center. Much of her research focuses on studies of drugs. Her work, which tends to be well funded by the drugs' manufacturers, attempts to determine the comparative effectiveness of drugs that are similar to a number of other products. Her ongoing work enables her, she finds, to maintain her professional reputation. She hopes this work will eventually involve investigation of the causes of the diseases in which she is most interested. One of the companies for which she does research, Pharmace, gives her consultant fees and has her on its speakers' bureau. Dr. H contends that such a relationship does not present a problem, since the studies she conducts are blinded—thereby preventing any bias.

   a. Does blinding eliminate all forms of bias? How or how not?

   b. When contrasted with findings for research with funders unknown to the researchers, studies have tended to show a strong correlation between researchers knowing the source of sponsorship of research and findings favorable to the sponsors' products. That is, if group X consists of researchers who know the identity of their funders and group Y is researchers unaware of their funders, Xs are much more likely to find that their funders' products are superior. Would it follow that knowing one's funding sponsor compromises scientific integrity? Would it follow that to have such knowledge is morally questionable?

   c. How might research be structured so that funding is provided without researchers knowing its source?

   d. If skewed findings affect health care practice, and hence public health, should scientific bias be punishable by legal means, which it presently is?

5.16   BIOWEAPON RESEARCH

Dr. A is a biological researcher who has extensive knowledge about viruses. Her career has moved in the direction of weapons research. By pursuing it, she would improve her chances of job security as well as ensuring substantial sources of funding. Also, she finds the work interesting, challenging, and important.

   She is confident that, if she does not do the research, someone else will; nevertheless, she has qualms about contributing toward an effort that might eventuate in the deaths of millions of people.

At a party, someone who knows of Dr. A's work confronts her about how she justifies her work. Dr. A finds herself formulating a response.

a. Can the ethics of her career choice be most productively understood as arising from utilitarian emphasis on likely outcomes (such as "the weapons will be developed anyway") or from virtue considerations, such as attention to integrity in one's personal participation (for example, "at least they will not be *my* creations")? Are both kinds of reasons available? Neither kind of reason?

b. In what ways do scientists who create biological weapons have a share of the responsibility when weapons they have created are used by governments (their own or others') and political leaders for political goals? Can your answer to this be generalized to the work of all scientists who work on weapons? To some scientists?

c. What is termed a "substitution" argument asserts that doing something apparently wrong can be permissible by the fact that, if one does not do it then someone else will. Is this plausible or implausible as applied to Dr. A's reasoning? Is use of such reasoning only a form of rationalization, or are there some contexts in which it can be justified?

d. How are citizens other than scientists responsible for their governments' development of such weapons, if it is known that research and development of the weapons is planned?

e. In terms of moral responsibility, is there a difference between working on conventional weapons and bioweapons?

f. How can weapons of mass destruction be used in a way that is *not* ethically questionable? Is it all right to threaten to use those weapons as long as one does not *intend* to actually use them?

CHAPTER 6

Pediatric Contexts

Many of the ethical issues applicable to adults apply as well to children. Some ethical problems, however, have special difficulty or poignancy in pediatric contexts. As was found true of other issues, many of the problems occur when conflicts of obligations, or rights, or goods, occur. These include the areas discussed in the following sections.

ABUSE AND NEGLECT

The notion and the systematic study of child abuse are, remarkably, very recent. These are mostly phenomena of the past thirty years. Although there is considerable agreement among those who study the area, some controversy remains about what constitutes child abuse. We have to distinguish between strict or traditional parenting methods and behaviors properly termed abusive and thus morally wrong. We need to balance the importance of ferreting out and identifying instances of abuse with that of protecting parents and guardians from the stigma of an unwarranted accusation.

MINORS' STATUS

Statute laws tend to specify a bright line, often age eighteen, for people's ability to consent to their health care. Adolescents are often conferred a legal right, in case law, as "mature minors," depending on the individuals' perceived level of maturity, to consent to their own care. According to American case law, a child is termed a *mature minor* if she or he possesses sufficient maturity, emotionally and cognitively, to consent to treatment and to be provided care with confidentiality. Often, this is interpreted as occurring at the age of fifteen, but it needs to be determined on a case-by-case basis.

Because of their developmental status, children and adolescents inhabit a type of limbo, legally and morally, in terms of their entitlement to have a say in their own care. They are often neither completely able nor completely unable to understand and make complex judgments of potentially momentous importance for their lives. We need to acknowledge their (developing) autonomy and at the same time paternalistically protect them from harm.

Family members of children usually have decision-making power for the children. Although they *usually* know and want what is best for the children, this is unfortunately not universally true. Whether because of ignorance, limited judgment powers, or less than complete altruism toward the child, parents may elect a course of treatment or nontreatment that is less than optimal for the child. Health workers and social workers in such cases find themselves in vexing situations.

CRITICALLY ILL NEONATES

Newborns with poor prognoses sometimes present parents and health workers with exceptionally difficult decisions. Several problems can become especially confusing and emotionally grueling for people trying to sort out their decisions. For example, how does one know what is in the child's best interests? How dependably can one judge guesses about the child's future with alternative treatments or nontreatments? What is in the best interests of the family, and may other family members' good be balanced against the good of the newborn?

OPINION CONFLICTS

Many sorts of conflicts of opinion occur in health care settings. Parents' judgment might conflict with that of health workers, parents might disagree with each other, staff might disagree among themselves (in a number of ways), or a child might disagree with parents and/or staff. All of these may present challenging problems.

6.1   SUSPICION OF CHILD ABUSE

A six-year-old boy, T, who was brought to an emergency room for abdominal pain, has multiple bruises on his back and the backs of his arms. T's father has what appear to be needle marks on his arm.

   a. How high should the threshold be for suspicion of child abuse?
   b. Do the father's needle marks increase your suspicions of child abuse? If so, is it based on knowledge that intravenous drug users (as contrasted with diabetic insulin injectors) are more likely to abuse their children?
   c. To what extent should you consider the potential harm to the parent caused by a false accusation of child abuse in deciding whether to report the parent to the authorities?

6.2   VACCINATION 1

Vaccination Scenario 1: Ms. C refuses pneumococcal vaccine for her two-year-old daughter. She states that the vaccine is "too new," and that it has not been tested sufficiently.

a. To decide this, it helps to know what studies *have* been done, and what the studies show about the vaccine's safety. (These are relevant *empirical questions* about the applicable science.) How might one decide this?

b. Has information about the vaccine studies been communicated to Ms. C in a way that can enable her to appreciate its significance? (While also an empirical question, this focuses on the facts relevant to the case's situation.)

c. What is the least harmful choice for her daughter? (An answer to this would combine factual information with normative value concepts.)

d. Consider, for each possible option available to Ms. C, both the *magnitude* of various harms/benefits and the *probability* of the harms/benefits.

   i. What is least harmful and/or most beneficial for Ms. C's child?

   ii. What is least harmful/most beneficial for *others* who are affected by Ms. C's decision? (See below also.)

e. *Physicians' attitudes.* There is a range of opt-outs allowed by physicians. Some insist on immunizations (at least threatening that they will not themselves keep the child as a patient otherwise), while others do not. Which approach is ethically preferable?

f. Who should have the right to make the decision about whether the daughter is immunized?

6.3   VACCINATION 2

Vaccination Scenario 2: Mr. and Mrs. W refuse all vaccinations for their children. They say they will use only herbal and "natural" means to keep themselves and their children healthy.

a. To what extent does each citizen have a *prima facie* obligation to contribute to the public health, part of the public good? More generally, how should parents balance the strength of their commitment to their children's interests with their obligation to society—in this case, to contribute to the immunity of the community's children?

b. How strong an obligation do the Ws have to educate themselves about these matters pertaining their children's health? How strong is the obligation to be persuaded by the best scientific evidence?

c. Is someone who opts for alternative medicine doing something comparable to someone who uses faith healing? Is it on a par with someone who just refuses all treatments, including preventive care?

d. In thinking about vaccination, we need to think in terms of *risks* as well as harms. It helps to recognize responsibilities in addition to those of avoiding di-

rect infliction of harm. Of almost as great significance is the avoidance of causing people *increased risk* of harm. Thus, to supplement the famous exhortation
from traditional medical ethics, "First, do no harm," we should consider
adding a new maxim, "Second of all, minimize risk." What are the implications of this for other areas of health care?

6.4   VACCINATION 3

Vaccination Scenario 3: Ms. D, the mother of an infant and a three-year-old, does
not trust makers of vaccines. She asserts that a number of those who advocate
vaccines receive money from the companies that make the vaccines.

a. An empirical question: To what extent are Ms. D's claims true?

b. An empirical question answerable by social/behavioral science studies: To what
   extent are people who influence medical opinion in positions that either are or
   appear to be influenced by financial considerations?

c. A very general question involving complex empirical and value dimensions:
   How can we determine the extent of compromise of scientific research and of
   clinical judgment by conflict of interest?

d. Should reasons count? That is, should people's reasons for their refusal of vaccination (or other treatments) be relevant to such refusals' ethical acceptability?
   Which of the following seems more plausible?

   i. *Reasons should count:* Religious and philosophical reasons are recognized,
      legally, in many states, as permissible exemptions to accusations of neglect—
      based on the importance of freedom of conscience and belief.

   ii. *Reasons should not count:* Reasons are not central to determining whether
       something is committing child abuse or neglect; only the behavior toward
       the child is.

e. The "free rider" problem and herd immunity. A valuable concept about infectious diseases is *herd immunity:* that a population can be safe from infection as
   long as most of the members of that population (whether a herd of cattle or a
   large group of children) are immunized, especially for live virus vaccines, such
   as polio and MMR (measles, mumps, and rubella). This allows for a few members to avoid immunization; but are those who do so—for whatever reasons—
   being "free riders," benefiting from the actions of others although they do not
   contribute?

6.5   REALITY TV: COVERT SURVEILLANCE
TO PROTECT A CHILD

Ms. A has generated suspicions because her hospitalized daughter has several times
become more seriously ill after Ms. A's visits. A nurse observed Ms. A giving a pill to
the child. The hospital's staff now believe that the mother is displaying Munchausen's
syndrome by proxy, a behavior pattern involving infliction of harm to a patient to
gain access to and attention from the medical system. To confirm their suspicions, the

hospital staff begins, unobtrusively, to observe the mother when she visits. Finally, they allow placement of a hidden video camera in the daughter's room.

a. Should the morality of observing the mother depend on the actual outcome? That is, would it be perceived as more justified if they caught her inducing illness and less justified if they did not?

b. Does either the unannounced extra observation or the use of the hidden camera represent an unacceptable violation of Ms. A's privacy?

c. Does one who authorizes health care treatments also, perhaps tacitly, assent to a decrease of privacy? If so, should the decreased expectation of privacy apply not only to the patient but also to visitors?

d. Would the permissibility of the surveillance depend on how serious the threat is to the patient's health (for example, to save the child's life)?

e. Suppose Ms. A begins to suspect that she is being observed and confronts the nursing staff about her suspicions. How should the nurses respond? Do the nurses at that point have a moral obligation to disclose their suspicions to Ms. A and the fact that they have been both overtly and covertly scrutinizing her behavior?

f. Should they confront Mrs. A before beginning the surveillance?

6.6   INCEST AND CONFIDENTIALITY

Mr. G, thirty-one years old, confides to his clinical psychologist that he has molested his ten-year-old daughter. He says that he no longer does so and would like help in controlling his urges. Should the therapist report the man? To what extent does the therapist have any *moral* responsibilities other than those required by the law?

a. Suppose the man says that the molestation occurred ten years ago. Three years ago. Six months ago. Suppose the man says that he is currently molesting his daughter.

b. Suppose the man is seeing the therapist for something unrelated to the molestation.

c. Suppose he has not molested his daughter, but admits that he has barely managed to restrain himself so far, and he is worried that he may do so in the future.

d. Suppose father and daughter are older: the daughter is twenty-one and consents to the relationship. In what sense is her consent problematic?

e. Suppose instead he confesses to having raped women. Would this confession be completely different with regard to the ethics of confidentiality?

6.7   A MOTHER DEMANDS CONTRACEPTION FOR HER DAUGHTER

Twelve-year-old N comes to the clinic with her mother. The mother requests that N be given a long-acting contraceptive (DepoProvera). She says that N has a boyfriend, that she found them kissing, and that she does not want the daughter to get pregnant. She has another daughter, age fourteen, who just had a baby. The twelve-year-old says that she does not need birth control and that she and her boyfriend have agreed not to "go all the way." The mother says that she will sue you if, as a consequence of your refusal to give her daughter DepoProvera, N gets pregnant. Should you give the DepoProvera? Why?

Suppose the following instead:

a. The case involves Norplant (effective for five years) rather than DepoProvera (good for three months).

b. N is fourteen rather than twelve, or N is sixteen.

c. N is sixteen and already has one child she has trouble caring for.

d. N is eighteen. Though she is legally an adult, her mother appears to be pressuring her into the idea.

e. The mother's boyfriend is pressuring her into obtaining the long-acting contraceptive for N.

f. If one rejects all abortions, should one also find contraception unacceptable?

6.8   AN ADOLESCENT ASKS FOR INFORMATION

J is a sixteen-year-old boy dying from cancer. The parents have strongly urged you not to tell the child of his poor prognosis. You feel some responsibility to the parents and to the child as well. Suppose now that you are alone with J in his hospital room and he asks you, point-blank, "Am I going to die?"

a. What *should* you say? What *would* you say?

Suppose the following instead:

b. J is fourteen years old. He is twelve years old.

c. J seems emotionally immature for his age.

d. He is of less than normal intelligence for his age (slightly or somewhat or significantly).

e. J does not actually ask you whether he is dying.

6.9   THE MORAL EQUIVALENT OF ADVANCE DIRECTIVES FOR CHILDREN

Advance directives—living wills and durable powers of attorney for health care—enable people to specify either what sorts of treatment to provide or withhold (if the former document) or who shall decide one's treatment (if the latter document) in the event of one becoming incapacitated. They thus enable one's wishes for oneself to extend past the point when one would ordinarily have such a power. Both types of legal instruments assume that one *was*, when completing them, fully competent to do so. What, though, of children—people who have not yet attained the legal point of competence? They are minors and so require proxy decision makers (parents or guardians) to decide for them.

Ten-year-old C has a form of lymphocytic leukemia quite likely to result in her death within the next few years. Her loving parents have always tried to provide the type of care that would be in her best interests. As a result of her numerous hospitalizations and other frequent exposures to the health care system, she has experienced tenfold, medically, what most people do during their entire lives. She understands her disease and prognosis and has a fairly clear idea of what each of the treatment (or nontreatment) options entails. She is intelligent and informed and wants to have a say in her own treatment plan. She completes, with the assistance of her parents and advice of her physicians and nurses, a document that she wants to stand as a statement of her wishes—her counterpart of a living will. All involved understand that, technically, it is not a legal document, but they want to view it as the *moral equivalent* of a living will.

- a. Is such a document meaningful and defensible, or is it merely a way of people indulging the dreams of a young girl?
- b. Suppose one or both of her parents change their minds about some aspect of the document. Although the document has no legal validity, should the parental wishes or the child's wishes be allowed, morally, to prevail? Or would this depend on what the wishes were?
- c. What are the pros and cons of having such documents?

6.10   A PREGNANT TEEN WITH HODGKIN'S DISEASE

Y, a sixteen-year-old in her first pregnancy, is carrying twins of fifteen to sixteen weeks' gestational age. After a few weeks of symptoms, she is diagnosed, upon biopsy, with Hodgkin's disease. Typical treatment includes both chemotherapy and radiation therapy. Treatment would result in spontaneous abortion or at least very likely serious anomalies for the twins.

The patient is given four options:

- ✦ Have an abortion and full therapy
- ✦ Keep the pregnancy and only a (shielded) form of radiation therapy
- ✦ Have the full therapy (both chemo-and radiotherapy)
- ✦ Withhold all treatments, and let nature take its course

Pursuing full therapy would almost certainly result in future infertility. The twins' father is unknown and, as far as can be determined, not involved in the situation. The patient decides to pursue only the shielded radiotherapy.

- a. Whose *interests* need to be considered in the health workers' decisions? Just the pregnant woman's? The fetuses'? The family's? The twins' father's? Why?
- b. Whose *wishes* need to be considered? Why?
- c. Assuming the girl is mentally competent, should she be given the final say in the decision making? Are sixteen-years-olds generally of sufficient intelligence and maturity to make informed decisions about their care? If so, should they be given the legal power to do so?
- d. Are all four options acceptable, or should one or more have been omitted from the list of permissible choices? Should a fifth choice have been added to the list?

6.11 RESUSCITATION OF A VERY PREMATURE INFANT

Baby F, a twenty-four-week gestational age infant, is admitted to the neonatal intensive care unit. She had been resuscitated at birth. Given the baby's level of development, apparent age, and various diagnostic signs, it appears that she has less than a 5 percent chance of survival. If she does survive, it is highly probable that she will suffer from bronchopulmonary dysplasia (a serious condition of the respiratory system), mental disabilities ranging from developmental delay to severe retardation, and quite possibly blindness. On the other hand, some infants in this category survive comparatively unaffected. (See also cases 14.10 and 14.11, page 125).

a. Should there be a cutoff point or threshold below which aggressive treatment ought not to be used, or does any situation with a possibility—no matter how slight—of benefit warrant full use of resources? If there is such a threshold, how should it be formulated: in terms of age, likelihood of survival, or likelihood of health or developmental problems?

b. If there is such a cutoff point (or collection of factors), how should it be implemented? Consider some possibilities. Is any of these best?

  i. No infants below that point may receive more than comfort care.

  ii. Parents should decide whether to have such children receive care.

  iii. Health workers should try to dissuade parents from using aggressive means to sustain the child.

  iv. Such care would not qualify for reimbursement.

  v. Parents should be provided with all the facts, but then allowed to decide without any further attempts to guide their decision.

c. Are parents equipped to make such difficult decisions? Might they decide for the wrong reasons, either for or against treatment?

d. Should parents be urged or pressured to make certain decisions, or should information just be presented to them in a "value-free" manner?

CHAPTER 7

Mental Health Contexts

PATERNALISM

In mental health contexts, questions about paternalism, or acting to protect someone independent of what that person wants, arise. This derives from the fact that the patients' disorders or problems may result in impaired autonomy, a diminished ability to decide what is in their own best interest. Because judgments about what health care options to consent to can be complex, they ideally require a fully functioning mind and a balanced personality.

Psychologists, psychiatrists, psychiatric nurses, and psychiatric social workers all find themselves in such complex, difficult problem situations. Some clients or patients have minimal apparent contact with reality in their thinking. The patients may also lack the ability to take care of themselves. This would apply, for example, to people with profound retardation or some psychoses. Others might be partly impaired, although not completely incapacitated. They present other dilemmas. They would benefit from treatment, yet forcing treatment on them represents a method of last resort.

WHICH SELF? WHAT RESPONSIBILITY?

Other vexing questions exist of how to make sense of concepts of personal identity, responsibility, and autonomy in people who have some unusual neurological, psychiatric, or psychological conditions that cause them to lack the ordinary unity of self or continuity of self-control. In which of their states, if any, should we accept their consent or refusal of treatment? To what extent should we hold them accountable for their actions if they are unable to understand or control what they are doing?

THE MENTAL AND THE PHYSICAL

We need to clarify how concepts of disease, illness, and health apply to the psychological realm. Although in an important sense mental disorders *are* at the same time physical, the causation and proper treatments in many instances can differ from those of most sorts of physical illnesses. In addition, it is vital to recognize the many and complex ways in which the mind and body influence each other, from psychosomatic symptoms and diseases, to placebo effects, to the value of psychotherapies. They also include disorders and diseases caused by neurochemical imbalances and neurological malfunctions, as well as psychotropic medications that can help manage mental disorders.

7.1 DIAGNOSING AND TREATING ADHD

Eight-year-old A seems to bubble over with energy. His parents are overwhelmed by his apparent inability to sit still and do quiet activities. He earns mediocre grades. His teachers report that he appears easily distractible and is "always on recess." Several of the other children in his grade have been diagnosed as having ADHD (attention deficit hyperactivity disorder) and so take daily doses of methylphenidate (Ritalin—a psychostimulant that helps most of those with that disorder). The boy's doctor, at the urging of the parents and supported by the teachers, prescribes Ritalin, and it seems to improve A's behavior in school and at home.

a. According to the official criteria, which are somewhat flexible, the person must often exhibit six of a list of the behavioral symptoms to be labeled as having ADHD. If A shows only four or five of those symptoms, does this mean that he is misdiagnosed?

b. How can we determine whether it is the parents' and teachers' concerns that are being "diagnosed" more than the child's behavior problem? Should the doctor investigate the home life for evidence of other factors that may contribute to the child's condition before prescribing a drug for him? If so, would this require that the physician become a social worker?

c. Should this condition be diagnosed only by specially trained psychologists or psychiatrists?

d. Does the fact that people too often seek exclusively pharmacological solutions to complex problems mean that the boy should not be getting the Ritalin? Does the fact that some drugs are abused or over-prescribed mean that the Ritalin is unwarranted?

e. Does the fact that the drug appears to improve the boy's behavior—to curb his bursts of energy and distractibility—mean that he does in fact have ADHD?

f. Suppose the parents allow A to constantly watch television and play video games, at least for as long as he concentrates on them. Would it be permissible for the doctor to require changes at home before he will treat the child with Ritalin?

7.2   PATERNALISM AND AGORAPHOBIA

Mrs. L has grown increasingly housebound during the past two years with agoraphobic symptoms. Agoraphobia, classified as an anxiety disorder, results in overwhelming feelings of panic at the prospect of leaving home. Mrs. L refuses any sort of treatment, including behavioral methods. Her situation has now begun to threaten her marriage.

   a. If her ability to understand reality seems largely unimpaired, does that morally prevent people from acting in her behalf against her wishes?
   b. Psychiatric paternalistic interventions, done to benefit people irrespective of their wishes, are based on likelihood of danger to self or others. Can the jeopardizing of Mrs. L's marriage be thought of as falling within this category?
   c. Suppose she has a job—presumably at her home—and it was also in jeopardy. In what sense are threats to a person's happiness or ability to function as he or she wishes properly judged "dangers" rather than merely significant harms?
   d. Is the standard of "danger," sometimes interpreted as risk to life or limb, too narrow? Or is it necessary to have such a narrow test to prevent others from meddling in life choices with which others may happen to disagree?

7.3   PATERNALISM AND A DANGEROUS ANOREXIA

T, age twenty-one, has a four-year history of anorexia. She is seriously underweight, exercises compulsively, uses laxatives, and has amenorrhea (has stopped menstruating). She refuses admission to the hospital and asserts that she is "too fat."

   a. Would you wait until her condition is imminently life threatening before hospitalizing her or treating her involuntarily? If so, why should that be the criterion for deciding when paternalism is acceptable?
   b. If her being twenty-one would deter you from treating her paternalistically, then at what lower age *would* it become acceptable? Seventeen? If so, why then? Does your moral judgment in this case correspond exactly to whatever your area's law specifies for people to be treated as adults?
   c. Should her family's opinions be considered in deciding how to proceed?
   d. Should the fact that this disorder is, in part, caused by society having an ideal of beauty that is unattainable for most women inform or affect your beliefs about other ethical aspects of the situation?

7.4   PATERNALISM AND SEVERE DEPRESSION

Mr. E suffers from severe depression but states firmly that he does not want psychiatric help, although it would very likely help him. Legally, he cannot be treated unless he is declared incompetent or poses a danger to himself or others.

   a. Should this legal condition be changed, or is it a helpful safeguard against abuse by those who would treat people involuntarily for the wrong reasons?

b. Suppose he has a psychotic disorder, such as schizophrenia, instead. As a result, he is unable to get or to keep a job. Should he then be involuntarily treated? Does inability to maintain employment constitute danger to self or others?

c. What is the difference between being partly incapacitated, or functioning in an impaired manner, and being a danger to oneself? How great must a harm be, and how imminent, to be deemed dangerous? Is the dangerousness standard too strict for involuntary treatment, or is it justified, given the importance of respecting people's autonomy?

d. To what extent should friends, family, and health workers pressure or otherwise try to persuade the person to try various treatments?

e. What should be done about a street person who talks to herself, sometimes shouts at passersby, excretes in alleyways, and scavenges in dumpsters to survive? Assume she poses no known risk to anyone, but makes people uncomfortable.

7.5   NOT GUILTY BY REASON OF INSANITY? EXPERT TESTIMONY

Mr. M, twenty-six years old, has a history of psychosis. For more than eight years, he has had difficulty thinking systematically for sustained periods of time. Almost daily he has had unpredictable outbursts of incoherent rambling. A few years ago, he was placed on an antipsychotic drug. His condition improved markedly, but only until he stopped taking the drug a few months later. Since that time he has received no sustained psychiatric treatment. A year ago, he assaulted someone at a bus stop. He had approached the man and accused him of trying to rob him.

At Mr. M's trial, the prosecution argued that he had been guilty of assault and deserved to be punished—partly because he had done something wrong, partly because he needed to be kept away from society, and partly because the court needed to send a message that assaulting people will not be tolerated. They added that, whatever his problems, he clearly knew that he was attacking and hurting someone and that he was not doing so in self-defense.

A psychiatrist, Dr. P, testifies for the defense. She argues that Mr. M's condition is a disorder arising from an organic brain malfunction. Mr. M simply did not appreciate the criminality of what he was doing, and, to the extent that he did, he could not control his behavior. He was in the grip of a neurochemical imbalance. Although society might see fit to impose a sort of treatment on him for its protection, it could not find him guilty of acting with a criminal intent since he was, under the law's concept, insane—and thus not properly criminally responsible.

a. Which side *should* prevail? Is the more persuasive side best understood as a clinical, social, moral, or legal reason? Or is it some combination of the preceding sorts of reasons?

b. What are the strengths and weaknesses of the arguments on each side?

c. Insanity defenses hold, more or less, that someone is not guilty of a crime if she or he, at the time, and due to a mental disorder, either could not appreciate the act's criminality or could not control the behavior. Is this notion basically sound? (Note that insanity is not, itself, a medical or psychological notion. It is a legal one, with medical judgments and diagnoses used to judge the defendant's mental state.)

7.6   PREVENTION OF A POSSIBLE (BUT NOT PROBABLE) SUICIDE

Mr. O suffers from bipolar disorder, which includes periods of deep depression during which he occasionally has thoughts of suicide. When he mentions to his psychiatrist, Dr. V, that he had earlier that day considered suicide, Dr. V. has him institutionalized for seventy-two hours. The psychiatrist has to judge the likelihood of a suicide attempt, as well as the likelihood of its success. He believes, without quantifying it as such, that there is about a 3 percent likelihood that Mr. O will actually attempt suicide. He also believes that there is only a 10 percent likelihood that the attempt would be effective. He believes, however, that the likelihood is sufficiently great that it is worth depriving Mr. O of his freedom temporarily to decrease the probabilities.

   a. Did Dr. V do the right thing, morally?
   b. The decision of balancing someone else's life with that person's liberty, each conditioned by probability estimates, is a clinical judgment that is also a moral judgment. How should those who have the power to judge about life and liberty decide?
   c. What threshold of probability sounds about right for involuntary intervention? Ten percent likelihood of suicide attempt? One percent? Less? More?
   d. Since suicide attempts also have other consequences, ranging from harm to a person's reputation to serious physical harm, how should those be factored in?

7.7   REFUSING INVESTIGATION OF POSSIBLE CANCER

Mrs. X, age forty-seven, refuses investigation of a breast lump discovered on a routine screening. She does not show evidence of any mental disorders except for the seemingly irrational refusal of further investigation.

   a. Does the fact that Mrs. X consented to the screening constitute evidence that she really does want further health information?
   b. Is her refusal of investigation sufficiently bizarre or irrational that she can be diagnosed as suffering from an incapacitating psychiatric disorder and thus labeled as mentally incompetent? Is her refusal evidence that she poses a threat to herself and so can be judged incompetent?
   c. Should family, friends, and/or health workers just accept the woman's wishes, or should they actively try to persuade her to have investigational workups?

7.8   FINE-TUNING THE PSYCHE

Mr. L works hard but is less productive than he would like to be at his job. He approaches his doctor with a request for a prescription for a drug that will affect his brain's chemistry in such a way that Mr. L will work more effectively. The doctor feels uncomfortable with this request, and so he refers Mr. L to a psychiatrist, Dr. G.

a. Is it morally wrong to prescribe a drug or treatment if a patient is not suffering from an illness or injury? Would the psychiatrist be indulging wishes rather than treating illness?

b. Is the enhancement of functioning an acceptable goal for health care professionals? Who should be permitted to determine which enhancements, if any, are acceptable? Should patients have some input about this?

c. Would it be unprofessional for Dr. G to diagnose Mr. L as having an anxiety disorder or mild depression to justify prescribing the drug? Why?

d. Dr. G needs to decide whether Mr. L has a mental disorder, and, if so, what his diagnosis is before he can prescribe any medication. Unfortunately, none of the standard classifications seems applicable to Mr. L's case. Should this automatically prevent Dr. G from prescribing anything?

e. Suppose Mr. L's work had been assessed as marginal, and he had reason to think that his continued employment depended on an increased performance level at work. Would this change the ethics of the situation?

f. Suppose instead of work enhancement Mr. L sought help for enhancement of his sense of well-being. Would that be less ethically acceptable? If so, why? If heightening one's sense of well-being seems questionable, then would it be wrong for the psychiatrist to recommend that Mr. L try a glass of wine after getting home from work?

g. How should we think about the rightness or wrongness of prescribing, recommending, or making use of the following?

   i. The drug Viagra.

   ii. Human growth hormones in people of different heights.

   iii. Germ-line treatments to eliminate diseases or to enhance people's lives.

h. Should only physicians be permitted to prescribe drugs? Some psychologists have argued that they should be allowed to prescribe for some sorts of mental disorders that they treat. Would this be acceptable or irresponsible? What factual information might enable one to decide these questions?

7.9 PSYCHOACTIVE DRUGS FOR YOUNG CHILDREN

Five-year-old K has an antidepressant prescribed for her, since she has moderately severe symptoms of depression. The drug has been tested on and approved for children, but not yet for children as young as K.

Six-year-old L has an antidepressant prescribed for him, since he is part of a trial of an antidepressant that has not yet been approved for use with children. The drug has, however, been tested on and approved as safe and effective for adults.

a. Is there something questionable about prescribing drugs for children when the drugs have not yet been tested or approved for that age group? Or would it be more ethically questionable *not* to prescribe the medication if in fact many people already prescribe it, with apparently good results, for children with the condition?

b. Suppose L goes through the "washout" period of two weeks without any medication, so that his system will not contain any significant amounts of other medications. Although this is an important part of the research methodology, is it ethically troubling to deprive the child of beneficial medicine if discontinuing the drug during that period will increase his unhappiness and his risk of attempting suicide?

c. Suppose L is in the control group that receives a placebo instead of the antidepressant being tested. This would probably prolong the time during which the child would suffer from the depression. Would that represent a wrongful neglect of the child's well-being?

d. If the circumstances mentioned above in (b) and (c) seem to make such research wrong, what alternative exists for proving the safety and effectiveness of drugs for children?

e. If the drugs have not yet been fully tested on children, then is their use less than fully supported scientifically?

f. Would the answers to these questions be different if the drug was an antibiotic and the illness a life-threatening infection known to be resistant to all other antibiotics? Why, or why not?

7.10   MENTAL HEALTH PARITY

Behavioral Wellness Associates provides mental health care with its staff of psychologists, psychiatrists, psychiatric nurses, and psychiatric social workers. They receive limited reimbursement under most insurance plans. Mr. W, a spokesman for one insurance company, Cosmopolitan Life, says, off the record, that the cost effectiveness and justifiability of such treatments can not be adequately assured. Members of a mental health advocacy group reject the claims of the spokesman and object that the insurers are discriminating against those who already suffer from stigmatizing illnesses.

Examine, with the use of the accompanying questions, the plausibility of each of the four reasons given by Mr. W to oppose mental health parity.

a. Mental disorders are more fuzzy than "medical" health problems, since psychological problems have less distinctive diagnostic criteria and are not as objectively definable.

   i. Clarify: Which psychiatric disorders? Which "medical" disorders?

   ii. Look at the latest DSM (Diagnostic and Statistical Manual of Mental Disorders) for lists of diagnostic criteria and decision trees. Are the diagnostic criteria indeed "fuzzy" for all mental disorders? For most? For many? Do only mental disorders have such fuzziness?

b. Treatments for many disorders, such as psychotherapies, might last for years with minimal effectiveness.

   i. Are there analogous situations for nonpsychiatric medicine?

   ii. If it is indeed true, what would follow, ethically, about these treatments? Which can be effective?

c. There are insufficient outcome measures, so we often can not evaluate the effectiveness of mental health treatments.

    i. Again, are there analogous situations for nonpsychiatric medicine?

    ii. Does anything prevent such outcome measures from being assessed?

d. Mental and behavioral health problems are often considered conditions that are self-inflicted and/or matters of character rather than pathology.

    i. Aren't mental illnesses matters of pathology rather than of flawed character?

    ii. Can something be both caused by one's behavior and also an illness in need of treatment?

    iii. Aren't sports injuries and heart disease often caused by risky behaviors? Medical therapies for these are covered by insurance. Is there a morally relevant difference between these two classes of cases?

CHAPTER 8

Valid Informed Consent and Compliance Problems

VALID INFORMED CONSENT

Authentic informed consent—both legally and morally—requires more than that one go through the motions of orally assenting or signing a written form. It also presupposes:

+ that the written and/or verbal behavior be given by someone mentally competent to consent,

+ that it occur after adequate disclosure of relevant information sufficient to enable a decision about treatment,

+ that the person consenting has actually understood the information, and

+ that the consent be given without compromised voluntariness of judgment.

Each of these conditions has been the subject of some unclarity and debate. As one example, the notion of mental competence is not completely unambiguous. Apart from the fact that there are legal and moral/conceptual concepts of competence, people have proposed a number of conceptual criteria, and legal jurisdictions have recognized different criteria for determining whether someone should be judged legally competent. Without presuming to disregard the controversies, we might think of it as having an adequate ability to comprehend relevant information and to make effective judgments about oneself.

As is seen in this book's chapters about research, pediatric contexts, and mental health contexts, each of these four necessary conditions of valid consent may fail to occur in a variety of ways. Indeed, given the importance of these four conditions, it appears that a significant portion of health care is delivered without true informed consent.

NONCOMPLIANCE

In health care, it often happens—some studies say between a third and half the time—that patients do not follow instructions, for example, to take medication as prescribed. This happens sometimes even when the person has a serious illness, such as tuberculosis. How to determine responsibility for noncompliance and how to encourage behaviors more conducive to good health without being excessively coercive are some of the difficult questions.

8.1   BEING ASKED "WHAT WOULD YOU DO?"

Nurse S has worked on a hematology/oncology unit for eight years and finds that she often encounters a difficult situation. The cancer patients, or their families, when struggling with a difficult decision about which of several treatment options to accept, will ask her, "What would *you* do?" The physicians and nurses with whom she works also find themselves confronted with this question. In fact, a few of them will even volunteer their perspective, without first being asked, when they think that their guidance of the patients' decisions would help.

- a. Should health workers offer their opinions in situations of this sort? Does it risk improperly influencing patients' decision making?
- b. Does it make a difference whether one has been asked for one's opinion?
- c. Is there a difference between saying, "What would you recommend for me?" and "What would you do if you were in my situation?"? Might there be at least some instances in which a person would recommend a course of action for someone else, even though she might not choose it for herself if faced with that situation?
- d. Should health workers be completely nondirective, mostly nondirective, somewhat directive, or very directive toward patients' decision making? Why? Might it depend on the sort of situation?
- e. Is stating what one would do in similar circumstances merely offering information? What might a physician or nurse reasonably infer about the influence of such information?
- f. Might the recommended decision be different if the patient's care is government funded and there are cost control incentives? Suppose compensation is related to the decision the person recommends. Might that encourage a conscious or unconscious bias?

8.2   IRRATIONAL TREATMENT REFUSAL IN AN EMERGENCY

A man, H, who looks to be in his thirties, appears in an emergency room. He is only partly helpful in responding to questions about his symptoms and health history. H is perspiring profusely, vomiting, and has low blood pressure and shortness of breath. When the team attempts to do various diagnostic tests such as drawing blood, he refuses to allow them to do so. The staff are unable to ascertain the reason for the refusal. H seems mentally competent in many ways but is behaving very irrationally, in a manner that could jeopardize his health or life if not quickly and accurately diagnosed.

a. Emergencies represent a class of situations in which usual informed consent expectations are decreased, because of the urgency, lack of time to attempt to persuade, and the potential for irreversible bad outcomes. For example, a person might die if he does not get the necessary life-saving treatment immediately. In what circumstances, then, should health workers be permitted to disregard patients' refusal of otherwise medically indicated treatment?

b. Should H be treated against his expressed wishes during emergencies only in imminently life-threatening circumstances? What about situations in which a body part, such as an arm or an ear, or the person's health condition would be placed in serious jeopardy instead?

c. Does the reason for the irrationality or the sort of irrationality matter? Suppose H's refusal of treatment does not reflect his or her usual values about wanting to remain alive.

d. Can the refusal be construed as strong evidence that the person is mentally incompetent? Or would that involve presumptuous, circular reasoning?

e. Is the combination of gravity and irreversibility sufficient to treat H involuntarily, at least temporarily?

f. Is his presence in the emergency room reason to presume that he wants care and thus de facto consents to treatment? What might be a problem with such an inference?

8.3   A MILDLY MENTALLY RETARDED PATIENT CONSENTS

Mr. J, thirty-one years old and mildly retarded, has a job and lives independently. Although he has learned to perform the activities needed to get by, he has difficulty performing cognitive tasks of some complexity. He takes his asthma medication daily and can get help when he suffers an acute episode. He has recently been diagnosed as having major depression but as yet has not received effective treatment for that disorder. One night Mr. J tells his neighbor that his "stomach hurts bad." The neighbor brings him to the emergency room, where health workers decide to schedule a gastroscopy, an invasive procedure. Mr. J must sign an informed consent for the procedure. The consent form specifies risks, benefits, and alternatives. Mr. J doesn't seem to understand all the information but is willing to sign the form to get on with the procedure.

a. Is encouraging Mr. J to sign the equivalent of railroading him into accepting treatment?

b. Should the health workers take special efforts to make sure he understands everything on the form? What if he has difficulty doing so?

c. If Mr. J has a lower level of cognitive functioning, then to what extent and in what senses can he provide truly valid informed consent?

d. Might Mr. J's mood disorder (the depression) further impair his ability to judge soundly?

e. Would people's judgment of Mr. J's ability or competence to consent depend on whether he made what seemed the right decision? Thus, suppose he refused a treatment that everyone agrees is medically indicated.

8.4 SUSPICIONS ABOUT SUBSTANCES

Nurse W notes that patient Y twice mentioned that she had taken an over-the-counter (OTC) appetite suppressant. Y has also shown evidence of nervousness, mood swings, and accelerated heart rate. Nurse W suspects that the physical and psychological changes may result from excessive, continued use of the drug. Y seems reluctant to discuss it, however.

a. Suppose, instead, Nurse W suspected Y of using controlled substances. Would that change the ethics of what should be done?

b. Assuming that Y is a minor, does nurse W have a moral obligation to disclose to Y's parents that Y is taking the OTC drug? Would it matter if Y prefaced her disclosure with a request for confidentiality?

c. Would it be acceptable for Nurse W to speak to Y's parents about Y's general health without mentioning her OTC drug use? Suppose the parents suspect Y is using diet pills and ask Nurse W her opinion as to this possibility. How should W handle her obligation to Y in this situation?

8.5 A RELATIVE'S CONSENT FOR AN UNWANTED PROCEDURE

Mrs. J, a seventy-eight-year-old with moderately severe dementia, says she doesn't want surgery to repair her broken left femur (in the leg above the knee). She does not seem to understand that she has broken a bone and thinks that she will be able to walk the next day. Her daughter says that her mother had tried to avoid going to doctors, had always especially opposed invasive medical interventions, and had said that she did not want to die in the hospital. The daughter, told by the surgeon that her mother is not mentally competent, reluctantly signs the consent form for the surgery. The surgery shortens the likely time until ability to walk from eight to three weeks, but it poses a 2 percent perioperative (around the time of the operation) death risk.

a. Consider two of the main standards for judgment as applied to Mrs. J:

i. The *substituted judgment standard*: People should decide based on Mrs. J's own values and her typical thought processes, from when she was fully competent.

ii. The *best-interests standard*: People should decide based on their informed beliefs about Mrs. J's best interests.

Does either of these standards seem preferable as applied to Mrs. J? What might be strengths and weaknesses of the use of each sort of standard?

b. Was the surgeon right to ask the daughter to sign the consent form?

c. Suppose Mrs. J was clearly competent—not suffering from dementia—and refusing treatment. Would that affect your judgment about getting someone to authorize the surgery?

d. Suppose the two alternatives are the following. How would you judge then?
  i. Without surgery she would require eight weeks of hospitalization.

  ii. With surgery she would be able to walk *at home* within three weeks.

8.6   OMITTING QUANTITATIVE MENTION OF DEGREE OF UNCERTAINTY

As part of the decision making for a patient with heart valve malfunction, various treatment options are presented. The alternatives are presented in qualitative terms: alternative X *might* have various risks and benefits, and alternative Y has other *possible* risks and benefits. There is minimal specific information about *probabilities* of the risks and benefits, and the physician does not mention that he has considerable uncertainty about the likelihoods of the possible results. These uncertainties derive partly from the complexities of this patient's situation and partly from the inconclusiveness of the studies that have appeared so far in the literature.

a. Assuming the patient could understand the quantitative information, is it acceptable to present the options only qualitatively?

b. How much specificity of information should a requirement of informed consent, when adhered to authentically, obligate one to disclose?

c. If the physician neglects to mention the range of uncertainty of the information because of a wish to avoid confusing or alarming the patient, is that an instance of paternalism? Are patients entitled to know about uncertainties?

d. Is some withholding information intended to be a sort of placebo effect? That is, might patients be assumed to do better if kept unaware of the uncertainty?

8.7   A PATIENT DOESN'T REMEMBER CONSENT SPECIFICS

Mrs. F, forty-one years old, has consented to a biopsy, signing an informed consent form. When she awakens from the anesthesia, she discovers that the surgeon had decided to perform a hysterectomy because he believed it should be done, because there was evidence of malignancy in her reproductive tract and because, at her age, she was unlikely to have further children. Mrs. F does not feel that she fully appreciated what it was that she had signed.

a. How much information about contingencies ought to have been disclosed to Mrs. F?

b. In what way should the information have been communicated? A written form? An oral explanation? A pamphlet? A video? Perhaps some combination of these?

c. How should those obtaining consent assure themselves that a patient truly understands and appreciates the situation and decision?

d. If the patient had been fourteen years old should she then have been excluded from the decision-making process?

e. What if she had been severely depressed, or learning disabled? Should there be additional safeguards then?

f. Might the patient have been more likely to have been informed if the decision had been a controversial one—with more than one course of action judged acceptable—within the profession? Ought she to have been? Should uncertainty be communicated to the patient?

g. How often do patients actually give truly valid informed consent? Is this a serious problem?

8.8   TREATMENT DECISION UNDER STRESS

Ms. K, who is forty-six years old and has four children ages five to fourteen, has recently learned that she may need to have surgery on her thyroid because of endocrine problems and a suspicious lump in her neck. Her illness has her very worried, which is compounded by the fact that some of the effects of the endocrine imbalance include mood swings. She now has the further anxiety about the prospect of having cancer.

Her companion, Mr. M, tries to help out with the children but does not prove very effective. The children are an energetic bunch who are uncomfortable with Mr. M. He communicates to Ms. K that the children are veering out of control. Ms. K has to decide what to elect: an experimental drug, surgery, or no treatment. She is worried, pressured, and uncomfortable and does not ask any questions about the alternatives that her doctor has tried to explain to her. Although her doctor, Dr. E, has recommended the surgery, Ms. K says that she can't afford to be away from her children that long.

a. If the combination of stress-producing factors creates a likelihood of an unwise decision by Ms. K, should her doctor try to counteract that by redirecting Ms. K's decision?

b. Does the sum of psychological and physiological forces acting on Ms. K render her less competent to decide about a proper treatment choice? How different is it from the situation of someone with severe depression, obsessive-compulsive disorder, or a decision-impairing brain tumor?

c. Would it be morally wrong for Dr. E to contact Mr. M and try to persuade him to guide Ms. K's decision? How ought we to distinguish between unwarranted intrusion in a person's decisions and helpful advocacy for a patient's health?

8.9   NONCOMPLIANCE AND PRESSURE

Mr. B, fifty-six years old, has moderate hypertension. Dr. A, who provides treatment for him at a clinic, prescribes a beta-blocker. When the blood pressure remains high, Dr. A increases the dosage. Meanwhile, Mr. B refuses to stop smoking. He has been told that it is important for him to give up smoking, yet he does not do so.

a. Should our judgment of Mr. B's behavior depend on how addictive nicotine is? On how vulnerable Mr. B is to this addiction?

b. If Mr. B is less than fully compliant with the regimen recommended for him, should we hold him morally blameworthy?

c. Would it be acceptable for Dr. A to make further treatment contingent on Mr. B's smoking cessation? On Mr. B's attempting to stop smoking?

d. How much pressure or urging by Dr. A is allowable?

e. Suppose Mr. B claims to have quit smoking, but his blood pressure remains high, and he smells of cigarettes when he visits Dr. A. Would it be acceptable for Dr. A to covertly monitor his blood for nicotine to determine whether he has indeed quit smoking? Would it make a difference if the drug Dr. A prescribes for Mr. B is dangerous when combined with nicotine?

8.10   RESPONSES TO NONCOMPLIANCE

Mr. Z, age sixty-three, has a prescription for a medication that has been found highly effective at preventing recurrences of heart attacks, provided it is taken regularly. Although the drug must be taken twice daily, Mr. Z takes it only intermittently. His physician, Dr. H, emphasizes the importance of taking a pill twice a day, explaining that, though not directly harmful, it is just not effective unless taken properly. Mr. Z says that he is sometimes "too busy" to do so, and it sometimes just slips his mind.

a. What options does Dr. H have? What sort of relationship does he have with Mr. Z? How extensively and clearly has Dr. H explained the situation to the patient? How aggressive should Dr. H be in his behavior toward Mr. Z?

b. Suppose the drug were an antipsychotic, and inconsistent use would result in Mr. Z losing touch with reality. What methods should Dr. H use to increase the likelihood of Mr. Z's compliance with the treatment plan?

c. Suppose Mr. Z only needed to come in for an injection every two weeks, but he doesn't show up for an appointment.

d. Suppose instead of placing Mr. Z at increased risk for a heart attack, it were insulin, and Mr. Z would almost certainly go into insulin shock, rather than just being at increased risk.

e. If Mr. Z were the sole means of support of a large family, would that support a different judgment than if he had no family or friends?

8.11 NONCOMPLIANCE OF A TUBERCULOSIS CARRIER

Although AIDS receives a lot of attention, other public health problems also confront us with ethical dilemmas. Tuberculosis, for example, presents society with difficult questions of how to balance public health and individual rights.

Mr. T has tuberculosis, an infectious disease a person can have without the person feeling ill (such as HIV infection or hepatitis). Because some strains of TB are highly contagious, they can be spread just by casual contact with someone infected—in sharp contrast to HIV infection. To have a chance of recovery, and to avoid spreading the infection, people need to take their medication regularly for a period of six months, but Mr. T does not do so. He vacillates between claiming that he is taking the medication and saying that he can't or won't do so. His physician, the courts, and public health officers need to decide what to do about Mr. T.

  a. At what point would consideration of isolating or quarantining Mr. T become plausible? If they were to isolate or quarantine him, would his home, a hospital, or a prison be most acceptable?

  b. Should Mr. T just be sent into therapy or counseling until he becomes able and willing to comply? Or would such means cross the line into excessively draconian, totalitarian measures? Should the degree of harshness that is acceptable be a function of how much Mr. T endangers others?

  c. How might each of these additional factual assumptions influence a moral judgment about how Mr. T should be treated?

   i. Suppose Mr. T works in the food service industry.

   ii. Suppose Mr. T works as an usher at a movie theater.

   iii. Suppose Mr. T works as an elementary school teacher.

   iv. Suppose, statistically, Mr. T's work and private lives combined caused him to be likely to infect five people with tuberculosis.

CHAPTER 9

Health Care Options, Culture, and Diversity

Controversies and ambiguities exist where patients or patients' families express a preference for a choice other than what their physicians or most practitioners recommend. How should we judge the amount of diversity that is commendable, or at least reasonably permissible? Are we willing to assert that instances of reckless, underinformed, or even superstitious choices exist? Does it all come down to a matter of one person's meaningful alternative being another person's ignorant superstition?

Most people these days at least pay lip service to cultural and religious diversity. Because of the value of diversity, difficult challenges exist for those who feel some responsibility for informing and encouraging others' sound health care decision making. A person may have strong religious or spiritual beliefs that happen to depart from the consensus of contemporary practitioners. When the consequences of choosing based on the spiritual beliefs reaches a level of sufficient severity or irreversibility, health workers may find themselves tempted to try to persuade, pressure, or even coerce people into doing what they think medically indicated. Again, we have a conflict of morally important values: here, respect for others' spiritual beliefs (and practices) and concern for protecting one's patients from avoidable harm.

The cases in this chapter encourage a search for a balanced view that will do justice to diversity and tolerance, on the one hand, and responsible health care choices and practice, on the other.

9.1   CHOOSING ALTERNATIVE HEALTH CARE TREATMENTS

Miss P, twenty-eight, says she believes in the effectiveness of products purchased in health food stores and also in the services of a massage specialist who makes use of what she describes as energy field loci she had learned from traditional healers. Some of Miss P's family members believe that she should be taking medication for her high blood pressure and diabetes instead.

   a. How much responsibility ought each of the following to accept for the woman's health level:

      i. The woman herself?

      ii. The alternative practitioner?

      iii. The friends and family?

      iv. The people who manufacture, distribute, and sell the health food store products?

   b. Is there some sense in which, although ultimately and legally it is up to Miss P to choose, each of the others has some moral responsibility? Does the practitioner have a responsibility to avoid allowing unnecessary harm, and are the family and friends obligated to try to help persuade Miss P? Does each of these in turn entail obligations to educate oneself?

   c. Do those who manufacture, distribute, and sell the products sold as health foods have any moral responsibilities to avoid unfounded claims or to prevent foreseeable misuse of their products?

   d. The effectiveness of any given treatment seems to be an empirical matter. What of a chiropractor who says that he can help a woman's ovarian cancer by manipulating her spine? Is this wrong?

   e. At what point does something for which (i) one claims effectiveness and/or (ii) one sells a product or service become an activity for which one must be held accountable?

   f. Should the urgency or severity of the woman's medical condition be relevant to your responses to the prior questions?

   g. Should insurance companies provide coverage for any or all alternative treatments and practitioners?

9.2   WHAT IS QUACKERY?

Quackery is a word with strong negative connotations. It is often applied to *the practices of* those who claim to be health care professionals and who knowingly and fraudulently deceive people. Because quackery is assumed illegal as well as immoral, those who accuse other people of it themselves risk being accused of slander, libel, or just exaggeration.

Dr. U has a family practice and tells most of his patients that they need more vitamins in their diet. He recommends organic vitamins, available at a local health food store or through his office. He believes many of the "alternative" health care modalities provide a better type of treatment than much of contemporary medicine. Dr. U often uses acupuncture for anesthesia and has a coworker, Miss V, who is trained in "traditional healing arts," and who provides therapeutic touch to supplement most procedures. "I've seen it help, and it certainly can't hurt," Dr. U says. He often discourages his patients from seeking conventional medical assistance. Most doctors, he says, are just pill pushers who don't appreciate the spiritual or psychological sides of their patients.

a. How should one decide what methods are safe, reliable, and effective and what methods are not? Might traditional practitioners too quickly reject legitimate, less expensive, lower-technology treatments? On the other hand, might nontraditional practitioners exploit patients' ignorance of the scientific knowledge needed to discriminate among proposed treatments?

b. Does Dr. U sound like someone who provides a harmless, possibly beneficial alternative to other providers of health care? Or does he seem to be either a knowing or an unintentional fraud?

c. Would knowing the profitability of Dr. U's practices provide some guidance to judging his legitimacy?

d. What sorts of scientific evidence might be helpful in determining the plausibility of Dr. U's claims and practices?

e. To what extent should Dr. U provide such evidence, and to what extent should consumers inform themselves about it? To what extent should governmental agencies regulate health claims and practices?

9.3   DIVERSITY AND LIMITS: FEMALE CIRCUMCISION

Some situations place people in conflicts of basic value priorities. In this case, Dr. J believes strongly in the rights of cultures to practice their own beliefs and traditions unimpeded by others' views of how they should live. The practice of circumcision of females, pervasive in some African, Middle Eastern and Asian societies, however, tests Dr. J's resolve to live and let live.

At around the time of puberty, most females in these societies have parts of their external genitalia removed or sewn shut. While opponents refer to this as "female genital mutilation," its advocates perceive it as a traditional ritual assuring female sexual restraint and hence protection of the young women's future marriageability.

Mrs. G brings her ten-year-old daughter, A, to Dr. J's office with the request that he perform the procedure on the daughter. Although traditionally female circumcision is done without anesthesia or antiseptics, Mrs. G says that she wants her daughter to have access to these, for the girl's sake, because she does not want A to suffer and she wants her to be safe. Dr. J does not find these concessions satisfactory, though. He believes that the practice, even when sanitized, reflects an unacceptable disfigurement, control, and repression of women. Mrs. G and her daughter insist that they want the procedure carried out; for them, the only alternative is the more painful and dangerous traditional method. The mother explains that she is convinced of the procedure's importance for reasons of hygiene, aesthetics, social standing, and the woman's marriageability, as well as for other reasons.

a. What should Dr. J do? What choices does he have? Does he have options beyond either complying with Mrs. G's wishes or turning the people out of his office?

b. Should Dr. J consider reporting Mrs. G to the police? If he does so, would such a report be likely to protect the daughter? Would performing the procedure represent a form of child abuse?

c. Suppose Dr. J relents and performs the procedure, and Mrs. G is so pleased that she recommends Dr. J to a number of her friends and family who have daughters, for similar procedures. Would this situation create more problems?

d. Suppose, on the other hand, that Dr. J refuses to remove A's clitoris, so her mother has it done the traditional way, and the girl suffers greatly and develops a life-threatening infection. Is there a sense in which Dr. J's refusal to participate in what he perceives as evil results in a greater harm being done? Does he keep his integrity at the expense of A's well-being?

e. Suppose A says that she doesn't want the circumcision. How should that influence Dr. J's decision?

f. Each of the following ethical *values and principles*—most in this book's glossaries—might be applied to this issue. Explain how. What action might each justify ethically? To the extent that more than one of these is applicable, how should their importance be weighed and balanced in judging this type of situation?

+ Nonmaleficence
+ Beneficence (including health promotion and health advocacy)
+ Respect for persons
+ Respect for cultures
+ Parental autonomy
+ Human rights
+ Best interests of the child
+ Confidentiality and its limits
+ Trust
+ Professional integrity
+ Professional competence

g. Several types of beliefs and claims are applicable to the issue. For each, what additional factual and value questions need to be asked and how ethically important is each category of belief to the morality of the practice? For those that are ethically relevant, what exactly is the relevance?

+ Health: What will be most beneficial for the child's long-term health? How is this determined?
+ Hygiene: What is most likely to enable cleanliness? How strong a value is cleanliness?

+ Aesthetic: What is most appealing, at least as judged by members of their group?
+ Social: What social and economic effects, for the family and the child, will occur if the child is (or is not) operated on?
+ Religious: What, if any, are the religious teachings about the practice?
+ Cultural—group identity, tradition: How strong is the practice as a part of their group's identity?

9.4   RELIGIOUS GROUNDS FOR REJECTING MEDICAL CARE: FAITH HEALING

Mrs. R, age thirty-three, becomes alarmed when she and her children all become violently ill. It appears to be food poisoning but that cannot be determined without further testing. Mrs. R, however, refuses treatment for herself and her children for the reason that her religion, a small group named the Servants of the Lord, believes that sufficiently strong faith and prayer can cure illness. Their conditions seem to be worsening.

a. Would it matter if, instead of belonging to an unknown sect, they belonged to a mainstream religion or denomination that accepted similar beliefs?
b. Would the acceptability of involuntary treatment depend on whether the woman and children were already in a hospital or were still at home?
c. Some would say that the adult can refuse treatment for herself but not for her children. Do you agree?
d. Is her sincere refusal of treatment for her children a form of abuse or neglect, or is it better understood as a type of exercise of religious freedom?
e. Should the national, cultural, or ethnic background of the people be considered a relevant factor in judging whether refusal of treatment should be permitted? If so, then how?

9.5   JEHOVAH'S WITNESS PARENTS REFUSE TRANSFUSION

A three-hour-old female infant, K, was transported to the neonatal intensive care unit (NICU) with gastroschisis, a condition in which the abdominal contents protrude externally at birth and which requires surgery. The mother is fifteen years old. The grandmother has legal custody of the infant. The family are Jehovah's Witnesses and so believe that transfusion of whole blood is contrary to God's commands. The surgical team agrees to use volume expanders instead of blood as long as this is medically feasible treatment for the infant.

In discussions, the grandmother, Mrs. L, had stated that she would consider allowing the use of blood in an emergency situation. Unfortunately, the baby developed sepsis (infection), was taken to surgery, and Mrs. L—under pressure from the other family members—refused consent for blood transfusions. After surgery, Baby K's hemoglobin declined to the point where a blood transfusion would be needed for her to survive. The family now refuses, however, and the medical team considers getting a court order for the transfusion.

    a. Should the mother have been brought more into the decision making?

    b. How should we balance respect for diversity of beliefs and cultures—in this case, religious diversity—with concern for patients' best interests?

    c. Are religious beliefs more important to respect than other beliefs? Why? In answering the preceding, what do you include within the scope of religion?

    d. Consider the following alternatives: (i) ignore the family's wishes, (ii) try to educate the family, (iii) try to persuade the family to make a different decision, (iv) respect the family's wishes, (v) ask others to assist, or (vi) report the family to the authorities. Have some options been omitted from this list of possible courses of action?

9.6 SEX SELECTION OF A PHYSICIAN: FOUR VIGNETTES

While people have loudly disputed the morality of allowing couples to select their children's sex, a very different sort of sex selection topic has remained comparatively overlooked: the sex selection of one's health professionals. Given that there are only two sexes, there are four possible kinds of requests patients can make.

    ✦ A female can request/demand that she be treated only by another female.

    ✦ A female can request/demand that she be treated only by a man.

    ✦ A male can request/demand that he be treated only by another man.

    ✦ A male can request/demand that he be treated only by a woman.

These requests/demands are likely to tend to come from different populations, such as the members of the first group being, on balance, younger than the second group.

    a. How might we begin to sort out the acceptability or wrongness of making such a request, pressuring people to honor it, encouraging it, or discouraging, perhaps even prohibiting it?

    b. Suppose we were to decide that all four sorts of requests ought to be honored in health care settings, although people's reasons for making the requests may range from any of a number of innocuous motives. More often than not, they have to do with a comfort or discomfort level, one that can be disregarded in sufficiently urgent circumstances.

    c. But what about physicians or nurses who behave similarly? Suppose, that is, a nurse refused to treat women or (more likely) men for certain conditions. Is such a refusal morally acceptable?

    d. What factual information might help us elucidate and decide these cases?

9.7 FORBIDDEN FOOD

Five-year-old A has eaten a hot dog containing pork, a food forbidden by her family's religion. Her father brings her to the ER and requests that the doctor "pump her stomach," i.e., pass a large-diameter nasogastric tube attached to suction to retrieve the hot dog. The emergency room physician, Dr. G, has reservations, because she does not find the procedure to be medically necessary. A's father thinks that Dr. G is insufficiently sensitive to his culture's beliefs and values. Dr. G considers contacting a clergyperson to clarify the religion's teachings.

a. Some medical procedures are performed due to the beliefs of cultures and religions. These include circumcision. Would the physician, in order to be consistent, either have to refuse to do both or be willing to perform both?

b. Does the fact that A is so young mean that she should not be held blameworthy for violating the dietary rule? Should this determination of the age of responsibility be made according to the rules of her parents' tradition? Is there a culture-independent way of developmentally specifying the age of responsibility?

c. Is the concept of "medical necessity" applicable to this case, or is it being used in a circular way, based on the physician's belief that medical intervention would not be justified? Can we specify a medical notion of appropriateness based on the known risks of stomach pumping?

d. Should a health care institution maintain that it will only treat people with conditions diagnosable by conventional medical criteria? Would doing so risk preventing the institution from responding to the diverse needs of members of their communities?

e. Would it be a good idea or a bad idea for Dr. G to contact the clergyperson? Would the morality of doing or not doing the requested procedure be a function of how helpful he or she proves to be? What are the advantages and disadvantages of consulting a clergyperson other than the one most closely associated with A's family?

f. In what ways do the ethical issues about culture-bound medical procedures apply to industrialized nations? Some possible examples are cosmetic surgeries, procedures caused by sedentary lives, and some sports-related and automobile-related injuries.

g. Can the physician refuse to go along with the father's request on the basis of the venerable principle, "*Primum, non nocere*" ("First of all, do no harm")—an early version of the concept of nonmaleficence? This, of course, assumes a clear risk of harm as a result of complying with the parent's request.

9.8 IS INTOLERANCE INTOLERABLE?

[Based on news reports from Nashville, Tennessee, in 2000.]

A couple requests that no black males be present in the operating room (OR) during a procedure the wife needs. When pressed, they confide their main reason: the husband is very uncomfortable about having his wife's undressed body seen by males of other races. Just before the operation begins, the surgeon notices a black perfusionist and asks him to step out of the room. He then locates another perfusionist. Afterwards, the hospital expresses its regret to the perfusionist and condemns the surgeon's action.

a. Did the surgeon do the right thing? Whether or not it was optimal (the best choice), did the surgeon take morally permissible action?

b. Did the hospital do the right thing?

c. The hospital has position and mission statements that affirm the dignity of everyone. Was the surgeon's behavior consistent with these statements? If not, does it follow that:

    i. The position and mission statements are questionable?

    ii. The surgeon's behavior was unacceptable, or at least dubious?

    iii. The statements were mostly valid generalizations but allowed for exceptions such as the present case?

d. To what extent should personnel at these institutions accommodate people's prejudices and biases, and to what extent should they not?

e. Suppose the couple had requested that no one in the OR be male. Would that raise the same kinds of issues?

f. Since many decisions are made based on people's comfort levels and preferences, when should these become viewed as decisive to the acceptability of treatment?

g. Suppose the hospital refused to comply with the couple's request, and there were no other facilities in the area that would treat them either. (In fact, in the Nashville case, they had sought care elsewhere, but were turned away because of their preconditions.) If the woman would in all likelihood die as a result of failing to have the operation, how would that affect the acceptability of the decision?

h. May we, *in some circumstances,* allow discrimination based on people's race, sex, or belief?

i. Could the surgeon have acted in some other manner that would respect the patient's wishes without violating the hospital's policy?

9.9 BY FAITH ALONE?

Parents A and B believe in the healing power of intercessory prayer. They believe that illness can be cured by praying and also by having a healer pray for the recovery of the ill person. Their son has Crohn's Disease—a painful, chronic disease of the intestinal system. The parents take him to a faith healer rather than to a medical practitioner. Sometimes the conditions being prayed about by the healer improve, and sometimes they do not. The parents have not attempted to ascertain how often each occurs.

a. Does such a concept of prayer assume that God is more likely to respond to parents' petitions than by the fact that the children are ill?

b. Would it make a difference, ethically, if the parents had witnessed people being healed by the faith healer? How should the parents distinguish seeing someone being cured versus merely *thinking* they were seeing the cure? Might these parents have a special moral responsibility to critically challenge claims about cures? How much should we ethically expect of parents in terms of their educating themselves about health care?

c. If the faith healer either does not encourage the parents to seek conventional medical help, or even actively discourages it, then is the faith healer morally culpable (and perhaps legally liable) for harm the child sustains?

d. Should the degree of urgency of the condition be considered in deciding about the ethics of this situation? Should the amount of harm caused, including pain and dysfunction, be factored in? Thus, if the child suffers much avoidable pain over the years as a result of the delayed medical intervention, would that be more serious?

e. Christian Science is a denomination of Christianity that discourages use of conventional medical science based on their affirmation of the spiritual as the highest reality. While they allow some latitude of choice by individuals, they strongly encourage use of prayer rather than medical interventions. How is such a perspective different, ethically, from that of less mainstream faith healers?

9.10   DEAF CULTURE AND COCHLEAR IMPLANTS

Scenario 1: Deaf parents have a congenitally deaf child. They oppose a procedure to give her cochlear implants, which is low-risk surgical procedure that almost always enables people to hear—especially if done at an early enough age.

Scenario 2: Deaf parents have a young child with normal hearing. The parents' culture has helped them to live full, rewarding lives. They want to put plugs in his ears to enable their child to acquire their deaf culture. (In contrast with Scenario 1, this is purely hypothetical.)

a. Is it permissible to allow a person to retain a remediable disability if it coincides with parental wishes and beliefs? Is there a moral difference between allowing a disability and inducing or causing it?

b. Do such wishes and beliefs have greater force if they are associated with a culture? If so, how does being associated with a culture make such a difference? Would this apply equally to all cultures, or only to some cultures? What is a *culture?*

c. *Consider possible analogy 1:* Parents choose to give their child improved appearance with rhinoplasty, liposuction, or breast augmentation. They argue that it helps the child adapt to the culture.

d. *Consider possible analogy 2:* Mentally retarded parents have a child with apparently normal intelligence, but choose to cause brain damage so that she can be part of their culture.

e. *Consider possible analogy 3:* Amish people wish to be able to remove their children from the school system as of eighth grade, several years younger than others in society. They argue that to keep the children in school after that would undermine their attempt to keep the children part of their community and to maintain their traditions. What are the proper scope and limits of parental judgment about their children's well-being? (This is based on a Supreme Court case, *Wisconsin v. Yoder.*)

f. Can something be *both* a disability (and so something that is, to that extent, a harm to be minimized) and at the same time a culturally valued characteristic (and thus, something with value and integrity to be respected and encouraged)?

g. Can the inculcation of a culture be, or result in, a form of neglect or abuse? Since one's culture can be important for purposes of group identification and values, how should an acceptable concept of *culture* be specified?

h. If inculcation can be viewed as a type of neglect or abuse, might there be a sense in which immersing children in a contemporary culture can be viewed as irresponsible, to the extent that it reinforces round-the-clock television viewing, violence as entertainment, and poor nutritional habits?

9.11 *WRONG ABOUT ONE'S OWN RELIGION?*

Mrs. G is an active member of her church. Her mother had a debilitating heart attack several months ago, and, maintained with tube-feedings and ventilation as well as a range of medications, drifts in and out of responsiveness. Mrs. G is her mother's legally-designated guardian. Although her denomination's theology does not assert that all medical interventions have to be used in situations of this sort, Mrs. G has somehow come to believe that death must come as a result of God's will. As she explains it, human agency in only in accordance with God's will if postpones a person's death.

a. Does the fact that Mrs. G believes as she does because of her religion have special moral force? Suppose, for example, she had formed a metaphysical belief that events, including deaths, should occur only as a result of fate. Would that be more questionable than if her belief were part of her religion?

b. Would a contrast of "accurate" vs. "inaccurate" religious beliefs help? Should one make efforts to try to sway Mrs. G's opinions to those more consistent with her own professed religion? Would that be (i) to arrogantly imply that she doesn't know her own religious beliefs, and to try to impose an orthodoxy, or (ii) to urge her to critically examine her religious beliefs? Are some people especially suited to do this?

c. Which of the following distinctions are applicable to this case?

i. Being correct vs. being mistaken empirically.

ii. Being correct vs. being mistaken morally.

iii. Being correct vs. being mistaken about what one's religion or denomination says.

9.12 *SOME HYPOTHETICALS ABOUT PAIN, PAIN MANAGEMENT, AND CULTURE*

A child is in pain from a broken arm (alternatively, from cancer; or post-operatively). The parents do not want you to use what you think of as adequate pain control.

For each of the reasons below, which response is most appropriate?

a. Allow the parents' view to prevail.

b. Try to educate the parents, so that they can re-think their opinions.

c. Refuse to honor the parents' wishes.

d. Report the parents for abuse or neglect.

Suppose the parents' reasoning consists of each of the following.

+ They just don't care whether the child is in pain.

+ They think that suffering is good in itself.

+ According to them, suffering is good as a means to something further, such as building character or getting to heaven.

+ They believe that their religion commands people to suffer.

+ Their culture allows suffering, even when it is preventable.

+ Their culture/religion denies the reality of suffering.

+ Their religion teaches that only "natural" means of healing are acceptable, and that drugs are "artificial."

9.13   PADDLING

Parents E and F use paddling—spanking with objects such as belts, sticks, wooden spoons, and paddles—as one of their preferred methods of discipline. They were raised by means of paddling. They believe that: (a) *their* having turned out to be good people shows that paddling is an effective method, and (b) paddling is *necessary* to provide adequate structure for their children's behavior.

a. Are they practicing child abuse, either legally or morally? How would one decide?

b. If it does not rise to the level of child abuse, can it still be viewed as less than optimal or as morally questionable?

c. How good is their reasoning?

d. Does the fact that they turned out all right—if indeed they did—*prove* that paddling is effective? Does it show that paddling is more effective than not paddling? How would one design a study to determine whether or not paddling is effective?

e. If the parents have indeed turned out well, does this show that paddling is *necessary?* Does the fact that their children sometimes seem to respond only to threats of paddling show that paddling is necessary for adequate parenting? What would constitute evidence that one thing (here, paddling) is necessary for something else (in this instance, growing up well-behaved and well-adjusted)?

f. Is the concept of *evidence-based parenting,* analogous to the new emphasis on evidence-based medicine, a good idea? Why or why not?

g. In what ways is the use of paddling a health-related matter? An ethical matter? A legal matter?

h. What additional facts—including what kinds of research—might help in deciding about the ethics of this case? Consider relevant factual consideration, including effectiveness of parenting techniques, the frequency of, severity of, and reasons for paddling, findings of psychological studies, their culture, and any other relevant factors.

i. How does use of inanimate objects differ from spanking with the open hand, physically or psychologically? How does the level of the parents' anger affect the rightness or wrongness of this form of attempted discipline? Suppose they used a single swat rather than prolonged beating? Are all forms of paddling equivalent?

j. Is parenting the kind of thing that is not the business of others to judge?

k. How much should intentions affect the morality of parenting? Would the fact that one loves one's child mean that whatever one does to the child is permissible?

9.14   OTHER CULTURES: OTHER FACTS AND OTHER VALUES?

Obviously, members of various cultures do not literally live in different realities. Yet people need to appreciate their different circumstances and their different value beliefs. This does not mean that all factual or value beliefs are equally correct.

For many societies, including perhaps billions of people, the contemporary Western notions of *informed consent* seem strange. In part, this arises from less individualistic worldviews; but it also has to do with the perceptions among many that the physician, by virtue of his or her education, knows what is in the patient's best interest.

Mrs. S spent her first eighteen years in an Asian nation. When asked about which of several types of birth control she would like, she tells Dr. D to give her whatever she thinks best. Before making a choice for Mrs. S, Dr. D considers trying to encourage her to participate more in the choice of contraceptive. She finally decides that she will not do to Mrs. S what Rousseau described as forcing someone to be free.

a. How, if at all, is Mrs. S's deference to her physician's judgment any different from willingness by people within one's own culture to let physicians act paternalistically (or at least expertly)?

b. Is something wrong with deferring to a physician's judgment about treatments? If so, then what or why? Should people be "forced to be free," at least about their health care? Does this assume that freedom is more important than health?

c. For many people in the late twentieth century, the concept of *autonomy* has come to play an important role in their moral judgment. Although there are various senses of autonomy (including free choice, self-determination, and rational deliberation about how to choose), is it something that people are *obligated* to exercise rather than merely permitted or encouraged to use?

d. Suppose Dr. D perceives that Mrs. S is choosing as she is because her husband has told her to do so. Should Dr. D try to encourage Mrs. S to choose what she herself thinks best, or should she refrain from intervening in a family situation that is conditioned by their culture? Suppose the relationship were not a product of their culture. Would urging greater assertiveness then be more acceptable?

9.15   RESPECTING CULTURAL DIVERSITY AND HEALTH

A family, the O's, has as part of their identity their heritage and traditions. Their culture accepts some, but not all, modern technologies. They believe, in part, that nature has healing qualities. They also believe that certain traditional practices, done by healers from their culture, are preferable to what they perceive as either less effective, harmful, or, in some instances, even profane activities of contemporary health care interventions. In many regards, their belief and value systems coincide with those of other cultures from much of the world.

One day, the concerned parents bring one of their children to their local clinic. The child has a fever and other signs and symptoms consistent with meningitis. Diagnosis and treatment would entail invasive tests that the parents reject.

a. Suppose, instead, the child has a form of neoplasm that responds well to chemotherapy.

b. Suppose, instead, the child needs a transplant to survive.

c. Suppose, instead, the parents reject routine immunization of the child.

d. Does the refusal of treatment or diagnostic tests based on cultural beliefs and traditions have a stronger force than a refusal that is not so grounded? Why? In judging about the weight of cultures' beliefs and values, should some cultures or subcultures have greater force than others? Should some traditions, value systems, beliefs, or religions? How might one justify distinguishing among these?

CHAPTER 10

Information: Communication and Confidentiality

Ordinarily, we have an obligation to communicate honestly with people. This obligation becomes especially strong in professional relationships because of the reasonable trust expectations that accompany professional-client or professional-patient relationships. In addition, clients or patients need information disclosed honestly so that they can make informed decisions about their care. Information ought, of course, to be communicated effectively and in a way sensitive to people's feelings. The presumption of confidentiality in professional relationships arises from respect for people's privacy and again out of the reasonable expectation of trust; it enables clients and patients to communicate more openly about matters they would otherwise keep to themselves.

Even so, some situations arise in which other factors may work against the true, full disclosure of information or against the confidential protection of information. Sometimes, then, there is strong reason either to withhold information from a patient or to disclose information about that person to others. This chapter's cases consider some problems about truthfulness in the disclosure of information to patients or about violations of confidentiality.

LIMITS TO CONFIDENTIALITY

Confidentiality is not an absolute, either morally or legally. First, laws in most states and countries allow or even require communication of information disclosed in a professional relationship between health worker and patient or client. Some examples include suspected child abuse, suspiciously inflicted wounds, sexually transmitted diseases, and the occurrence of births and deaths. More controversial, both legally and ethically, are some other sorts of information: HIV infection (to whom may or should it be disclosed?), potential serious danger to others, and, perhaps, use of patients in teaching or research work.

WITHHOLDING OF INFORMATION

Sometimes, the opposite occurs. The problem exists because of unclarity concerning whether, or how, to convey information to a patient. In such cases, analogous to the sort mentioned earlier, the balance must be struck between others' wishes (for instance, parents' or the state's) and the patient's right to information. Another sort of balancing might have to occur between the patient's right to information and what one perceives to be in the patient's best interest.

At first glance, one naturally thinks of truth very simply. That is, people should always tell the truth to others and ought never to lie to them. Immediately, however, complexities arise. Consider the following:

+ *All the truth? Always?* Is the truth the whole truth? What if it might be destructive or very hurtful to someone if you tell the truth? Should truth always trump other moral considerations? Does it never conflict with them? Don't we have other duties to people that may override the duty not to lie?

+ *Even if not asked?* Does telling the truth mean volunteering information whether or not asked? Or does it only mean not deceiving people *if* they have asked for information? Aren't there forms of wrongful withholding of information that are not instances of lying? Suppose, for example, you know that someone believes something that is false, and you know that the false belief is harmful to the person. Suppose further you knowingly allow the person to continue to hold the destructive false belief, although you could easily correct the mistaken belief.

+ *None of others' business?* Does a person's right to informational privacy mean that others do not have a right to truth about that person?

+ *Neither truth telling nor lying?* Is telling a partial truth, selectively disclosing information, or "bending the truth" an instance of truth telling, or is it lying? Or do lying and truth telling not exhaust all the options?

+ *Changing the subject?* Suppose someone asks you a question and you do what many (most?) people sometimes do: rather than lying, you attempt to finesse the situation by changing the subject. Because it is not lying, it is morally acceptable, you think. But is it? Or might it depend on other factors such as how important it is for the person to obtain the requested information?

The preceding should give some indication of a few of the complexities arising from the simple distinction of thinking that (a) lying is always wrong, (b) telling the truth is always right, and (c) all statements we make to others are either instances of lying or instances of truth telling. Having observed all this, though, it should also be emphasized that many of the greatest problems in people's lives have always been caused by people's casual manipulation of truth and their excessive comfort at deception.

10.1 *WITHHOLDING IMPORTANT GENETIC INFORMATION FROM A FAMILY*

Mrs. H, forty-four years old, presents with what seems to be an early stage of Huntington's disease, an incurable genetic disease resulting in gradual deterioration of the brain and other neural tissue, which she inherited from her parents. The rest of her family is unaware of the Huntington's disease in their relatives. The woman does not want them told.

   a. Do the relatives have a right to information that concerns their health?
   b. Does the fact that the relatives would not be able to prevent the disease by being informed of it militate against informing them?
   c. Does the obligation to preserve confidentiality extend to genetic information applicable to others? By analogy, suppose one person's blood tests enabled diagnosis of a disease in another person who did not suspect that he or she had the disease.

10.2 *PRESSING SOMEONE TO ADMIT SPOUSAL ABUSE*

Dr. W works in a clinic. Mrs. I has come into the clinic twice before with injuries, each time saying they were the result of an accident. This time, she has two facial contusions. Her husband, who brings her to the clinic, smells of alcohol and is impatient and belligerent. The woman rejects any suggestion that Mr. I might have caused her injuries.

   a. Should Dr. W report her suspicions to the authorities if, and only if, she believes that the police will persuade Mr. I to refrain from his violence? Should health workers be bound by mandatory reporting laws for suspected cases of domestic violence as they are in suspected cases of child abuse and abuse of the elderly? Are adult women who are subjected to continual abuse less vulnerable than children and the elderly?
   b. Would it be acceptable for Dr. W, as a health care provider, to suggest to Mrs. I that she consider getting out of her apparently abusive environment? Would she be meddling in their relationship or attempting to protect the patient's safety?
   c. Is Dr. W morally obligated to direct Mrs. I to social work, psychological, pastoral care, and/or other resources, or should such referrals be thought of as optional?
   d. How much should Dr. W and others pressure Mrs. I to report the violence? What if Mrs. I has young children at home? May Dr. W threaten to have the children taken away if she doesn't report the violence?
   e. If Mrs. I remains unwilling to press charges, should anything else be done?
   f. Would different laws and policies better enable protection of victims of domestic violence? If so, what should they allow or require?

g. Is part of the role of a health worker to protect people from violence? In what senses are prevention and treatment of violence health matters? Does this involve health workers too much in politics, or does it provide evidence that politics is inseparable from health promotion?

h. Suppose the woman says that the fights between her and her husband are a private matter and that she wants to be left alone. Morally, is she within her rights to do this? Suppose there is strong evidence that her refusal of help is a consequence of acting under duress or because she has been so brutalized or intimidated that she has become incapable of seeking help. Short of kidnapping and "deprogramming" her, what can be done for her?

10.3   ELEVATOR AND CAFETERIA CONVERSATIONS

Dr. K and Nurse L were chatting on their hospital's elevator. While in the room of one of their patients, they began a discussion of that patient's challenging case. They continued the intense discussion as they walked through the hallway to the elevator, into the cafeteria line, and when seated at the lunch table. Their institution discourages its staff from discussing cases in public spaces.

a. What would we need to know to decide whether Dr. K and Nurse L were doing something morally wrong in having their conversation? Suppose, for example, the discussion concerned only the most effective way to perform a procedure.

b. Should health care facilities strictly prohibit public discussions of cases? How might they enforce that policy? Should such a rule depend on other factors, such as the sensitivity of the topic?

c. Does the behavior of Dr. K and Nurse L constitute a violation of confidentiality?

d. Suppose they were whispering or speaking in hushed tones. Would that matter?

e. Which location or locations were inappropriate for their conversation? Would anywhere they might have been overheard be inappropriate?

10.4   A PATIENT'S HISTORY IN PRINT

One of Nurse M's patients presents an especially interesting case. The patient, Mr. J, has HIV infection, kidney disease, and a complicated psychosocial picture. Mr. J seems very conscientious about some aspects of his health, such as taking medications as prescribed, yet he smokes cigarettes and drinks three bottles of wine a day. The nurse writes up his case and submits it to a journal. As published, a number of personal aspects of Mr. J's life, health status, and family dynamic appear, although Mr. J is not mentioned by name. An acquaintance of Mr. J reads the article and wonders whether the person described is in fact Mr. J.

a. Suppose Nurse M were confident that Mr. J would not read the article. Would that affect the acceptability of submitting it?

b. If it is important to include actual cases in health care professions' literature, how can patients' privacy be protected?

c. Must Nurse M ask Mr. J for permission to write the article? Must she inform Mr. J that she has written the article? Does the fact that Mr. J is not named absolve Nurse M of the need to inform or ask permission?

d. Should the case be revised and made partly hypothetical to avoid the possibility of harming, embarrassing, or offending Mr. J, or would modifying the case compromise its authenticity?

e. The American Nurses Association (section 2.3 of its 1985 version of the *Code for Nurses with Interpretative Statements*) said, "If the nurse wishes to use a client's treatment record for research or nonclinical purposes in which anonymity cannot be guaranteed, the client's consent must be obtained first." What is involved in guaranteeing anonymity?

10.5   SHARING PATIENT INFORMATION WITH ONE'S SPOUSE

A nurse, Mrs. R, tells her husband during supper about some of the patients she saw at the clinic where she works. She mentions a few of them by name or gives descriptions of the people that could enable the husband to identify them. Mrs. and Mr. R have found that their relationship works better when they can share information about their working lives.

a. Although confidentiality is assumed as part of the privacy and trust relationship between professionals and clients/patients, does this mean that a professional such as Mrs. R must keep secret virtually everything challenging, interesting, stressful, or unusual from the work setting? Is bottling up all this information consistent with healthy relationships and professionals' own mental health?

b. At what point does making conversation cross over the line to gossip? What constitutes potentially damaging or humiliating disclosure?

c. Between the opposite views of barring all mention of patients, on the one hand, and accepting sharing of information about patients, on the other, might criteria exist for judging which information would be ethically permissible to disclose?

d. Suppose a close friend tells you something about herself "in strict confidence." You tell another friend, asking him to tell no one else. Have you done something wrong, or have you merely done something that occurs often as a natural part of the structure of many intimate friendships? Should the rightness or wrongness of telling your friend be a function of how likely it is that the person *will* keep the information secret?

10.6   WHO SHOULD KNOW WHAT?

Ms. N, forty-one, is being treated for pre-menstrual dysphoric disorder. She has, in the past, been treated for two sexually transmitted diseases (chlamydia and herpes) and two mental disorders (adjustment disorder and chemical dependency). She had an abortion at eighteen. Her cholesterol level is high, and she possesses a gene that predisposes to a one-in-three risk of breast cancer. She has had several precancerous cervical lesions.

Ms. N recently applied at a large corporation that requires a physical examination and history. In her opinion, her health history is none of their business. From their point of view, they want to know what kind of person they would be hiring—and paying to insure.

   a. How much of the information about Ms. N's medical history should her prospective employer rightfully have prior to their decision to hire her?

   b. If the insurer should be entitled to most of the information, are there any areas that should be considered private and to be protected from their access?

   c. Suppose the corporation has phased in DNA profiles as a condition of employment. Would that be too intrusive or a reasonable expectation on the part of the employer?

   d. Should Ms. N's insurer and employer have *all* the information her primary care physician has? If not, what exceptions are reasonable?

   e. Are there some kinds of health information that Ms. N would be well advised not to disclose even to her primary physician—either because they are not necessary for treating Ms. N or because they are too sensitive and the guarantees of confidentiality are too weak?

   f. Suppose her health history were directly and obviously related to the duties of the job she is applying for. Would that be decisive?

10.7   A DUTY TO WARN?

Dr. C is a clinical psychologist who has Mr. D as a patient. Mr. D's wife recently admitted that she had become romantically involved with her husband's best friend, and filed for divorce. She wants custody of their children. While in therapy, Mr. D has expressed feelings of rage, and has stated that sometimes he feels like using his gun to kill his wife, her lover, or both. The state in which Dr. C practices does not require by specific statute that potential victims be warned.

   a. Given that legality is not the same as morality, in what ways should knowledge of the state's law be considered in making ethical decisions?

   b. How would the *ethics* of the situation vary if the state law

     i. Required warning those in danger?

     ii. Allowed (without requiring) warning those in danger?

     iii. Prohibited warning those in danger?

   c. Since decisions about whether to warn potential victims are based on estimates of likelihood of risk, among other factors, would a 1 percent likelihood of homicide suffice to justify warning potential victims? Suppose a 1 percent risk of suicide (or serious *self*-harm) were judged sufficient to paternalistically hospitalize someone. Should that be the same threshold applicable to predictions of serious harm to *others*?

   d. How should the importance of protecting innocent third parties be balanced against other factors? Consider:

i. About the *individual* therapeutic relationship:

   (a) The *promise* (tacit or explicit) of confidentiality made to the patient.

   (b) The importance of maintaining *that* patient's *trust*.

   (c) The likelihood that Mr. D will *discontinue* his relationship with the therapist.

ii. About therapeutic relationships *generally*:

   (a) The likelihood that people will *seek* mental health treatment if they are distraught.

   (b) The importance of *therapists* being able to assure their patients that their communications will be kept confidential.

10.8   TRUTH-TELLING AND TERMINAL ILLNESS: LYING ABOUT DYING

In order to be admitted to hospices, patients have to be diagnosed as having less than six months to live. Dr. X tries to decide what to tell his patient, Mrs. Y, who is being admitted to a hospice, about how much longer she will live.

a. If the news to be given is unpleasant, how might that influence Dr. X's willingness to tell?

b. Since hope is usually valuable, how should that be considered in deciding about withholding information about the prognosis?

c. What kinds of uses (such as "putting her affairs in order") might Mrs. Y have for the information?

d. Suppose the physician refuses to estimate, and instead says, "Only God knows." Is that a good strategy? Is it honest?

e. Suppose Mrs. Y has asked about her situation; alternatively, suppose that she has not. Would that make a difference, ethically? Suppose she has expressed a strong wish *not* to be told.

f. How should one balance the importance of maintaining honesty and candor in a professional relationship with that of protecting people from what seems to be very hurtful information?

g. If Dr. X believes it right not to tell Mrs. Y very hurtful information, should he *over*estimate or *under*estimate the amount of time he believes she probably has remaining? Why?

10.9   PATERNITY INFORMATION EMERGING IN GENETIC COUNSELING

Nurse G, a genetic counselor, reviews the results of a series of prenatal diagnostic tests. One of the tests produces an unanticipated result: the woman's husband cannot be the genetic father of the fetus. There is no evidence that the husband knows of this. The counselor tries to decide what may, ought, or ought not to be disclosed to the woman and her husband.

a. Would it matter if the patient or client of the counselor were just the woman rather than the couple?

b. May the counselor, ethically, urge the woman to disclose the paternity information? May she, ethically, urge the woman to keep the information secret?

c. Should the counselor try to anticipate the consequences for the fetus of the husband being not told at all, not told yet, or told immediately? In what sense is the fetus also a patient or client of the genetic counselor?

CHAPTER II

HIV/AIDS

Few, if any, health subjects in the past century have created as much fear and anger as AIDS. Also, few, if any diseases have generated such vehement ethical and public policy debates. This chapter's cases will focus some of these ethical and public policy issues.

CONFIDENTIALITY

As with many ethical questions, deciding about the appropriate amount of confidentiality for those with HIV infection requires *balancing*. Without recognition of the importance of balancing, discussions quickly deteriorate into nondiscussions; they become instead assertions by each side of an absolute right that must prevail. If we begin, instead, with the acknowledgment that neither individual privacy and freedom nor public health is an absolute, we can then explore how to *balance* the strengths of the relevant claims on each side.

In favor of protecting the confidentiality of HIV infection information are some strong arguments, including one that emphasizes the high likelihood that disclosure would not be confined to those who claim a need to know. Given the stigma associated with AIDS, they say, it would subject the infected person to various forms of discrimination.

Those who advocate selective disclosure of HIV infection information also have several strong reasons. For example, some argue that, because of AIDS' severity and high fatality rate, people exposed to any nonnegligible risk of it are entitled to know of the risk and thus to be able to take whatever precautions they deem necessary.

TESTING

The question of who should and who should not be tested for HIV antibodies should actually be divided into several questions. Also, for those who should (in some sense of "should") be tested, the questions remain of how coercive governments, health care institutions, and individual practitioners may be. To say that someone *should* do something, in the sense that it would be for the best, is not necessarily to say that the person morally *must* do so or that others may threaten or coerce the person into doing the right thing. Who, then, ought to be forced to submit to testing for the HIV antibodies? (The "AIDS" tests are actually tests for the antibodies to HIV, the virus that causes AIDS. As with any diagnostic test, the positive or negative test results may be correct [true positives and true negatives] or incorrect [false positives and false negatives].)

Who, then, should—in either the strong or the weak sense of "should"—be tested for HIV? Everyone in society? No one? All patients at hospitals? Some patients at hospitals? All people with high-risk behaviors? To answer these questions, we need to be able to balance not only the effects on privacy and health on each side but also other considerations.

REFUSAL TO TREAT

To decide about the acceptability of refusing to treat someone, it would help to know the extent of risk to health workers. Although needle-sticks immediately after blood draws occur from time to time, and so the risk is not zero, it seems to be so small, especially in comparison with other risks both to life and to health (for example, from hepatitis B or C) from working with patients that refusal to treat HIV-infected patients appears unwarranted. Nevertheless, some health workers assert that they can make such a refusal, just as some people, de facto, avoid exposure to HIV by choosing as a specialty or subspecialty a sort of work, such as radiology, that would keep them free of any possible exposure to the virus.

FUNDING

At least two major sorts of funding questions exist about HIV-related conditions. The first concerns the amount of money that should be allocated for those conditions compared with the amount allocated for other health care priorities. The second focuses on what proportion of AIDS funding should go for prevention, what percentage for treatment, and what fraction for research. Asking the questions this way tends to oversimplify these issues, since they make it seem as though there is a fixed total amount being divided up. Nevertheless, having some idea of the ratios may well be necessary both for planning and also for morally evaluating allocation decisions. And such moral evaluation of allocations must be done. Economics does not exist in a moral vacuum.

11.1   A PATIENT'S REQUEST NOT TO TELL PARTNERS

Mr. W, an HIV-infected man, is reluctant to disclose information about past or present sexual partners to health workers who inquire. He says that he will be safe in activities with future partners. Most of those who know of his attitudes and behaviors strongly disagree with Mr. W's approach, but he contends that it is his own business, and his relationships, and furthermore, he fears the isolation likely to follow from his disclosure of partners' names.

  a. To what extent should he feel morally obligated or even be forced by law (either civil or criminal) to disclose that information?
  b. Should HIV be treated differently than other sexually transmitted diseases? If so, then how and why?
  c. Should the potential for discrimination against people with AIDS or who are HIV-positive be a consideration in formulating policy?
  d. Given the life-threatening nature of AIDS, should there be required partner notification?

11.2   HOPE AND POWER: HIV PATIENTS' ACCESS TO UNAPPROVED DRUGS

Some HIV patients have decided to press for expedited access to drugs for their conditions. Person A is seropositive (has the HIV antibodies indicative of infection) but has no symptoms, person B has recently begun to experience symptoms, and person C is in the advanced stages of AIDS. They argue that it is their own bodies and that they should be given the opportunity to take as-yet-unapproved drugs since they don't have much to lose. They say it provides them more power and at least more hope than otherwise.

  a. Do you agree or disagree with the reasons advanced by A, B, and C? Why?
  b. Why do governmental agencies prohibit the public from gaining access to drugs prior to the completion of studies concerning their efficacy and safety? Is it merely paternalism—protecting people from themselves?
  c. Are those who sell unapproved products to HIV-infected people sources of hope or exploiters of desperate, vulnerable people?
  d. Given that almost any form of health fraud can be marketed by means of arguing that it provides people hope, how should people distinguish the acceptable from the unacceptable instances of allowing access?
  e. If the government makes special provision for expedited approval and/or access to drugs for AIDS, should this be viewed as a worthwhile responsiveness to a real need or as caving in to the political pressure of an activist, highly vocal constituency?
  f. If HIV-infected patients are deemed deserving of such access, then what relevant difference would justify denying it as well to those who have cancer or other diseases?

11.3   FUNDING FOR AIDS VERSUS FOR OTHER DISEASES

Citizens debate how much funding HIV-related conditions, including AIDS, should receive. Opinions range from those who believe it should not receive any public money to those who believe it should receive more than any other health priority.

Nurse R overhears two seriously ill patients arguing about this matter in the hallway of a hospital. Patient A, with AIDS, defends his staunch advocacy of greater funding for HIV/AIDS. Patient C, with throat cancer, equally vehemently defends more funding for cancer. A asserts that the government has long underfunded AIDS research because of people's perception of the disease as associated with behaviors they find distasteful, sinful, and/or illegal. C contends that far more people suffer and die from cancer than from HIV-related conditions, so cancer research deserves more money.

   a. Suppose it turns out that there is not a fixed pool of funds (so that allocating more for HIV would not entail less for other illnesses, and conversely). Would that eliminate a basis for the disagreement between A and C?

   b. Suppose, instead, the total for health is more or less constant. What percentage should be allotted for HIV conditions? More than or less than for heart disease? Cancer? Kidney disease? Other health priorities?

   c. How should one decide whether a health priority, such as HIV-related conditions, is overfunded, underfunded, or funded just enough? What kinds of reasons might be most persuasive for defending funding? The number of people affected? The number of deaths? The amount of suffering? Other factors?

11.4   HIV RISKS TO PATIENTS?

Many dental and medical patients express their concern about AIDS. They worry that they might be at some risk of infection by HIV.

Mr. I fears infection by his dentist. He notices that the dentist now wears gloves and a mask, but he worries that these might not assure his safety. He wants to know whether his dentist is infected with HIV. His fear arises in part from the reports in the early 1990s of a Florida dentist who appeared, at the time, to have infected five or six of his patients.

   a. Do dentists (or physicians or nurses) have a moral obligation to report their HIV status to patients? To refrain from practicing if they are HIV infected?

   b. Given that no cases have been documented of a health worker infecting a patient (with the possible exception of that one dentist), to what extent do HIV-infected dentists (or physicians or nurses) pose a risk to patients?

   c. If dentists (or others) do have an obligation to disclose their HIV status, then do they also have an obligation to disclose other *possible* (versus probable) risks to patients?

   d. Do health workers have the same (or perhaps more or less) responsibility to disclose their HIV status to patients as patients do to their health workers?

11.5   LESS-THAN-UNIVERSAL PRECAUTIONS

Some health workers, including Dr. B and Nurse C, wish to gain further information about patients, such as their HIV status, to protect themselves. Others argue that consistent adherence to universal precautions assures maximal realistic safety.

a. What is the significance of the fact that fewer than half of health workers at most health care settings practice universal precautions such as consistent use of gloves? Does it follow that they should be held to a more demanding standard or that the patients ought to be tested so that health workers will be better informed about who poses a risk to them?

b. If, other than by sexual activity, HIV can only be transmitted by the passage of sufficient amounts of blood into an open wound, why would a health worker who does not have a large wound fear becoming infected?

c. Is there too much emphasis on AIDS/HIV, given that health workers are at greater risks to life and health from other sources?

d. Suppose giving health care workers more information about the HIV status of their patients led to an increase in the selective use of (what are called) universal precautions. Would that fact be a good reason for withholding such information from the health care workers?

e. Suppose information about HIV status increases the likelihood that health care workers will deliver substandard care to these HIV-positive patients. Would this fact be a good reason for withholding HIV status information from the health care workers?

11.6   TESTING FOR HIV AND HEPATITIS: THREE VIGNETTES

Scenario 1: A hospital considers testing all its employees for HIV and hepatitis. A school system considers this also.

Scenario 2: The nurses, phlebotomists, orderlies, and others who work on a hospital's inpatient unit want to be informed of all patients who are HIV positive.

Scenario 3: A general surgeon wants all patients to be tested for HIV before surgery without specific consent so that the staff can take extra precautions.

a. Does it matter whether it is a hospital, a clinic, a private physician's office, or a school system? Are there relevant differences such that testing at some of these but not at others is justified? Or should none be allowed to require testing? Should all require testing?

b. Should only some patients be tested? If so, which ones and why those?

c. Should only some employees be tested? If so, which ones and why those?

d. If it turns out that confidentiality is frequently breached, would that influence judgments about who ought to be tested?

11.7 REFUSAL TO TREAT: CHOICE OR DISCRIMINATION?

Dr. L is a physician in private practice. He wishes to treat only people who are not HIV infected. Some of his colleagues try to persuade him not to refuse patients based on their seropositivity status, but Dr. L argues that he is not preventing those people from receiving *any* care, only from receiving *his* care. He does not oppose the provision of care to HIV-infected people. Rather, he believes only that not all members of the medical profession must be obligated to do so.

a. Suppose Dr. L wishes to treat only white people. Only black people. Would either of these be analogous to the HIV situation? Why?

b. Suppose he wishes to treat only heterosexual people.

c. Suppose he wishes to treat only females. Only males.

d. Which are instances of permissible professional choice, and which are examples of impermissible discrimination?

e. Is the fact that he is in private practice relevant to the morality of his decision? Suppose he worked at a public facility but asked his coworkers to provide treatment for the HIV-infected patients. Would that be acceptable?

f. Suppose he argues that, as someone with a great aversion to HIV, he would be unable to provide care as adequately as one without the aversion; therefore, for the patients' sakes, he ought not to treat them. Is this persuasive or unpersuasive?

CHAPTER 12

Reproduction, Genetics, and Abortion

REPRODUCTIVE TECHNOLOGY AND GENETICS

It seems reasonable to predict that, in the next century, just as it has in the second half of this century, scientific work in genetics and reproduction will create some of the most momentous challenges to our lives and worldviews. Perhaps only neural science compares in terms of the obvious significance and promise for affecting our views about our human identity and potential. Thus, as the new reproductive technologies have become available, they have inspired fascinating, profound conversations in which we try to decide which of these technologies are permissible and which are not. Such technologies, mentioned in some of this chapter's cases, include the following:

Artificial insemination

In vitro fertilization

Frozen embryos

Surrogate pregnancy

Prenatal diagnosis

Prenatal treatments

Experiments with cloning of humans

Experiments with gene replacement therapies

Experiments with embryonic stem cells

In addition to questions about the acceptability of various technologies or reproductive practices such as selective reproduction (negative and positive eugenics), further complicated concerns exist about the proper involvement of commerce in these activities. Those concerns also appear in some of the cases.

A number of ethical issues about science have an aura of science fiction. They concern very recent or prospective scientific developments. The moral evaluation of a cutting-edge technology or area of knowledge can be difficult because of the novelty of many of these technologies. People respond to novelty in the only ways they know: by constructing analogies with existing technologies or by suggesting slippery slope arguments.

We mobilize *slippery slope arguments* in attempts to defend all sides of most moral and legal controversies. There are two main sorts of such arguments:

> *Justification* slippery slope arguments challenge whether a plausible, nonarbitrary line can be drawn, distinguishing justified from unjustified instances of an action once a first assumption about the action's rightness or wrongness is granted. (For example, if very early abortions are justified, then all killings of humans would be permissible; or if very late abortions are prohibited, then so would the earliest ones.)
>
> *Causal* slippery slope arguments suggest that an uncontrolled sequence of events would likely follow from allowing a first event. (For example, if you implement [or outlaw] regulation of guns, then tyranny [or chaos] would be very likely to occur.)

Some such arguments are persuasive and some are not. It depends on the specific slippery slope being asserted.

Among the great number of subjects for which people use slippery slope arguments is the implementation of new and prospective reproductive technologies. When scientists announce or leak news of some new reproductive technology, we can anticipate promptly reading both justification and causal slippery slope arguments on each side—that is, arguments from both defenders and condemners of the technology.

ABORTION

Abortion is probably *the* most volatile issue today. Because it is, in a very important sense, an ethical issue as well as a legal, political, medical, and social one, its ethical dimensions must be addressed. How might we go about judging the justifiability/ unjustifiability of various sorts of abortions? What theories and criteria have the most and the least plausibility? One conclusion increasing numbers of people have reached in recent years is that informed, compassionate, intelligent people stand on all sides of this issue.

There are three main sorts of approaches to abortion, frequently termed the conservative, the moderate, and the liberal views. These labels do not necessarily correspond to the political classifications. Conservatives believe that no or almost no (less than 1 percent) abortions are permissible. Liberals believe that all or almost all (more than 99 percent) abortions are morally permissible. Liberals tend to emphasize the effects on the woman and to grant the fetus no or minimal moral status. Conservatives tend to focus on the fetus as either an actual or potential person, to assume that all biological humans are on a par, and therefore believe that any other considerations must be subordinate in importance to the fetus's right to live, much as they would think of newborns.

Abortion moderates, in contrast with those who oppose all abortions and those who accept all abortions, believe that the reasons—the relevant circumstances—for an abortion help determine its rightness or wrongness. Thus, knowledge that (for example) a pregnancy resulted from incest with a twelve-year-old makes it easier to approve of that abortion. Most moderates claim that abortion for sex choice is less acceptable, particularly if the abortion occurs fairly late in the pregnancy.

12.1 POSTMORTEM SPERM "DONATION"

Mr. and Mrs. D had talked often of their plans to have children. Mr. D died suddenly from an accident. Mrs. D then put to the hospital an unusual request: that she be permitted to authorize someone to harvest sperm from Mr. D's now brain-dead body, with the hope that she could thereby become pregnant. She said that Mr. D would have approved and that she, as his next of kin and executor, could dispose of his remains and his property as she saw fit. The hospital and many of the staff felt uncomfortable with the request. Their reactions varied. Some described it as bizarre, ghoulish, unnatural, and outrageous, whereas others perceived it as an expression of love, devotion, and a use of medicine for supporting the family values and enhancing the life of Mrs. D.

a. Would the situation seem more, less, or equally acceptable if Mr. D were still alive but irreversibly comatose?

b. How does this situation compare with that of a request to use the body of a brain-dead (or irreversibly comatose) pregnant woman to complete a pregnancy?

c. Suppose, in the next century, scientists develop the capability of determining an individual's DNA identity—the person's genomic information. Suppose further that some or all of this DNA could be combined with the remaining material of a sperm or egg cell (perhaps by renucleation, sometimes termed "cloning") so that it could become part of a fertilization process. Would such an activity be morally permissible? Why?

d. What is the difference between donating one's organs (or having them "harvested") upon one's death and donating (having "harvested") sperm or eggs?

12.2 QUESTIONED REQUESTS FOR ASSISTED REPRODUCTION: FOUR VIGNETTES

Scenario 1: Mrs. R is being treated for depression. She has three children (two of whom have been in trouble with the police) and is unemployed, as is her husband. She requests assistance to become pregnant again by receiving current infertility treatments.

Scenario 2: Mr. and Mrs. S ask a GP for help to reverse a sterilization and for in vitro fertilization so that they can produce a pregnancy. They seem to the doctor to be less than optimally qualified parents. He cites as reasons for discouraging their use of the reproductive technology their history of activities that he judges questionable: a history of drinking too much, dabbling with drugs, going to rock clubs on motorcycles, and breaking up every few years.

Scenario 3: Miss T, twenty-nine, is unmarried. She earns a comfortable living and is a stable, mature person. Although she lives alone, she wants very much to have a child biologically her own. She asks for assistance in becoming pregnant.

Scenario 4: The W's, both fifty-eight, have raised three children who now live on their own. They would like to have more children and would rather not adopt. So they explore the possibilities of in vitro fertilization or having a woman go through a surrogate pregnancy (artificially inseminated with Mr. W's sperm) for them.

a. Is the assisting of reproduction a medical treatment that ought to be universally accessible? If not, then what should constrain its availability?

b. If lack of qualifications for optimal (or for adequate?) parenting constitutes grounds for refusing to "treat" such people, then does that also mean that such people should not be allowed to be parents at all? What is the difference?

c. Does assisting reproduction involve indulging whims rather than alleviating illnesses? Why?

d. Which of the people in scenarios 1 through 4 should be entitled to assistance and which should not? Why?

12.3   FROZEN EMBRYO BROUHAHA

In Britain in 1996, a problem arose. Several thousand four-celled embryos—created from human sperm and eggs in petri dishes for in vitro fertilization—had been frozen for five years. Although that was the original maximal duration granted them by government policy, the clinics where they were stored either could not find their (genetic) parents or could not get a response about whether the parents wanted the embryos to be kept frozen or thawed, destroyed, and disposed of. This created a controversy, with religious and nonreligious reasons offered on each side. Some suggested other courses of action, including permitting other people to "adopt" the embryos, so that they could be implanted in the uteruses of women who would bring them to term and raise them. Others have said that, inasmuch as the embryos are forms of human life, they should have been provided decent funerals if they were to be destroyed.

a. To what extent should people's thinking about this issue mirror their judgments about the abortion controversy? What are relevant similarities and contrasts?

b. Should four-celled embryos (sometimes described as preembryos) be thought of as tiny clusters of cells, as potential persons, as actual persons, or in some other way?

c. Some argue that these embryos possess the same human dignity everyone else has. Because there seem to be various understandings of the term *dignity*, what might be meant in this context by ascribing dignity to the embryos?

d. Are the embryos property that is owned by their genetic parents, or is the concept of property not applicable to humans? What about the concept of custody as applied prenatally?

e. What reasons, secular or religious, might be most relevant to this debate?

f. One way to see the conceptual and thus the moral ambiguity of the situation is to inquire about the *age* of the embryos. Which of the following are they?

   i. One day old?

   ii. Five years old?

   iii. Minus nine months old?

   iv. None of the preceding?

12.4 IN VITRO FERTILIZATION: HELPFUL OR WASTEFUL?

The T's, an infertile couple, seek help. A reproductive specialist informs them that in vitro fertilization (IVF) offers them the opportunity to have their own baby. Drugs would induce superovulation in the woman. The harvested eggs would then be combined with the man's sperm in the laboratory and the resulting embryos implanted in the woman's uterus. Because the procedure might need to be done several times to produce a pregnancy, it would probably cost $30,000 or more.

a. Is such an expenditure morally unjustified?

b. Some argue that the practice is questionable, because plenty of babies are already available for adoption. Is that a good criticism of IVF?

c. Does IVF treat babies as objects or products with less than human worth and full dignity?

d. Can the procedure be questioned on the grounds that it is not designed to treat an illness but is only a way of indulging people's desires? Do people have a right to reproduce?

e. Should infertility be classified as a disease? If so, should attempts to cure it be covered by private insurance or government health care programs? Should postmenopausal women be allowed to undergo the procedure? Is being infertile due to the onset of menopause properly viewable as a medically treatable disorder?

12.5 REPRODUCTIVE ASSISTANCE FOR A SAME-SEX COUPLE

Ms. H and Ms. I are lesbians who have lived together for ten years. They come to a clinic that specializes in assisting reproduction. The clinic has previously only helped married couples in which the husband or wife is infertile. Ms. H and Ms. I explain that their problem is not one of infertility, because they are, they assume, both fertile. Rather, they want some help with artificial insemination. The clinic's director—Dr. F—to whom they are directed, feels uncomfortable about helping them, explaining that he has doubts about the effectiveness of parenting in a household with two parents of the same sex.

a. Is there a distinction between Dr. F's personal beliefs and value judgments and his professional judgments? If so, does that apply to this situation?

b. In what sense, if any, can factual opinions, such as beliefs concerning the effectiveness of people to parent, be properly termed personal?

c. How would one distinguish between denying services based on defensible value judgments and unacceptable discrimination?

d. May the clinic refuse to assist the two women on the basis of its being privately owned?

e. Can the clinic just assert that they apply similar criteria to those of adoption agencies? Or would that merely raise the issue of adoption agencies' criteria?

12.6   PRIVATIZING THE SALE OF SPERM AND OVA

A startup business offers sperm and eggs for sale. It argues that fees are already being charged by those involved in the treatment of infertility and that people can also earn money for donating blood or donating sperm for artificial insemination. It asks, rhetorically, why it is all right to profit from facilitating a service but not from supplying a product. It also asks why the "suppliers" can be reimbursed but not the "distributors."

a. How strong or weak are the business's arguments? Why? Has it omitted any relevant disanalogies?

b. Does such a business run the risk of creating what might be termed a "eugenopoly"—that is, a disproportionate amount of genes from those whose genes are deemed desirable?

c. Is something morally questionable about charging for body parts or by-products? If so, then what exactly would be the wrong-making factor?

d. In what sense do people own their bodies? In what sense do they not have proprietary control over their bodies?

12.7   PERFORMING SURROGATE PREGNANCY AS A LIVING

Ms. R earns a living performing surrogate pregnancy, a practice popularly referred to as surrogate motherhood. Usually the people who use her service are married couples, with the wife unable to go through pregnancy owing to physical limitations such as having had a hysterectomy. Yet they want a child who is at least partly biologically theirs.

   a. If such a source of income seems questionable, then why is it so? Some have argued that surrogate pregnancy is the equivalent of baby selling, or commodification of children. Are they right?

   b. Is there a moral difference between surrogate pregnancy done once for a fee versus as a primary source of income?

   c. Is there a moral difference between the practice done for free versus for a fee?

   d. In general, how should one decide what sorts of services are permissible when done for a fee and what sorts are not?

   e. Suppose a couple, the M's, are willing to pay for Ms. R's service because Mrs. M does not want to go through the discomforts, inconveniences, and risks associated with pregnancy. Is this reason less morally acceptable than the usual one? Should it be outlawed?

12.8 DNA BANKS: TWO VIGNETTES

Much about a person is a function of that person's DNA. This includes substantial parts of one's appearance, predispositions to health or illness, and—more controversially—even, to an extent, some psychological and behavioral traits. Each of these is, to a greater or lesser extent, an expression of one's genetic identity. For a variety of reasons, many people have a wish to learn whether they have a specific gene, such as for an inherited disease, but also to preserve the genetic information about themselves and their family members. That technology is now available. DNA repositories, sometimes in conjunction with cooperating funeral homes, can collect and store one's DNA.

Miss X and Mr. Y both want to make use of this service, while others believe that such a practice is pointless.

Scenario 1: Miss X wants her descendants to have access to the information coded in her DNA "in case they want to know more about me," she says. She fears that her medical records might not be accurate, complete, or accessible and that, moreover, there is more to her genetic makeup than her medical history would contain.

Scenario 2: Mr. Y has obtained a (noninvasively obtained) DNA sample from his mother. He wants, he states, for her to survive not only in people's memories and photographs but also in this form.

   a. If one will be able to determine one's risk for hereditary disorders by having one's own DNA tested, would there be any medical reason to have information about one's ancestors' DNA?

   b. What sorts of valuable information might emerge from knowledge about one's parents' or one's great-great-great grandparents' DNA? What sorts of harmful information might emerge?

c. Some have argued that, although there are good reasons for storing samples of DNA from those who have inherited conditions, since that would make possible the discovery of the genetic basis of those ailments, it is wasteful to store other people's DNA. Does this practice seem to be a frivolous use of a new technology or a meaningful new extension of an expanding area of knowledge? Both? Neither?

12.9   EUGENICS: POSITIVE OR NEGATIVE?

Mr. and Mrs. S, both twenty-nine years old and well-to-do investors, have two children, A and B. A, an eight-year-old boy, has hemophilia, a genetically transmitted disease. B, a six-year-old girl, is physically healthy and has average intelligence and abilities. The S's want to have more children. They place a phone call to a well-known obstetrician, Dr. M, and begin to probe about some reproductive options they would like to explore.

Their inquiries concern eugenics, or selective reproduction of humans. Whereas *negative* eugenics involves elimination of undesirable characteristics, *positive* eugenics is the breeding-in of characteristics thought to be desirable. Mrs. and Mr. S want to make sure (by artificial insemination using an anonymous donor, if necessary) that their future children will not have hemophilia. They do not want to prevent hemophilia in their other children by going through a string of pregnancies, prenatal diagnoses, and abortions. They want, they say, to "get it right" every time. They want to "invest conservatively," as they put it.

Their next request sounds more unusual. The S's say they believe in excellence, although not perfection, and want to give their children every possible advantage, both culturally and genetically. Accordingly, they want to be able to get donations of sperm and eggs from people who exemplify outstanding physical strength, health, character, intellect, and other talents. Dr. M approves of their wish to avoid hemophilia but wants nothing to do with the S's second proposal, which, he confides to a colleague, strikes him as "Naziesque."

a. Many people would agree that negative eugenics, such as that facilitated by means of genetic counseling, is morally acceptable, perhaps even commendable, but they reject positive eugenics of any sort. If they are right, then what exactly *is* the essential moral difference that would make *all* positive eugenics morally wrong?

b. Might the difference between positive and negative eugenics result from the greater ease of specifying what is undesirable than of identifying what is desirable? If so, then are all instances of bad traits clearly so, and all examples of good traits purely arbitrary?

c. Suppose one selects a mate at least partly because of the person's desirable traits, with the intent to have children equally worthy of admiration or with a maximal likelihood of success. Is either of these a form of positive eugenics?

d. Opponents of eugenics frequently express the fear, based on frightening historical precedents, of governmentally imposed programs of involuntary eugenics, with a single model of desirability in mind. If eugenics were voluntary and individually decided, would it still create an excessive risk of central enforcement?

12.10   CLONING

Dolly, the ewe, became a celebrity of sorts when the circumstances of her birth became known in 1997. Scientists brought her into existence by cloning the genetic information of a somatic (nonreproductive) cell. Dolly contained the same DNA as her mother. In that regard, her mother was like her identical twin. Many found that feat of reproductive biology troubling, especially when they contemplated the application of similar techniques to humans.

Within a year, a scientist announced that he could, would, and should offer the technology as a service to infertile people. The news fueled the controversy about human cloning. Many called for regulation outlawing such practices. People in government, ethics, and medicine went on record in opposition to human cloning as unnatural, unproven, too risky for the cloned children, or a risk to genetic diversity. Others thought that the initial opposition seemed overstated or, because technologies can't be prevented, unrealistic.

a. Which of the reasons for and against cloning of humans apply to the cloning of other species?

b. Might reasons for opposing or regulating cloning of other species depend on the species? Should the acceptability of cloning animals depend on its uses? For example, suppose someone clones cattle to develop consistent quality of meat, versus to produce a medically valuable drug.

c. What enforceable restrictions or regulations, if any, for the cloning of humans are most important?

d. Cloning resonates with many stories and anxieties in culture.

   i. Identity issues, in metaphysics and literature, have always intrigued us. Can we effectively distinguish someone from a simulacrum, a twin, a doppelganger, an alter ego?

   ii. Given that two clones—particularly if gestated or raised separately—should turn out different from one another, might they also be very similar in ways beyond the superficial resemblance?

   iii. How much risk exists in the production of multiple clones of individuals?

   iv. Would clones be more likely to be exploited or accorded less respect than other persons?

   v. Might some of the concern actually involve the same issues as eugenics?

e. Because all new biotechnologies require testing, how (if at all) should experimental creation of clones (perhaps compared with in vitro fertilization) deserve special caution?

f. Because the creation of Dolly required hundreds of attempts before one was actually born, what problems does this technique raise about the cloned cell clusters or fetuses that do not survive to birth?

g. Would the design of effective prenatal tests for potential health problems help or create further problems?

12.11 OBJECTION TO AN ABORTUS-DERIVED VACCINE

Dr. G, who is firmly opposed to abortion, refuses to use an effective new vaccine because it is made using a line of cells derived from an aborted fetus (abortus). Some of his colleagues believe him guilty of providing substandard care to his patients in this regard. People describe him in terms ranging from "principled" and "courageous" to "zealot" and "fanatic."

a. Does Dr. G have an obligation to his patients to explain to them his conscientious refusal? If so, does he have an obligation to make available to them information about where they can find the vaccine?

b. Suppose Dr. G refuses, because of his views of abortion, to make vaccine information available to patients who could benefit from it. Is he guilty of providing substandard care to these patients?

c. To what extent does the source or origin of something—in this case, the fetal cells—affect the morality of using it? Might there be a moral difference between using the cells themselves and using the cells' cloned "descendants"?

d. To what extent might the acceptability of using abortuses for the development of medical treatments depend on either of the following factual questions?

i. Was the woman's choice to have the abortion influenced by her belief that the fetus's tissues would be used for medical purposes?

ii. Would refusal to use the vaccine cause the number of abortions to drop?

12.12 USE OF EMBRYONIC STEM CELLS TO HEAL

Medical researchers have experimentally transplanted tissue from embryonic stem cells to animals with various conditions. Stem cells, because undifferentiated, have more adaptability of function. They are also less likely to cause immune system rejection in the host. Ethical questions have arisen, however, because of the *source* of the cells.

Mrs. H, sixty-seven years old, has Parkinson's disease, and she consequently has tremors and difficulty using motor skills such as walking. Because her disease is progressive, she can anticipate worsening of the symptoms in her remaining few years. Her doctor informs her of a highly experimental program at a nearby medical center, but when she learns of the nature of the treatment, she feels uncomfortable about it because the therapy uses embryonic stem cells.

a. If the stem cells would be discarded otherwise, does this represent a better use of them? Compare, perhaps, the harvesting of tissue from people whose bodies would otherwise be buried or cremated. On the other hand, many people would not, if asked, allow their tissues to be harvested and used. Should, then, there exist a presumption in favor of or against harvesting from cadavers?

b. If the abortions generating the embryos were morally questionable, would that taint their products? Is it morally wrong to view anything derived from an aborted embryo as a product?

c. Does the fact that the embryos did not consent to use of their tissues render that use improper? If so, then would it follow that *any* decision about—or even for—a fetus or young child is improper, because none of them can give consent?

12.13   STEM CELLS, POTENTIALITY, AND MORAL STATUS

Dr. S, a researcher, plans to create some four-day-old clusters of human cells by in vitro fertilization. She will then attempt, by biotechnology, to transform their stem cells into liver cells that could be cloned and then implanted into people with liver diseases. Ms. W challenges this type of work: such a process, she argues, takes something that is on its way to becoming a person and alters it. Surely, she says, just as no one would dream of turning a child into a giant liver just to help people with liver disease, so too, we must avoid doing this with a very early human. Dr. S argues that since the embryonic (termed "pre-embryonic" by some) stem cells have such research potential, the research should go forward. Ms. W believes that the defenders of such research are sophists or that they are morally blinded by their enthusiasm for science and their hope for cures.

a. Is Dr. S or Ms. W more justified? Why?

b. At what point in development of an embryo or fetus would use of it for research become questionable? Or should the ethical focus not consist of a point in time? If there is a time or developmental stage, what is that time or stage, and why is *it* decisive?

c. If differentiation has not yet occurred, then in what sense is it (he? she?) a human, rather than a pre-human—or is it perhaps a pre-person? If it is not yet implanted?

d. What of a sperm cell and an egg cell just prior to fertilization? What type of potentiality do they possess?

e. Suppose a four-celled cluster is teased apart, and each of the cells becomes a human. What was the moral status of the cluster? How would this be ethically different from the intentional formation of identical twins?

f. Would it affect the morality of the situation to use blastocysts from IVF that would not have been implanted?

g. Would it affect the project's morality if the stem cell research seemed promising toward benefitting those with Alzheimer's, Parkinson's, diabetes, and other serious conditions? Would this depend on *how* promising it was (that is, how probable its good results would be)?

h. We have elsewhere referred to the use of utilitarian and deontological reasons to support moral judgments. These are mobilized as well to think about stem cells. Does either seem especially useful for illumination of these issues?

  i. *Utilitarian:* The research is likely to have good consequences for humanity.

  ii. *Deontological:* Since it is wrong to kill humans, and since the embryonic stem cells are humans—albeit in their early stage of development, destruction of them is morally wrong.

  iii. How should we balance the importance of performing research on "adult" (differentiated) stem cells versus researching embryonic stem cells? While there remains insufficient information about either type, what follows ethically about the amount of research appropriate for each type?

12.14 CONSIDERING AN ABORTION

Miss M, age twenty-two, learns she is pregnant. She wants to continue working and going to graduate school without the responsibilities of raising a child at this time. She contemplates having an abortion.

 a. Suppose her husband (or her boyfriend) does not want her to have an abortion at this time and offers to help raise the child.

 b. Suppose the husband or boyfriend wants her to have the abortion, but Miss M has second thoughts about it.

 c. Suppose she finds that the pregnancy is eight weeks along. Twelve weeks? Sixteen weeks? Twenty weeks? Twenty-five weeks? Thirty weeks? Thirty-four weeks?

 d. Suppose Miss M learns, from prenatal diagnosis, that the baby would probably have Down's syndrome.

 e. Suppose the baby would have trisomy-13, which is lethal within the first year.

 f. What are reasons that Miss M should or should not consider adoption instead?

 g. Would it be morally acceptable for her to contract with a couple willing to compensate her if she gave the child to them after it was born? Would this be belated surrogate pregnancy, preadoption, baby marketing, or something else?

12.15 SEEKING PRENATAL DIAGNOSIS FOR A POSSIBLE SEX-CHOICE ABORTION

Miss J, twenty-eight, has her regular appointment with her obstetrician, Dr. O. The three-month pregnant Miss J wants to discuss having a test performed to determine the sex of the fetus. She wants this information, she explains, because her boyfriend wants a son and has made it clear that any other outcome would have an adverse effect on their relationship. Thus, a female fetus would "have to" be aborted. Dr. O thinks, although she refrains from saying so, that Miss J should not be involved in a relationship involving such manipulation.

 a. If abortion for career choice is permissible, why is abortion for sex choice (of the fetus) less so?

b. If abortion for reason of sex choice is wrong, should it also be illegal? Which wrong abortions should be prohibited by law? None? Some? All?

c. Suppose Miss J only learned that the fetus was female as of the twentieth week of the pregnancy. Would that make a difference to the acceptability of the abortion? If so, why?

d. Suppose Miss J asks Dr. O for her advice about what to do. What should Dr. O say? Consider some further alternative suppositions:

   i. Dr. O thinks that all abortions after four weeks are completely impermissible, but she recognizes that many would disagree with her. What should she say to Miss J?

   ii. Dr. O thinks that all abortions until viability, regardless of the other reasons or circumstances, are permissible, but she recognizes that many would disagree with her. What should she say to Miss J?

12.16 MORAL OR LEGAL RESPONSIBILITIES DURING PREGNANCY?

Ms. Z, a pregnant twenty-four-year-old woman with two children, takes various illegal drugs that have been shown to greatly increase the likelihood of birth defects and children's susceptibility to illness after birth. She also smokes, drinks a lot, and eats mostly junk food. She has not sought out any prenatal care or advice. When she was growing up, this was, more or less, what she had seen at home as well.

a. Would it be acceptable for society to regulate Ms. Z's behavior?

b. If so, does the justification for regulating her conduct have to do with anything other than her illegal drug use? Is any of it based on the interests (or future interests) of the fetus?

c. Is there a prenatal counterpart of child abuse?

d. Are women's responsibilities to their fetuses exhausted by their rights to have (or not to have) abortions? Or are there other responsibilities that are contingent on the expectation that one will bring a pregnancy to term?

e. If regulation is permissible, exactly which risk factors and behaviors should be monitored? Consider, for example, skiing, sky diving, riding motorcycles, or working as a server in a smoky bar.

f. Would it be permissible for a private employer to require all pregnant employees to take prenatal classes to reduce the incidence of preterm labor, which has cost the company a great deal due to increased insurance premiums?

g. Some object to regulation of women's behavior during pregnancies as not workable. Would the difficulty or impossibility of consistently enforcing prenatal responsibility by means of the criminal law make it a misguided approach?

h. Would prenatal accountability create a slippery slope leading to the acceptance of something like a pregnancy police?

12.17 AMNIOCENTESIS: RISKS AND INDICATIONS

Mrs. W, a pregnant, healthy thirty-year-old, requests amniocentesis, a prenatal diagnostic procedure usually considered "indicated" (that is, advisable) only for women of at least age thirty-five—although women younger than thirty-five are often informed of its availability. She does not have any of the risk factors usually associated with recommending earlier amniocentesis. She asserts that even though rates of certain birth defects rise more steeply at about age thirty-five, she wants to rule out any foreseeable chance of "problems" with her fetus. Her obstetrician, however—Dr. O—does not approve of Mrs. W's reasoning. She thinks that the probability of any detectable birth defect is negligible and that there is a slight (half of 1 percent, or 1/200) probability that significant harm, such as loss of the fetus, might result from the procedure. (This 1/200 probability is, incidentally, controversial.) Mrs. W insists that her balancing of the risks and benefits, including the probabilities, has led her toward requesting the "amnio."

    a. If the age of thirty-five is usually recommended for consideration of amniocentesis because of an increasingly steep rise in the incidence of some birth defects in women in their midthirties, does that justify such a cutoff point? Why should the steepness of the rise matter rather than, say, some specified percentage of birth defects?

    b. Is Mrs. W's thinking flawed, either morally or scientifically?

    c. Is the obstetrician's thinking flawed, either morally or scientifically?

    d. Suppose Mrs. W states that she herself would not request the procedure except that her husband is pushing her to have it done, and she wants to put his mind at ease. What is the nature of Dr. O's responsibility in such a case? Should she request a meeting with the husband to explain why she believes the procedure is not indicated in Mrs. W's case? If Mrs. W opposes such a meeting, should the doctor refuse to perform the procedure, which she believes not to be "indicated"?

    e. How much weight should be placed on a patient's request for procedures such as this that are judged not medically required? How might one distinguish between what is and what is not "medically required" without bringing in value judgments?

12.18 RU-486 AND ABORTION

The abortion drug, RU–486, may alter the abortion debate. RU–486 is a medical, rather than surgical method, one that can be used at home by taking a few pills—although its proper use requires supervision and monitoring by a physician. In some countries it is legally available, in others prohibited, and in yet others gradually being phased in, sometimes with considerable opposition.

    Miss P, eighteen years old and unmarried, finds that she is pregnant. Although she regrets not having been more consistently conscientious about contraception, she decides to have an abortion. Her physician can prescribe RU–486, which is more than

95 percent effective at terminating a pregnancy if used as indicated within the first seven weeks of pregnancy.

    a. Would an abortion done by this method be either better or worse, morally, than one done by other methods?

    b. Some factual issues need to be resolved:

        i. Will the number of abortions increase?

        ii. Will the time of the abortions shift (so that, perhaps, more will be done before the seventh week of pregnancy)?

        iii. What percentage of abortions will be affected by increased use of this method?

        iv. What are the effects on the woman and the fetus by the alternative methods?

    c. Consider some alternatives:

        i. *If* almost all abortions are morally permissible, then how should we view the introduction of RU–486, morally?

        ii. *If* earlier abortions are preferable to later abortions, then how should we view the introduction of RU–486?

        iii. *If* almost all abortions are morally impermissible, then how should we view the introduction of RU–486?

12.19 PARTIAL BIRTH ABORTIONS (OR WHATEVER THEY SHOULD BE CALLED)

J is six months pregnant. Cramps have troubled her for the past month. Her obstetrician just informed her that the pregnancy is not proceeding well. The fetus had, whether because of genetic causes or due to factors present while it was in utero, received inadequate nutrition and oxygen. Its nervous system and limbs had sustained patent, extensive damage. J's family and boyfriend tell her what they think she should do. Her parents want her to continue the pregnancy, and the boyfriend urges her to have an abortion. She agrees with some, but not all, of their reasons. She is torn about whether to further consider having an abortion. Because of the stage of the pregnancy, her doctor has told her that the abortion might be—although he does not put it this way—a "partial birth" abortion. This would entail partly delivering the fetus and, to ease the extraction for the woman, removing the skull's contents.

    a. The logically polar opposite stances of "pro-life" and "pro-choice" advocates are reflected in debates about what is termed either "partial birth abortions" or "a certain type of (late-term) abortions." What *empirical* or factual considerations seem relevant to the ethical issue? (For example, how safe are the alternatives? Does the fetus experience pain?) Which *conceptual* and *value* factors should be emphasized or clarified? (For example, how should we understand the fetus' moral status at this stage of development? If the fetus is viable, would that make the procedure more wrong than it would be otherwise? Significantly so?)

b. If it is especially troubling, exactly why is it so? Because of the fetus' developmental stage? Because of the crushing of the skull? Because of the removal of the brain-matter as part of the procedure? If the procedure is more objectionable than other abortion methods, how is it so?

c. Can the circumstances of the pregnancy (such as medical risk to the mother or a fetus with a lethal defect) be relevant, or does the stage of the pregnancy and/or grisliness of the procedure override the possible reasons for allowing an abortion at that point? For example, suppose J's life depended on the procedure. Would that affect its moral justifiability?

12.20   BUILDING A BETTER MOUSE

In Daniel Keyes' science fiction classic, *Flowers for Algernon,* scientists produce a mouse with greatly increased intelligence, and then apply that technique to a human with low intelligence. Science produced an example of science imitating art, when it was announced in 1999 that Joe Tsien led a team that engineered increased intelligence in mice. Compared to others of their species, the mice had dramatically higher learning abilities.

It is the near future. Three individuals are presented for consideration. E, who has lower than average intelligence, and C, who has normal intelligence, have both been given an intelligence-boosting pill. A, on the other hand, has by all accounts been *bred* with high analytic intelligence, creativity, physical dexterity, and emotional acumen.

a. Is increasing learning of some skills to be equated as learning in general? Is it to be identified with increasing intelligence?

b. Increasing intelligence in other species seems not to be morally troubling. Would engineering learning-improvement or intelligence-increase in *humans,* by either genetic or pharmacalogic means, be morally questionable? If so, then why? Would it make a difference if the engineered change occurred in adults or newly conceived individuals?

c. What sorts of enhancement of human function are morally questionable? What sorts might be praiseworthy? Why?

12.21   A REPRODUCTIVE STRATEGY: PRE-TESTS AND POST-TESTS

Mr. and Mrs. C, an affluent couple who reside in the not-too-distant future, have close friends whose child suffers from many developmental and physical disabilities. They wish to avoid these problems, and so seek the help of people who will reassure them that they need not worry about such a situation. With the help of several people, they design a strategy that will draw upon a range of expertise. A reproductive specialist will be able to eliminate some of the sperm and eggs most likely to result in defects. Then, the specialist will fertilize eggs with the sperm and again test the several-celled embryos (or pre-embryos) for suspicious signs. Optimal embryos will be implanted, and Mrs. C will undergo tests during the pregnancy. Finally, the fetus will be subjected to batteries of pre-natal tests and monitoring until birth. Just after the baby is born, it will be given the legally required tests plus additional tests.

a. Consider the questions about fetal moral status raised in connection with the cases about abortion.

b. Should prenatal genetic counseling be prohibited for some conditions? If so, why those? Should it be required in some instances?

c. Should pre-conception counseling be prohibited or regulated for some (or for all) conditions? Why?

d. Should pre-implantation counseling be prohibited or regulated for some (or all) conditions? Why?

e. Should the costliness of such a strategy represent an ethical objection to it?

f. Which elements of the Cs' strategy should be covered by insurance?

g. Is this an offensive-sounding scenario? Is it an inspiring one? Explain.

h. What options are available to the couple if the child is discovered only after birth to have serious defects?

CHAPTER 13

Life and Death Decisions, Part I

Assisted Suicide and Other Patient Requests About Dying

In many people's opinion, the most pressing, difficult, and poignant sorts of questions have to do with decision making about life and death. How might one make a justified decision about the end of a life? That very general question needs to be divided up into a number of more specific questions.

ASSISTED SUICIDE

Whether health care workers should be allowed to assist people in committing suicide has become a major area of debate. The well-publicized actions of Dr. Kevorkian focused greater scrutiny on this issue. People in a number of countries and states have recently proposed methods for legalizing the practice, along with certain sorts of voluntary euthanasia. In the wake of two circuit court decisions in 1996, it appears that the United States Supreme Court will address these issues.

DRAWING DISTINCTIONS

Lately, citizens of many countries have tried to arrive at conscious, reflective laws, public and institutional policies, and individual decisions about the end of life. Health care workers have, at the same time, struggled to find lucidity and a level of moral comfort in their beliefs and practices. To what extent can some of the often invoked concepts help us decide, and to what extent do those concepts not provide helpful moral guidance? Consider the following distinctions, many of which can be found in the book's glossary.

Active euthanasia is one of the hottest of the hot-button issues in all of ethics. Contrasted with *passive euthanasia,* in which one lets someone die, active euthanasia involves killing someone for reasons having to do with that person's benefit. As with passive euthanasia, active euthanasia is (a) voluntary (done with the person's consent), (b) involuntary (done to a competent person without that person's consent—a form that is universally rejected), or (c) nonvoluntary (performed in circumstances such that a person cannot give consent—for example, a baby).

Additional issues are as follows:

Not initiating versus discontinuing treatment

Ordinary versus extraordinary means of treatment

Natural versus artificial means of treatment

Medical means versus nonmedical means

Invasive versus noninvasive means

Intended (directly intended) deaths versus not (directly) intended deaths

Assisting suicide versus performing euthanasia

This and the next chapters' cases review and inquire about all of these distinctions and more.

13.1   THE CASE OF DR. NEKROVIAK

Dr. Nekroviak, unrelated except by anagram to the more celebrated Dr. Kevorkian, believes in assisted suicide. He has not publicized his beliefs and has only assisted in the suicides of those who have already been his patients. He goes to considerable lengths to avoid participating in suicides of those who might merely be depressed. He expresses some ambivalence about the scope of privacy as applied to the justification of suicide decisions. Instead, he prefers to think of it as an exercise of people's liberty, a freedom that, in these instances, also coincides with those people's interests.

Mr. T, one of his patients, has AIDS. He does not yet show any signs of dementia but has increasingly frequent infections and wasting. The new combinations of drugs have not reversed the disease's ravaging effects. Mr. T has asked Dr. Nekroviak several times about the possibility of helping him commit suicide when the AIDS reaches a sufficiently advanced stage.

   a. Would Dr. Nekroviak be doing something morally wrong if he helped Mr. T commit suicide? If it is wrong, why is it wrong? Might it be any of the following reasons?

   i. Such a practice could not be adequately regulated to protect the vulnerable.

   ii. Because killing is wrong, killing of oneself is wrong, and so the facilitating of such self-killing is also wrong.

   iii. The patient only needs assurance that care at the end of life will be provided to keep him comfortable.

   iv. Such an activity would demonstrate and encourage a lack of respect for life.

    v. Such an activity values freedom too highly.

    vi. Some other reason or reasons.

  b. To what extent is each of these reasons persuasive or unpersuasive?

  c. How might one decide whether adequate safeguards could be established to prevent abuses of assisting suicide? What sorts of empirical evidence might help one decide this? What might make it difficult to gather such evidence?

13.2   ASSISTING A DYING PATIENT'S SUICIDE

Mrs. O, a dying patient, has pain that is not being satisfactorily controlled by medication. She requests help in committing suicide. Recent legal trends and public opinion, Dr. T realizes, have increasingly shifted in favor of allowing assisted suicide. Dr. T has also, however, heard that all instances of pain can be satisfactorily managed and that people just require such treatment and proper psychological support through those difficult times. Dr. T has also heard that health workers should not become takers of life—that it violates their role responsibilities. He is inclined to accept these latter notions.

  a. If medical and nursing practitioners disagree about a factual matter—in this case, about whether all pain can be managed—what should patients do?

  b. How should one understand the claim that it violates the health worker's role to assist a patient in dying? Is the role responsibility basic, and not derived from a further reason, or is it justified by something further, such as the risk of a slippery slope to killings everyone would agree are clearly unjustified?

  c. What additional role responsibilities do health workers have besides that of keeping patients alive? Might any of them, such as respecting patients' wishes, dignity, and right to be free of unnecessary pain, conflict with the life preservation obligation? Might the other responsibilities in some cases potentially override—that is, be morally weightier than—the responsibility to keep patients alive?

13.3   ASSISTING THE SUICIDE OF A CHRONICALLY ILL PATIENT WHO IS NOT DYING

Mrs. S is a sixty-three-year-old patient who has ALS (Lou Gehrig's disease), a degenerative neuromuscular condition. She has no history of depression but asks to be helped to die. Although her prognosis is poor, she is not expected to die within the next six months. She maintains that it is her decision and finds her own condition, plus the effect she is having on others—not to mention its economic effects on her family—has made her life, on balance, more unacceptable than acceptable. She does not subscribe to the view that as long as there is any happiness or love remaining it is more worthwhile to live than to die. Nor is she willing to completely ignore the financial consequences for her family.

  Which of the following are acceptable options? Which are the best choices?

  a. Dr. N, the physician in charge of the case, says that, because suicide is unnecessary and misguided, she will try to prevent it.

b. Dr. N says that she will not participate in the suicide but will not try to interfere with it.

c. Dr. N says that she will neither directly assist nor hinder the suicide, but will instead refer the patient to someone who would provide the requested assistance. (Is this perhaps assisting after all?)

d. Dr. N says that the patient needs to go through counseling and to draw up a statement explaining her situation. Only then will assisting be acceptable.

e. Dr. N says that she will respect the patient's wishes and will do everything possible to help.

f. Are there legal factors that ought to be considered as well? What weight do legal factors have in this case?

g. If Mrs. S considers the economic cost of her care as relevant to her suicide, could this sort of factor also justify many other suicides, including those by people who suffer from any expensive condition?

h. What does it mean when comparative poverty becomes an "indication" for allowing treatment termination? Or is this a natural consequence of an increasingly expensive health care system?

13.4   IGNORING A LIVING WILL AT A DAUGHTER'S INSISTENCE

Mr. G's daughter disagrees with her father's wishes as expressed in his living will, so she approves when the hospital workers intubate and resuscitate Mr. G after his massive stroke and place him on a respirator. He spends ten weeks on the respirator before dying. His attempts to remove the tubes are described by his daughter alternately as either not intentional or unacceptable, and so his wrists and ankles are placed in restraints. The hospital does not want to contend with the adamant daughter, who says that she would feel like a murderer if the living will were followed.

a. Are the hospital's actions only explainable purely prudentially, based on their own interests as interpreted by hospital attorneys, or can they also be defended as acting morally properly toward Mr. G and his family?

b. Is the use of restraints morally acceptable in this sort of situation? What alternatives do the health workers have?

c. If Mr. G somehow manages to indicate rational-seeming wishes during that time, should they then prevail? Suppose he refuses treatment. Should he then be perceived as a competent adult refusing treatment or as someone hastily trying to die prematurely?

13.5   INTERPRETING ADVANCE DIRECTIVES

An advance directive is either (a) a living will or (b) a durable power of attorney for health care (a health care proxy). People sign these documents while they are mentally competent, able to understand their situations and to think clearly about themselves.

The living will authorizes treatment to be withheld if one should become terminally ill/injured or "permanently unconscious." A durable power of attorney for health care (the name for such a document varies) designates someone (such as a spouse, child, or close friend) as a health care proxy to make health care decisions for one, including end-of-life decisions, if one should become unable to decide for oneself.

Mrs. B signed both sorts of advance directives. Several years later, she became completely incapacitated by a massive stroke. Her husband, Mr. B, is given conflicting interpretations of the notion of a "terminal" condition. These range from death expected within a matter of days to eventual death from the condition even if more than a year in the future. Although Mrs. B shows no signs of recognition of anyone or anything and is almost completely paralyzed, she is not imminently dying and is also conscious.

She develops several potentially life-threatening medical conditions, including increasingly severe heart and liver disorders. The prognosis of when her heart or liver will completely stop functioning is a matter of probabilities. When internists are asked for a quantified prediction, they estimate a 90 percent likelihood of death within the year and a 50 percent likelihood of death within six months.

a. Is Mrs. B's condition terminal? Is it a matter for decision?

b. Suppose Mr. B, based on conversations with his wife, knows that Mrs. B would not have wanted to be kept alive in her present condition. Would it be morally permissible for him to urge the health team to withhold everything except palliative means (comfort measures)?

c. Suppose the estimate were of a 25 percent likelihood of death within the next twelve months. Should Mr. B's decision to refuse life-prolonging treatment means be viewed as acceptable?

d. Do the notions of terminal condition and permanent unconsciousness seem, morally, to exhaust the circumstances in which people should be allowed to refuse (in advance or by decision of a proxy) life-sustaining treatments? What is there about each of these two that makes it morally permissible to hasten the moment of death?

13.6   DISCONTINUING NUTRITION AND HYDRATION

Mr. C, a seventy-four-year-old with metastatic bone cancer, wants to be allowed to die. His illness may take another few months to claim him. He wants to be able to die on his own terms. Some members of his health care team have said to him that he should try to stay alive for as long as possible and that they will do everything possible to keep him comfortable. He does not want to take them up on their offer. One apparently legal way to enable him to die would be to sedate him and discontinue his nutrition and hydration.

a. In what sense(s) are nutrition and hydration medical treatments, and in what sense(s) are they not? Might it depend on the type of nutrition and hydration, on the route of administration, or on other factors?

b. Would discontinuation of nutrition and/or hydration be more accurately characterized as killing or letting die? Does that matter for the ethics of this case?

c. Should Mr. C's mental competence affect the moral acceptability of the decision to discontinue nutrition and hydration? Why?

d. Does the presence of pain or the use of pain medication compromise the patient's mental competence?

e. Can this case be illuminated by means of the distinction between not initiating and discontinuing? Thus, some people have claimed that there is a much stronger obligation not to discontinue treatments once begun than there is to initiate the use of treatments. Others, however, have strongly challenged this view. Does either side seem more plausible?

f. What *moral* distinctions, if any, exist among the following?

   i. Discontinuing food and liquids given PO (by mouth).

   ii. Discontinuing nutrition and liquids given by NG (nasogastric) tube, a second type of enteral feeding (that is, via the digestive tract).

   iii. Discontinuing nutrition and liquids given by a tube directly into the stomach.

   iv. Discontinuing nutrition and hydration given intravenously (IV) by parenteral nutrition (infused other than enterally), either into a peripheral vein, such as in an arm, or into a central vein, in the neck or chest.

13.7 VOLUNTARY ACTIVE EUTHANASIA: UNTHINKABLE? ABOUT TIME?

Mr. V is dying of a painful disease and has always maintained that he did not want his life prolonged "unnecessarily." He reaffirms this even from his hospital bed, although he finds it awkward and humiliating to have to ask repeatedly to be released from his suffering.

Meanwhile, his doctors and nurses, for a number of reasons and causes, find it unthinkable that they should be asked to dispatch their patient. They offer Mr. V and his family a variety of options but refuse to be parties to something that they think goes contrary to their professional responsibilities. They tell him that, though he has the right to refuse treatment, he has no right to request that they murder him; for they perceive it as little better than any other murder.

a. If active euthanasia (AE) and passive euthanasia (PE) differ essentially in some crucial ways, what exactly are those ways? Is AE always more wrong than PE, is it usually so, or is it impossible to generalize about the morality of these practices?

b. In what respects is AE like the usual examples of unjustifiable homicide, and in what respects is it different?

c. If a euthanasia is voluntary, does that make it more acceptable? If it does, then is the greater acceptability sufficient to permit legalization of the practice?

d. Many people have argued that, even if in some cases voluntary AE were justified, it should not be legalized, because the practice would be too likely to be abused. Does this view seem plausible or implausible? How can we decide about these predictions, since they are empirical claims? What sort of investigation, study, or other evidence might be relevant to deciding such predictive claims?

e. Some advocates of AE have said that people's rejection of AE as killing is inconsistent with those same people's approval of killing in self-defense or in the defense of others. Is this view plausible or implausible?

CHAPTER 14

Life and Death Decisions, Part II

Deciding Limits of
Life-Prolonging Treatments

LIFE STAGES

Approached in terms of life stages, some decisions involve babies, others entail children past infancy, others are about young and middle-aged adults, and still others concern the elderly. In this chapter we explore cases with each age group.

DNR STATUSES

How should DNR (do not resuscitate) orders be used properly? These instructions, placed on the medical charts of many patients by their physicians, can set limits on the aggressiveness of certain sorts of care. Some cases discuss these.

TECHNICAL TERMS

How can people better understand and use concepts such as "medical futility," "not clinically indicated," "persistent vegetative state," "invasive," "death," and "brain-dead"? A number of the cases explore these matters.

14.1   LIMITING CARE BY AGE

An eighty-one-year-old man has advanced kidney disease. He requires hospitaliza-tions every few weeks, many sorts of medications, and kidney dialysis to stave off precipitate deterioration of his condition. Increasingly complicated, invasive, and uncomfortable forms of treatment have become necessary, progressing in complexity almost by the week.

   a. What care would benefit him? What is meant by "benefit," and how should it be determined?

   b. Should unlimited funds be allocated for the person's treatment from his insur-ance company? From his HMO? From Medicare? From his own or his family's savings?

   c. Should there be no limits on the amount of treatment the person receives? If limits are necessary, what should those limits be? How should they be deter-mined, and by whom?

   d. Suppose, instead, he has a condition that might respond to some costly treat-ment. Is his age a relevant consideration? To what extent may responses to questions a, b, or c be affected by the person's age?

   e. Should someone be morally obligated to discuss his condition, his options at each point, and, if he probably only has weeks or months to live, end-of-life plans with him?

14.2   SOMEONE ONCE RECOVERED: A SINGLE INSTANCE

Sixty-seven-year-old Mr. V has been comatose for a year. His wife has heard of a single instance of a recovery from such a condition. She believes that *any* chance of recovery, even if *almost* zero, is preferable to giving up hope. Mr. V's neurologist does not agree. He believes that Mrs. V's unrealistic perspective prevents her from allowing Mr. V to die and from getting on with her life.

   a. How should statistical information of this sort be presented by clinicians and evaluated by decision makers?

   b. Is Mrs. V's reasoning defensible, or is it more like that of the person who con-tinually buys lottery tickets on the slim chance that he might win the super prize?

   c. Suppose that looking after her husband provides meaning for Mrs. V. Does that, then, add credence to her view? Can the opportunity for devoting oneself to something—when considered independently of any possible benefits to the patient—justify use of health care resources? Could this open the door to al-lowing anything at all, including use of resources on delusions or proven frauds?

   d. Would this situation be significantly altered if Mr. V were on life support and Mrs. V had to decide about discontinuing life support?

14.3   *JUST VENTING?*

Miss E has undergone brain death, but a nurse argues forcefully for the ventilator to be kept on so that Miss E's far-flung family, most of whom cannot get there until the following week, can say goodbye to her. The medical interventions will cost $3000 per day, including use of the hospital room, as well as staffing. Some question this use of hospital resources, since the patient has already been pronounced dead.

a. Can one justify using "life support" when a patient is no longer alive? Has the family now become "the patient?"

b. Would it be justified to bill either the family or the insurance company for the continued use of hospital resources?

c. Would the propriety of billing the family or insurance company depend on whether or not they have been consulted and have agreed to the continued life support?

14.4   *TREATMENTS JUDGED "NOT CLINICALLY INDICATED:" THREE VIGNETTES*

Consider three situations, each involving a seventy-five-year-old person.

Scenario 1: Coronary bypass surgery is deemed "not clinically indicated" for Mr. B based on his age.

Scenario 2: Mrs. C has carcinoma of the breast with widespread metastases— irreversible spreading of cancer to other parts of her body. She develops cough and fever and seems to have pneumonia. She is not confused. Her oncologist deems that only comfort measures should be used for her, because other means are "not clinically indicated."

Scenario 3: Cardiologists and cardiac surgeons decide that Miss D, who has shortness of breath from moderately severe aortic stenosis-caused heart failure, should not be offered or recommended for valve replacement surgery since the surgery is "not clinically indicated."

a. Does the concept of "clinically indicated" or "not clinically indicated" have a clear meaning? Does it have clear criteria?

b. Is it a descriptive sort of judgment or an evaluative one?

c. If it is evaluative, what moral elements are contained in the determination of a decision as being indicated or not indicated?

d. Would consideration of the moral dimensions of such a judgment be performed best by clinicians? Why?

e. Many people believe that *futile* treatment is either not morally required or morally wrong. How should medical futility be determined? How does it differ from labeling a treatment "not clinically indicated"?

f. Which of the three patients (if any) should receive treatment? If treatment should be denied to any, is it because the treatment is not clinically indicated? If that is the case, then what is meant by saying that treatment is not clinically indicated?

14.5   "WE DON'T HAVE TO BEGIN THIS TREATMENT, BUT ONCE WE DO . . ."

Mr. B, eighty-four years old, suffers from multi-infarct dementia and has become mostly incoherent and immobilized from the brain damage. When he had had one episode of difficulty breathing, the health care team placed him on a respirator. His doctor, Dr. E, advises Mr. B's family that they must continue to provide that care since it is already in effect. Only the decision to begin the treatment involved a real choice, Dr. E states.

a. Some people maintain that there is an essential difference, morally, between not initiating treatment and discontinuing treatment. Do you agree? On what, exactly, is that distinction based?

b. To the extent that such a distinction is useful, is it based on something further, such as the difference between killing and letting die?

c. Should the children's opinions be considered as much as the wife's?

d. Would withholding treatment involve making unacceptably value-laden judgments about quality of life? Should quality of life be taken into consideration at all? If it can be considered, how should the frequently invoked concepts of "quality of life" and "acceptable quality of life" be understood?

14.6   DO-NOT-RESUSCITATE PROBLEMS: TWO VIGNETTES

Scenario 1: Legally, a competent adult has the right to refuse treatment. Nevertheless, for a number of reasons including financial risk management, physicians and hospitals often defer to the wishes of family members who do not want to see their loved ones die. Mrs. Z, a thirty-year-old woman dying from AIDS and still mentally competent, has asked not to be resuscitated if she should suffer a cardiac or respiratory arrest. Her husband, Mr. Z, disagrees with her about this and wants everything possible done for her.

Scenario 2: Mr. Y, eighty-eight years old, has congestive heart failure. His family has asked that he not be resuscitated if he stops breathing or if his heart stops, and the physician has agreed to this. Mr. Y has not, however, been informed of the decision.

a. If Mrs. Z's expressed wishes are not formulated in a legal advance directive such as a living will or a durable power of attorney for health care, do they have less moral force?

b. If a close family member, or even most of the person's family, disagree with the patient's decision, what is the morally best thing to do? Does it depend on the nature of the patient's decision?

c. Although a mentally competent person has the legal right to refuse treatment, does the person also always have a corresponding moral right?

d. Has Mr. Y's family made a good decision in protecting Mr. Y from knowledge of his "code status" (in this case, not to resuscitate)? Might it depend on the sort of person Mr. Y is and its likely effects on him?

e. Suppose Mrs. Z or Mr. Y is ruled mentally incompetent. Should health care teams factor in the pain and suffering of those close to the patient when deciding whether to issue a DNR order? If so, should those family and/or friends be able to influence the physician to assign a DNR order as well as to release the patient from it?

14.7 INVASIVENESS

In decision making, including those about life and death, people's ethical judgments are based on what they believe to be morally relevant factors. One of the most important such factors in many people's, including many clinicians', decision making is *invasiveness*. Other things being equal, noninvasive treatments are universally assumed preferred to invasive ones. Invasive procedures intrude on anatomical boundaries. Thus, injections, catheters of all sorts, intravenous lines, nasogastric and tracheostomy tubes, and surgeries are all invasive means of treatment.

Mrs. A, eighty-six years old, thinks of herself as being fortunate to have avoided much illness or disability during her life. She lives in an extended care facility and gets around with the use of a cane. Based on her observations of the deaths of friends and relatives, she has concluded, and stated to anyone who will listen, that she does not want to end her life "with a bunch of tubes in me."

a. Might there be degrees of invasiveness as well as something's being either invasive or not? Thus, for example, heart surgery would be more invasive than an injection.

b. Should Mrs. A be forced to clarify exactly what she does and does not want done, or would pressing her about such possibilities be unnecessarily stressful and cruel? Given the importance of making decisions that she would agree with, how might people obtain more specific information about her values and wishes to be able to provide the amount of care she would want? (Some of the advanced directives now allow for people to specify their values and wishes in at least some contingencies.)

c. Is it possible that Mrs. A fears becoming incapacitated at least as much as she does the tubes?

d. If we take her at her word, does this mean that one or two tubes would be acceptable to her?

14.8 MENTAL RETARDATION AND QUALITY-OF-LIFE JUDGMENTS

Miss U, age twenty-four, is transferred from an extended care facility to a hospital. The woman, who was transferred because of respiratory distress, has profound mental retardation and cerebral palsy. She has neither verbal nor nonverbal means of communication. As the respiratory distress worsens, the staff decides that intubation and mechanical ventilation are needed. The parents had, some years before, signed a do-not-resuscitate (DNR) order.

a. Would it be acceptable for the decision makers—whoever they may be—to consider the patient's mental and physical disabilities in judging the acceptability of a satisfactory outcome? Or would consideration of either sort of disabilities as relevant constitute a form of discrimination against people with disabilities?

b. Who should make the decision about treatment or nontreatment of Miss U: the hospital medical team, the parents, the medical team at the extended care facility, the ethics committee, or the legal system?

c. Suppose the parents thought Miss U should be allowed to die but the medical teams disagreed. Suppose the parents thought she should be kept alive but the medical teams disagreed. Should the parents' or medical team's judgments prevail?

d. Are these decisions best understood as *primarily* medical, ethical, or legal?

14.9 DECIDING WHETHER TO OFFER OPTIONS: METASTATIC CANCER AND PNEUMONIA

Mr. N, a sixty-three-year-old man, has metastatic cancer and pneumonia. The health care team discuss what options to offer him. At this point, treatment does not include further chemotherapy, but they consider the possibility of intubation by tracheostomy, so that he could be placed on a respirator. They realize that this approach would not reverse his terminal illness and that it would commit them to a protracted, comparatively uncomfortable course of treatments, quite likely ending with him unconscious or stuporous. They know that some people do elect this option anyway.

a. Does the fact that all or most of the health team, including the attending physician, find the tracheostomy route undesirable mean that they ought not to offer it to him?

b. How harmful must an option be for it to be permissible not to offer it to a patient?

c. How beneficial must an option be for it to be offered to a patient?

d. In general, what criteria should determine which options may be offered to patients?

14.10   *LIMITS OF PREMATURITY*

Baby N, born at twenty-five weeks' gestational age, weighs six hundred grams (about one and a quarter pounds). Although the technology in neonatology of keeping very premature infants alive improves yearly, Baby N has less than a 10 percent probability of surviving. Because of her extreme prematurity and very low birth weight, if she survives she will probably sustain physical or developmental damage. The parents and health care team have to decide how aggressively to treat her. (See also the pediatric case "Resuscitation of a Very Premature Infant" on page 151.)

a. Is the fact that 10 percent is greater than 0 percent central to deciding the issue?

b. Should the high probability of physical or developmental harm be a factor in deciding how aggressively to treat Baby N? Suppose Baby N were one year old instead. Should the decisions be arrived at in a similar fashion? Why?

c. If decisions about life and death are slightly different for newborns than for older children, does that mean that we view newborns as having slightly less moral status than the older children?

d. Is it permissible to consider the expense of treating the child and/or the effects it will have on the parents/family when making decisions about whether to treat Baby N?

e. Suppose the health care team and the parents disagree about how aggressively to treat Baby N. Should there be a presumption about whose wishes should prevail in such a case? That is, should one be the default decision maker in the event of a disagreement?

14.11   *TRISOMY QUANDARY*

Baby B has a trisomy, which is usually (75 percent) fatal in the first year. She also has several congenital anomalies (birth defects) of varying degrees of severity. Her care costs hundreds of thousands of dollars during the first year. The cost will likely be shared by her parents, her insurance company, the pediatric hospital, and possibly also eventually the state—when the others run out of ability or willingness to pay.

a. Suppose the parents ask that treatment be discontinued. Is that an acceptable option for them? If it is permissible for them to request, how strong an obligation would it impose on the health workers and their institutions?

b. Suppose the parents insist that "everything" possible be done. To what extent should their wishes be honored? To what extent should there be limits on the granting of their wishes?

c. In what ways is it acceptable to consider costs in making decisions about Baby B? In what ways would it be unacceptable to consider costs? What weight do economic factors have in this case? (This is, of course, a question applicable to many cases.)

d. Should an upper limit on health care expenditures be set per person, especially if the money does not seem to produce adequate benefits? Or is raising such a possibility morally impermissible?

14.12 CONJOINED TWINS

In 2000, a Maltese couple brought their conjoined infant twins to England for treatment. When the children's condition began to deteriorate, the parents were confronted with the difficult decision of whether to authorize a procedure to surgically separate the twins. Since the twins shared some organs, only one of them would be able to survive the procedure. Without the surgery, it was highly probable that both children would die in a matter of months. The parents refused permission for the surgery. This was based on their belief that, as Catholics, to give permission would impermissibly entail killing one—who would (only) have survived a few more months—as a means toward saving the other. Eventually, a British court ordered the surgery, and it resulted in one twin dying sooner than otherwise, while the other twin survived.

Several types of analysis emerged during the public debate. At one level, utilitarian reasons contrasted with deontological reasons.

a. (Primarily) *utilitarian reasoning:* Minimize harm by doing the procedure. To withhold surgery would have the foreseeable and preventable result of allowing the deaths of both, rather than preventing one death.

b. *Formalist deontological reasoning:* Intentional killing is, in itself, always morally wrong. Killing would not be made acceptable by its having good consequences.

Some discussions of the situation focused on other matters, such as the following:

c. The children's best interest should be respected, so the courts could rightfully intervene and override the parents' wishes.

d. The parents have the right to make the decision, since it is not among the few classes of possible legal exceptions.

   i. Might utilitarian reasoning about life and death decisions justify killing of some people in order to save others?

   ii. Might formalist reasoning, which discounts consequences as morally permissible considerations, lead to inflexible judgments?

   iii. How would one decide what is in the children's best interests?

   iv. Who should have made the decision? The parents? The courts? The medical team? An ethics committee?

   v. How should we decide what should be legal exceptions to treatment otherwise viewed as medically necessary?

Although it was not mentioned in the media at the time, the parents' religious tradition contained a notion termed the *Doctrine of Double Effect,* which seems applicable. According to that doctrine, an action that is otherwise bad can be permitted under certain conditions:

a. It is not wrong in itself.

b. What is intended is the good effect; the bad effect is foreseen, but not directly intended.

c. The evil is not a means to the good.

d. The good must be proportionate to the harm (roughly put, the good must be more defensible).

In the case of the conjoined twins, the four conditions seem applicable as follows:

a. Was the surgery life-saving, and so not wrong in itself, or was it lethal for one, and so wrong to that extent?

b. What was intended? Seemingly, the saving of the one child who would otherwise have soon died; the death of the twin, while foreseen, was not what was intended.

c. The death of the one twin was not a means to the life of the other; rather, the surgery resulted in both.

d. Exactly how to judge the respective goods and harms is unclear. Those in favor of the surgery would say that it would be more likely to result in a reasonably happy, normal life for the surviving child; opponents would argue that the premature death of one baby was too high a moral cost.

14.13   PERSISTENT VEGETATIVE STATE

Seventy-nine-year-old Mrs. C has been in a persistent vegetative state (PVS) for eight months. In that condition, she has lost all conscious and cognitive function, since her brain cortex has shut down. Only the brain stem, which maintains some involuntary responses and reflexes, is functioning. After such a length of time, recovery is virtually unprecedented. Mrs. C's family is torn about what to do and how to feel about her.

a. Would discontinuing her artificial feeding constitute active euthanasia or passive euthanasia?

b. Is there some reason other than its being classified as active euthanasia that would help you decide whether it is morally acceptable?

c. Would removing Mrs. C from a mechanical ventilator (if she is on one) be active euthanasia?

d. Should the family be given full power to decide her medical fate, or should there be some guidelines (legal, ethics committee, or other) as to what they may or may not decide about her? If there are constraints, what should they be?

e. At what point should her family be offered, encouraged, or allowed the option of withholding or discontinuing life-sustaining measures? Within a few weeks of the PVS beginning? A few months? A year? More than a year? Never?

f. May cost considerations be relevant? If so, should they be mentioned to the family?

g. Is it morally permissible for financial considerations to be considered in decisions about how to proceed?

h. Should *any* nonzero probability of recovery (that is, if anyone in such a situation has *ever* recovered) be considered sufficient reason to continue treatment?

14.14   REFUSING TREATMENT FOR A PATIENT WITH BRAIN DAMAGE

A man had sustained severe brain damage some years ago, to the point that he had lost his ability to recognize people and to perform any cognitive tasks. His wife, who was his legally authorized decision maker, requested that he be taken off life-support systems even though (a) he was not in a persistent vegetative state or coma, and (b) he had left no documented written evidence of his wishes. According to legal precedents, the presence of these conditions would have made the decision clearer. The wife (with the support of other family members) claimed that he had indicated he would not want to be kept alive with "tubes" and unable to communicate. One family member, as well as a disability-rights advocacy group, argued against allowing the withdrawal of life support.

a. If a competent adult has the right to refuse treatment, should the legally designated decision maker for an incompetent adult have a similar right? Why or why not?

b. Would allowing withdrawal of treatment be wrong in itself? Would it be wrong because it would risk beginning (or continuing) a slippery slope?

c. If the laws about withdrawing treatment cover primarily irreversible consciousness and imminent death, does it become too questionable to consider such withdrawal in other classes of cases?

d. Should the family be allowed to prolong treatment by means of providing financial support?

14.15   THE SEARCH FOR MEDICAL FUTILITY: NOT NECESSARILY HOPELESS

Each of the following situations has been mentioned in discussions of the concept of *medical futility*.

♦ The *Wanglie* case: The husband of eighty-seven-year-old Helga Wanglie refused to allow withdrawal of life support from his wife, even though she was in an irreversible persistent vegetative state. The staff at Minnesota's Hennepin County Hospital thought that continued use of those means was unwarranted.

♦ The *Scoon* case: The parents of a brain-dead child would not allow withdrawal of life support machinery from their daughter, even after she had been pronounced brain dead.

♦ An eighty-seven-year-old woman is found in asystole (with no heartbeat) at the nursing home where she resides.

♦ *Palliative care* and *comfort care*, including hospices, are used when other, more aggressive, means are judged inappropriate due to incurability.

a. Concepts about "futility" are still in great debate. Each of the following has been put forward as a definition or criterion of "futility." How might an advocate of the criteria reply to the questions accompanying them?

 i. Futility as *zero probability of benefit* from a medical treatment. Question: Can't something be futile because it has too low a likelihood, even though it is not impossible?

 ii. Futility as *zero quality of life* resulting from a medical treatment. Question: Can't something be futile because the resulting quality of life is too low rather than zero? Also, doesn't probability level matter?

 iii. Futility as a type of treatment that is *never beneficial*. Question: Can't something be futile because it is insufficiently beneficial (or probable, etc.)?

 iv. Futility as *absence of all vital signs*. Question: Why must a patient actually be dead in order for treatment to be futile?

 v. Futility as a type of treatment that goes *contrary to fate*, that is, to what is destined to happen no matter what anyone does. Questions: If it is indeed fated to occur, then how could anyone change the outcome? Wouldn't attempts to prolong life, as well as those resulting in the end of a life, equally violate fate?

b. How would these features of a concept of *medical futility* be combined to enable judgments?

 i. Futile for a purpose. (For example, antibiotics are not futile per se, although they are futile for viral conditions.)

 ii. Level of futility. Futility might be more-or-less rather than either-or.

 iii. Some confounding factors. Information can be formulated or evaluated imprecisely; loved ones sometimes grasp at vanishingly small odds, even when great burdens might be entailed.

 iv. Although mentally competent adults have a right to refuse treatment, they can not demand treatment.

14.16 BE STILL, MY HEART

Ms. F has sustained massive brain injury, with destruction of her cerebral cortex precluding any future conscious activity. The hospital has a transplant team, and can make use of her organs and tissues. These body parts can best be obtained, however, if the heart is kept beating until the last possible moment. One possibility is to make use of a "non-heartbeating donor" (NHBD) protocol, which would allow life support, including ventilators, to be discontinued and the organs removed a few minutes after the ensuing cardiac arrest. A number of organ procurement centers now make use of such protocols, which are associated with a significant increase in the number of viable donations. Ms. F's family wants to donate her organs to help the recipients. Usually, however, in order to allow removal of organs for transplantation, the person must have undergone *total* brain death, including the brain stem, as well as the cortex.

a. Would use of the protocol constitute killing Ms. F? If so, is it wrongful killing or justified killing?

b. Is Ms. F being used as a means to someone else's good? If so, then is that morally wrong?

c. At what point should we judge that Ms. F has died? Based on what criterion or criteria?

d. Does Ms. F, rather than her body, no longer exist? If so, what would be the ethical relevance of that fact? For those who believe that a soul survives, is there a case to be made for claiming that her soul has already departed? What reasons might be helpful for deciding this metaphysical claim?

e. Since Ms. F will never again experience anything, can it be argued that she is not being harmed by being taken off life support?

f. Does use of such protocols mean that the concept of *death* can be crafted to meet transplantation needs? If so, is that a good or a bad idea?

CHAPTER 15

Allocation and Access

Often the demand for health care resources exceeds the supply. In conditions of scarcity, decisions have to be made about how to allocate the limited resources. Several important value norms tend to inform people's moral judgments about allocation. These include justice, freedom, and quality of life. Each of these, however, requires clarification. In Chapter 4 about managed care and the health care business, there are related topics in several of the cases.

CRITERIA FOR ALLOCATING SCARCE RESOURCES

Because decisions have to be made in which some people will receive certain sorts of care while others will not, these decisions should be as morally plausible as possible. We need consciously to seek out guiding principles and criteria that best structure a decision procedure for this sorting or rationing process.

In some societies, physicians work strictly for the state. In others, they work strictly for themselves. Just as there are mixed economies, so too there are complex and multiple combinations of incentive structures and degrees of independence and obligation for physicians. In systems allowing physicians and medical institutions such as hospitals some latitude of choice in these matters, the exercise of those choices often has a profound impact on people's lives.

Whether a society should have universal access to an equal level of health care leads to questions and problems of great complexity. First, universal access to *at least some* level of care—perhaps a guaranteed floor meeting basic health care needs—differs from universal allocation of an *equal* level of health care. Second, people need to decide whether all care treatments should be used regardless of how costly it is and how much good it would do. Third, we need to clarify whether personal responsibility for health, illness, or injury may be considered in deciding about allocating resources. Fourth, we must decide whether all health workers would be part of the same plan or whether there can be alternative plans with alternative methods of funding, costs, and incentives. Fifth, we should look for a structure that will maximize values of health, quality of care, affordability, convenience, fairness, satisfaction by both providers and patients, and other important priorities. Governments are all experimenting with, and modifying, a variety of systems.

TRANSPLANTATION ISSUES

Organ and tissue transplantation create many ethical problems. For one, society, professionals, and individuals need to decide what are permissible and impermissible methods of obtaining organs. Suppose an impoverished person offers to sell blood, tissue, or a body part. To the extent that any of these is found objectionable, the reasons must be made clear. A second area of concern has to do with people not competent to consent: fetuses, anencephalic newborns, and cadavers. How might we distinguish the morally permissible from the impermissible sources of tissues, organs, or blood? A third sort of question concerns the methods of procurement of organs and blood from those who die. Should organ donation, procurement, and harvesting be (a) a purely voluntary system, (b) encouraged by requiring a health worker to request authorization from the next of kin, or (c) optimized by automatically harvesting under a system of presumed consent, barring only those who have registered objections of conscience? Each of the three methods is already in place in some countries.

Even the notion of "medical suitability" for transplantation is controversial and value laden, since prosperity, social class, and psychological factors may be included in people's lists of medical criteria.

PRICING, VALUING, AND RATIONING

Cost-benefit reasoning can be applied in thinking about litigation and policy areas. Some lawsuits require assigning an economic value to lives, experiences, or aspects of lives. While pain and suffering may seem roughly calculable in cases about accidents, how would one apply cost calculation to someone's existence? How should individuals' responsibility for their circumstances modify such financial estimates? How should disease-funding be calculated? For example, how would one compare funds to be allotted for AIDS vs. the amount for strokes?

How can one place monetary value on lives? How can we weigh one value, such as a life, against another, such as freedom or happiness? How should considerations of justice affect our perceptions of health care pricing—including drug prices in developing nations, lawsuit settlements, and appropriate levels of insurance coverage?

15.1   ACCESS TO HEALTH CARE

The Z's, a family of five, have a low income. Their insurance coverage is insufficient to pay for the treatment required by Mrs. Z, who is chronically ill. She has diabetes, suffers from frequent infections, and also has severe major depression. As a result, her symptoms frequently get worse rather than being resolved, and she experiences additional discomfort.

a. How should we understand the value-infused notion of treatment being "required"? Is it restricted to treatment needed to stay alive? Suppose the insurance covers insulin, but not depression treatment.

b. Would it matter if one of the children were uninsured instead? If so, does that mean that adults' lives and health are of less value than those of children?

c. Should the mental disorder (the depression) be viewed differently, in terms of worthiness of reimbursement, than the other health problems? If so, then why? The controversy about parity of health care coverage for mental health deals with this sort of problem (among others).

d. Should Mrs. Z have access to the health care system regardless of ability to pay? To what extent should ability to pay be relevant to the quantity and quality of health care one receives? Does society, collectively, have an obligation to every citizen to provide or insure some level of health care? Is there such an obligation to provide adequate police protection to citizens or education to its children?

e. Suppose Mrs. Z's health problems are exacerbated by her financial worries. Would this fact give her greater moral justification for access to health care independent of her ability to pay?

15.2   POOR ACCESS TO THE SYSTEM

Miss G, thirty, has two children, ages two and five. Both children have cystic fibrosis (CF). Miss G has a very low fixed income and relies on governmental support to make ends meet. Although government programs, social workers, and a local clinic would, in principle, enable her to provide much of the children's needed medical care, she has developmental problems herself and lacks parenting skills as well as the support systems, emotional resources, and stability necessary to care adequately for the children.

a. Suppose Miss G finds it difficult to get to the clinic with both children. Who should take responsibility for her transportation?

b. If she seems to lack the resources necessary to provide for the children's medical needs, should an agency remove them from the home? Should they threaten Miss G with this measure? Since *neglect* is defined in terms of failure to provide for the basic needs of a child, is Miss G guilty of medical neglect or any other sort of neglect?

c. If Miss G's poverty exacerbates her inability to provide adequate care for her children, then is society partly responsible for their less than optimal care?

15.3   A PLAN TO RATION CARE

Whether intentionally or unintentionally, whether by plan or by outcome, all societies ration health care. In a place where everyone cannot afford all forms of health care service, some people receive some forms of health care and others do not. The national (or regional) government of X has decided to fund treatment for some cases of pneumonia and not others. If a patient has metastatic cancer or advanced AIDS or was born weighing less than five hundred grams, the pneumonia will probably not receive funding; whereas if the patient can be restored to a standard of health, judged by some criteria, the government will pay for antibiotics and other treatments beyond comfort care.

Mr. M has partial paralysis from a stroke, some coronary artery blockage (not life-threatening at this point), and pneumonia. The formula established by the government places this situation in the borderline-case area.

a. Should Mr. M be entitled to receive government-funded care for his pneumonia?

b. If not all instances of all illnesses and injuries can be covered, then what kinds of criteria should be used in determining a scheme for rank-ordering the provision of care? Which of the following seem most plausible?

  i. Urgency of the situation.

  ii. Justice of distribution.

  iii. Effects on a person's likelihood of survival.

  iv. Effects on a person's duration of survival.

  v. Effects on a person's level of function.

  vi. Effects on a person's comfort level/happiness.

  vii. Opportunity to have some say in deciding the service.

  viii. Expense of the service.

  ix. Ability to contribute toward cost.

  x. Extent of responsibility in causation of condition.

  xi. Social status or social value.

  xii. Other factors (specify).

15.4   REFUSAL TO ACCEPT PATIENTS: FREEDOM OR DISREGARD?

Dr. R has a private practice in endocrinology. As a private practitioner, she feels free to accept or refuse anyone as a patient. She screens potential patients not only for medical suitability (proper referral or explanation of symptoms), but also for financial suitability (adequate insurance, health plan coverage, or ability to pay). Her situation, she believes, is like that of almost everyone else who provides a product or service for a living: one has a right to expect that in the marketplace of supply and demand, those who supply can specify a price that consumers are free to accept or reject. In this way, both sides have freedom.

Miss S has an adrenal condition that, for optimal management, should be assessed and treated by an endocrinologist. She works at a low-paying job that does not provide health insurance coverage. In her geographical area, Dr. R is the only endocrinologist.

a. Should Dr. R consider lowering her fees to accommodate Miss S's limited ability to pay?

b. Would the morality of the situation depend on the availability of other endocrinologists in that region? Suppose three practice there, and they all have the same policies as Dr. R.

c. Is the moral acceptability or wrongness of Dr. R's stance a function of the seriousness of the bad consequences if Miss S only receives treatment from a nonspecialist?

d. The legal profession assumes that all attorneys have an obligation to do some pro bono (free) work for clients unable to afford their services. Should physicians view themselves as having a similar professional obligation? Why?

e. Suppose Miss S has Medicaid coverage, which would reimburse Dr. R, but not to the extent that Dr. R believes she is entitled. Is it morally justified for Dr. R to refuse to accept Miss S because of the lower Medicaid reimbursement rates? What if Medicaid required more paperwork and reimbursed less consistently?

f. Some argue that health care (or at least a "decent minimum," or floor of health care) is not a good or service comparable to a luxury. As a necessity, it is something to which people have a right, and so it may not be denied to a person. Is this view correct? If it is a right, does it follow that specific people have corresponding responsibilities to provide care such as, in this instance, the only endocrinologist in an area?

15.5   SECOND AND THIRD TRANSPLANTS

Ms. D, forty-seven, received a kidney transplant three years ago. After two years, her body rejected the kidney. Soon thereafter, she was given a second kidney. That lasted less than a year. Now she will receive a third kidney. After preliminary discussion, three main sorts of perspectives emerge. (Their proponents would, no doubt, reject the irreverent labels given here.)

♦ *"Investments first"*: Ms. D's transplant team reasons that, since they have invested so much time and effort into saving her, she should be placed at the head of the line for another kidney.

♦ *"Losers last"*: Others disagree. They think that, because Ms. D was fortunate enough to receive one opportunity at a kidney, she should now be placed at the bottom of the list.

♦ *"Blind equality"*: A third group believes that her history should count neither for nor against her, because all kidneys should be distributed among the eligible recipients by means of a lottery-like system. Anything other than a random method among medically eligible candidates would represent a form of discrimination, they argue.

a. What are the strengths and weaknesses of each of the three views?

b. What are some additional possible criteria or procedures for judging among candidates? (For more possibilities, see the cases about rationing care and ranking candidates.)

c. Earlier, we had occasion to examine the value-laden notion of "clinically (not) indicated." Might not the concept of "medically eligible" similarly have built-in value assumptions? For example, is psychological stability, which improves compliance, a purely medical criterion of eligibility? What about developmental or physical disability? Are these relevant or irrelevant to "medical eligibility"? How, if at all, should age factor in the decision making?

15.6   AN ANENCEPHALIC BABY AS AN ORGAN DONOR

Representatives of a transplantation organization persuade the Q's, parents of an anencephalic baby (one born with virtually no brain tissue and unable to survive more than a few days or weeks) to request discontinuation of life-sustaining treatment to enable donation of the baby's organs. This way, the Q's agree, the baby's death will become more meaningful and worthwhile.

a. Is this baby, who will never become conscious or may not even have sensory experiences, most comparable, ethically, to a normal baby, someone who is irreversibly comatose, an invertebrate organism with similar neurological development, or some other being?

b. If discontinuation of life support would result in death earlier than otherwise—to make possible transplantation of sufficiently viable organs—then several issues and questions arise.

i. In earlier chapters, we encountered some of the conceptual and moral complexities of the distinction between killing and letting die. Suppose the anencephalic baby would only live a few more days. Would discontinuation of life support constitute killing or allowing to die? Would the answer depend on the sort of life support? Would the morality of the decision depend on whether it was killing or allowing to die?

ii. Is the baby being exploited as a source of organs? If so, is it wrong in the same way that exploiting other members of the human species is wrong?

iii. Is the baby beyond being helped or harmed because it has no or minimal awareness?

iv. The criteria and definitions of death are very much contested. There are many theories of death, and yet this may be central to deciding the nature and morality of killing (or allowing to die) anencephalic babies. What is being assumed in claiming that it is a wrongful killing, and how might one argue both that such a killing is and that it is not morally objectionable?

15.7 A FAMILY'S MEDIA CAMPAIGN

The A family conducts a massive media campaign to raise funds for their seven-year-old son, B, who desperately needs costly liver transplant surgery to have a chance of survival. The child happens to be photogenic. The family raises a million dollars within a few weeks.

- a. In what ways is this method of financing needed medical procedures at the same time morally praiseworthy, morally permissible, and also morally questionable?
- b. Apart from the fortunate child who is the beneficiary of such methods, what of those whose families lack access to the media?
- c. Is it the obligation of a community or society to provide all needed treatments to children regardless of ability to pay? To all adults, regardless of ability to pay?
- d. Is it proper to use the fact that one is a celebrity, or has some other way to "leverage" public opinion, to affect the outcome?
- e. What issues of journalistic ethics arise in connection with this case? If the practice is at all questionable, then do the media have some responsibility for facilitating it?
- f. How, if at all, should the likelihood of a favorable medical outcome affect one's moral judgment about the propriety of each such practice?

15.8 CELEBRITIES AND ADVOCACY

Celebrity actor and singer C testifies before legislatures and appears in public service announcements and magazine advertisements to draw attention to the seriousness of heart disease.

- a. Keeping in mind that a person's circumstances may not be that person's primary motive, how would the *justifiability* of C's actions be affected if each of these were true of him?
  - i. He has heart disease.
  - ii. Although he does not have heart disease, he has a relative who suffers from it.
  - iii. Although he has never known anyone who suffered from heart disease, he is an advocate because he became persuaded of its importance.
  - iv. He receives a fee for his endorsements.
  - v. His agent has told him that the publicity will help his career.
- b. Suppose he uses his fame or charisma, rather than the presentation of information about the disease, to create more funding. Some would argue that use of fame is vulgar. Are they right?
- c. Suppose the disease is already funded more than others of its severity and pervasiveness. Would that make his efforts less morally justified?

d. If the advertisements are effective would it be wrong for C to accept money as payment or as a gesture of thanks for doing the advertisements?

e. Are his efforts morally justified only if any information he presents is accurate?

15.9   ONE LAST QUESTION: ASKING FOR ORGANS

Mr. F, a forty-three-year-old, otherwise healthy man, has suddenly and unexpectedly died of a heart attack. Some of his organs and tissues seem suitable for harvesting so that they could be transplanted, thereby helping those in need of corneas, kidneys, and a liver. His immediate family—a wife and teenaged son and daughter—is overwhelmed with grief. Local law requires a physician to request that the next of kin make available the body of the person who just died for purposes of harvesting the usable organs. Because of their own discomfort and concern for the family, however, the physicians do not approach the bereaved family about organ donation.

a. Should organ donation be based solely on the expressed voluntary wishes of the donors?

b. Apart from the legal responsibilities, do physicians and/or hospitals have a *moral* obligation to request the next of kin to allow organ donation?

c. Suppose the initial suggestion of organ donation upsets the relatives of the deceased. May the doctor persist further by reminding the family how others' lives may be saved?

d. How much persistence is acceptable? Would it be going too far to provide Mr. F's family with details of the lives of patients who would benefit from the organs of the deceased? In emotionally charged circumstances, how might one distinguish among altruistic persistence, offensive persistence, and coercion of the bereaved?

15.10   ESTATE SALE OF ONE'S ORGANS

Mrs. B, a fairly healthy forty-seven-year-old, inquires about the possibility of selling some of her organs in the event of her death, with the proceeds to go to her family. She is told that such a practice is illegal, whereupon she asks why. Her doctor states that, as she understands it, such a practice would place a price tag on body parts, which is unacceptable, and that it "just isn't done; it's too ghoulish to contemplate." Mrs. B replies, "It's *my* body, isn't it?"

a. Suppose Mrs. B were in failing health, but many of her organs would remain viable when she died.

b. In what sense is one's body one's property, and in what sense is it not like (other?) property such as a house or a painting?

c. Suppose Mrs. B is in failing health and wants one of her organs to go to a particular individual in need. Should organ donors in cases like this have control or at least some say over who receives their organs? Would it make a difference if the individual to receive the organs were a relative of the donor?

15.11   SELLING ORGANS

Twenty-nine-year-old F lives in a south Asian country. He supports his four young children and wife on the equivalent of a few hundred dollars a year. With the $10,000 he can get from selling one of his kidneys, he will have a once-in-a-lifetime opportunity for his family to become economically self-sufficient.

Kidney broker G earns $20,000 for each transaction. The purchasers pay him $50,000 per kidney. G believes his work is morally justified. He argues that, in contrast with many who sell or distribute expensive yet largely useless consumer goods, he enables both buyers and sellers to benefit greatly.

At present, only a third of those in the United States who need kidney transplants will receive them. People in developing nations sell organs for needed money. Although the sale and purchase of organs are legally forbidden almost everywhere, these laws are not enforced. A few brokers procure and distribute such organs. Yet the need keeps outpacing the supply. So far, a black market goes part of the way toward filling the gap.

a. Is F or G doing something wrong? If so, why is it wrong?

b. Should the laws (including their enforcement) pertaining to sale of organs be changed, so that they are either more or less strict than they are now?

c. Should we view the procurement or purchase of organs from starving, desperate people as unacceptable exploitation? Or is it properly thought of as a sad, yet permissible, opportunity for these people to earn some money—albeit in a way that has some physical risk to them?

d. Should the recipient be told (if he or she asks) the source and circumstances of the donated organ?

15.12   PLASMA "DONATION" AND JUSTICE

Mr. E is unemployed and gets a substantial part of his income from selling plasma at local blood/plasma centers. Although he would rather not do this, he finds it a preferable choice to some of the alternative, possibly illegal, sources of money. While well-organized and well-publicized campaigns occasionally generate donations from segments of the public, Mr. E and other financially strapped people turn out to contribute a considerable portion of the plasma supply.

a. Some societies find it morally unacceptable to pay for blood. Others do not. Which seems morally preferable, and why?

b. Does the system described here place an unfair burden on the poor? Is the fact that the poor supply a disproportionate amount of the plasma that is needed a burden different in kind from other burdens the poor may experience? Suppose it is qualitatively different. Does this lead to a moral conclusion about the morality of the practice?

c. How might an adequate supply of blood be obtained without basing it on momentary, unpredictable altruism of donors or great financial exigency?

d. Suppose an adequate supply of plasma could be obtained by voluntary means. Is meeting demands for plasma by relying on the altruism of certain members of society acceptable, or is it in some way unjust?

e. Suppose we could, by an easy-to-perform chemical treatment, use animal blood in humans. Would it be acceptable to take blood from cows, pigs, dogs, and/or cats? Would you place the same volume (percentage of blood supply) limitation on the animals as there currently is on humans?

15.13   SALE OF TISSUES AND ORGANS

Mr. T is a thirty-five-year-old indigent man who often sells his blood. He asks one of the technicians at his local office of Hemagift Ltd. about the possibility of selling bone marrow to those who would benefit from it. They tell him to speak to the director of the facility, Miss M. He tests the waters by asking her about the possibility of selling a kidney to someone who would benefit. She informs him that this is illegal, but Mr. T persists in demanding a reason that, in a country that claims to value the market and initiative, his offer is being refused. Miss M responds that it isn't for her to decide; all she needs to know is that it is illegal.

a. Suppose the potential recipient were a relative of his. Would Mr. T's sale of the organ seem (more) morally acceptable then?

b. Why does society permit the sale of some body fluids (such as blood for transfusions or semen for artificial insemination) but not of body parts?

c. How does one draw the line between exploitation and permissible exercise of bodily self-determination?

d. How morally plausible is Mr. T's case?

15.14   RANKING RECIPIENT CANDIDATES: FOUR VIGNETTES

Four transplant candidates need hearts:

♦ Mrs. X just got on the list but is the most likely to die soon without the transplant. She is unemployed and resides in another state but is the mother of a resident of the area.

♦ Mr. Y has been on the list for a year-and-a-half but is comparatively stable, medically. He resides in the area and works as a clerk. He has two children in their teens.

♦ Mr. Z lives in the area, has been on the list for five months, and is gradually deteriorating. He is a married executive with a family of five.

♦ Miss W has been on and off the list for two years, as her health care institution has changed criteria. She works locally for the state government and smoked until four years ago.

A heart becomes available, and all four candidates are tissue-compatible. We are asked to recommend a ranking for distribution of the heart.

a. In ranking recipients, exactly which factors are valid criteria? (See questions c–f.)

b. If these questions may be considered, why wouldn't a similar allocation decision procedure exist for contexts other than transplantation in which resources are scarce?

c. Should extramedical criteria for transplantation differ from those for other clinical allocation decisions? If so, exactly how would one distinguish between "medical" and "nonmedical" factors?

d. Should constituency (living in the immediate area, region, or country of the hospital) be considered as relevant? Does this conflict with treating people based on need? Is this need an unstated moral principle in transplantation cases?

e. Should the number of dependents count? What about social value? Or the ability to pay? Do these *factors* also conflict with the ideal of allocation based on need?

f. Should the amount of time on the list be considered as relevant? Some argue that discriminatory policies can be avoided only by using a first come, first serve policy. Is this plausible?

15.15   WAITING FOR A TRANSPLANT

Tens of thousands, perhaps hundreds of thousands, of people die each year while waiting for organ transplantation. E is a fifteen-year-old candidate for a kidney. He will soon die if a kidney does not become available. During this time, a number of people who might have been suitable donors have died without donating their organs.

a. How should we understand the morality of letting someone die whose life could have been saved? Would it only be wrong if the person who died knew that there was a specific individual who needed his or her organ(s)? Consider, as a few possibilities, the following situations. In so doing, reflect on the extent of the analogy to these rescue situations:

   i. You are in a theater, know CPR, and someone is in distress whom you could save, but you do not know of it.

   ii. You do know of it, but would rather not be bothered.

   iii. You could have taken a CPR course, but neglected to do so.

   iv. You failed to take the refresher course.

b. Suppose it is common knowledge that thousands of people are dying, but could be saved with sufficient donation. Is the situation of the nondonor more like that of the person who lets someone drown in shallow water or that of the person who turns down a request for a donation to a worthwhile charity?

c. How does the need of the transplantation candidate compare with that of many others who die each year because of lack of other adequate resources?

d. Would different societal policies help solve the problem of the discrepancy between supply of and demand for transplantable organs?

15.16   A SMOKER'S CLAIM TO HEALTH CARE RESOURCES

Mr. W, fifty-four, has smoked for the past forty years. He began at age fourteen when a number of his friends took up the habit, and he has not quit more than briefly since then. Mr. W gets frequent colds, has a persistent cough, and has recently developed lung cancer. He believes his insurance company or, at least, the government, should provide coverage for his health care expenses. (Assume for now that the insurance company covers his condition.) Others disagree. They believe that he is responsible for his own illness and so ought to pay for his own care. They maintain that the costs should not be passed along either to the others covered by his insurance company or to the taxpayers.

   a. Is there a difference between the plausibility of the objectors' reasons when applied to insurance companies and when applied to a government-funded program? If so, what is it?

   b. To what extent should people be held responsible for the consequences of their own risky behaviors? Is denial of health care coverage or treatment a morally acceptable option? Is our moral obligation to treat illness, if there is such an obligation, independent of the origin of the illness?

   c. Does the fact that Mr. W is addicted to nicotine lessen his responsibility for his illness-causing (or -exacerbating) behaviors? Does it completely eliminate it? Should the level of voluntariness of people's actions be considered in judging people's moral or financial responsibility? Should we think differently about Mr. W if he began smoking and became addicted at age thirty-four rather than at age fourteen?

   d. How does Mr. W's situation compare and/or contrast with that of an alcoholic? A heroin addict? An athlete with a sports-related injury? A motorcyclist who suffered a head injury after refusing to wear a helmet?

   e. Although this is not always the case, suppose providing health care to Mr. W— and to all others in similar circumstances—would entail an increased expenditure of health care dollars that would limit the amount of resources available to treat other health problems. Does it make sense to distinguish between illnesses for which individuals bear some responsibility and those for which they do not?

15.17   TOBACCO LITIGATION AND RESPONSIBILITY

Mr. T, a lifelong smoker, developed lung cancer at age fifty-three. He joined a lawsuit filed by a number of smokers. After his death at age fifty-five, his family continued its commitment to participation in the suit.

   a. Discussions of moral and legal responsibility for smoking often focus on several factors as relevant. In particular, how should the respective moral responsibilities of Mr. T and of the tobacco company be affected when we assume a range of different facts? Suppose, for example:

    i. Mr. T began to smoke more recently instead of much earlier (for example, in 1991 vs. in 1951).

    ii. He started smoking as an adult rather than at a younger age (for example, at age twenty-three vs. at eighteen vs. at thirteen).

    iii. He began after the Surgeon General's report rather than before that report appeared.

    iv. He began after mandatory package warnings appeared instead of before they began.

    v. He began after, rather than before, tobacco company admissions that smoking is bad for health.

    vi. He stopped smoking for a while (vs. he smoked consistently over the years).

b. What responsibility (either legally or morally) should the manufacturer (and distributor, etc.) have for a product that is legal? Are the responsibilities for alcohol and legal drugs comparable to cigarettes?

c. Might tobacco companies be morally responsible even if not legally liable, or should they only be held morally blameworthy for the harm to smokers if they can be found legally guilty of making and selling a dangerous product?

d. How can one establish causation of individual cases for a disease like cancer?

e. Does the addictiveness of tobacco mean that smokers are less responsible for their conditions? Does it mean that the manufacturers are more blameworthy?

f. In public policy and legal circles, some have tried to make a case that tobacco should be regulated as a drug. Should tobacco be thought of as drug and regulated as such?

15.18 COSTING KIDS

A mother sued her former gynecologist for having botched a tubal ligation, a procedure informally referred to as "having one's tubes tied." The gynecologist had explained that the procedure, performed to cause sterility, has a 1/100 to 1/200 rate of failing to prevent pregnancies. The plaintiff was suing for $160,000 to compensate her for the costs of raising her six-year-old daughter, who was the result of an unwanted pregnancy. The woman said that she was opposed to abortions, but that she could not afford to have a third child and had suffered health problems from the pregnancy. Experts who testified for the plaintiff estimated that food, medical care, and clothing, plus "quality-of-life" costs, such as dance lessons and toys, would cost $110,000. Tuition at a private college would add another $50,000.

    The jury was charged—if they found for the woman—with determining damages caused by emotional distress, and also, as a counterbalance to the harms, to financially value the happiness brought by the child to the parents.

a. Is the notion of pricing emotional suffering and pleasure morally questionable? Juries do often assign damages based on suffering. Given this, can it then be applied to the suffering caused by a person's existence?

b. Can the case be dismissed if the woman had been informed and was aware of the slight risk of becoming pregnant? Would it depend on what professional standards for tubal ligations specify?

c. Would a finding in favor of the woman mean that the jury was placing a price on the daughter's life? Are juries who award damages for wrongful death placing a price on people's lives? Is pricing of lives always wrong? What makes it wrong when it is wrong?

15.19   NEGLIGENT BIRTH?

A woman sued her family practitioner and obstetrician for $143,210, which she claimed was the amount necessary to raise her two-year-old son. She charged that the physicians had not notified her that she was pregnant in time to have an abortion. Although the child is healthy, she had not wanted the pregnancy. The jury decided against the plaintiff.

a. Should the physicians have been found not responsible if the woman could reasonably have inferred from her own physical changes that she was pregnant?

b. Was the woman's case weakened by the fact that the physicians were not responsible for the child's conception—which, some maintain, should be the only proper locus of responsibility?

c. Did the case lack sufficient merit because other people could and would have adopted the child?

d. Is filing such a suit morally wrong because of the likely effects it would have on the child when he became aware that he had been unwanted?

e. Is the suit justified to the extent that missing a diagnosis of pregnancy is an error like any other diagnostic error?

f. Is the case weak since pregnancies (and children) are not illnesses or injuries, and they are not sufficiently analogous to illnesses or injuries?

g. If the child had been born with a serious disability, would it have justified a higher settlement?

h. Could the case be considered a "wrongful life" suit? Medical malpractice? Suppose the physicians did not practice in accordance with the standard of care for detecting pregnancies. Would it follow that the physicians were negligent?

i. Is the woman's case comparable to that of a suit against either

i. A manufacturer of ineffective contraceptive products, or

ii. An abortionist who does not perform well enough to assure termination of the pregnancy?

j. Could the stage of pregnancy at which the woman learned of it have been relevant?

15.20 *DALYS AND QALYS*

Criteria need to be identified for judging the comparative value and impact of different health care resource allocations. Two such devices, which have become influential in thinking about allocation of resources, are abbreviated DALYs and QALYs.

DALYs are *Disability Adjusted Life-Years*. These take into consideration the age of those affected by the condition or disease in question, the degree of disability resulting from the condition or disease, and the number of deaths from the condition or disease.

QALYs are *Quality Adjusted Life-Years*. The value assigned to a year of healthy life is one, and zero is the value if one is dead. Negative quantities are assigned to lives that are judged to be worse than death. Most people, most of the time, would fall between zero and one, depending on how healthy they are. According to this, health care should aim at increasing both the number of years and the quality of life during those years.

Policy makers want to decide how valuable and effective treatments are in deciding about planning diagnostic, preventive, and therapeutic procedures. If outcomes are a function of many variables, how should they count each of the following?

- R is a seventy-year-old female and is healthy except for treatment-resistant depression.
- S is a fifty-year-old male with diabetes and arthritis.
- T is a thirty-year-old with schizophrenia and asthma.

a. Are DALYs *ageist* as formulated? In other words, is it discriminatory to take a person's age into consideration in judging the value of that person's life for purposes of allocating resources?

b. How would one judge the QALY values of treatment-outcomes, since evaluation of such outcomes seems to be part of the reason for proposing the concept of QALYs in the first place?

c. Assuming also that QALYs can be associated with monetary values, how would one do so? Might such an activity be likely to result in discrimination—for example, against people with lives deemed less desirable, or against older persons?

d. When John Stuart Mill wanted to defend his notion of qualitatively higher and lower pleasures, he said that it is better to be Socrates dissatisfied than a pig satisfied. How, then, would one compare the QALY of an older (perhaps even a dissatisfied) Socrates with that of a younger, satisfied swine? Or do only humans count?

e. Is QALY a concept that is too subjective?

f. How could one assign numerical values, other than for amounts of time, in ways that do not appear substantially arbitrary? What aspects of a person's life and health might be omitted from these ways of calculating?

g. About weighing, rationing, tradeoffs, and forced choices: Is it acceptable or correct (other things being equal) to decide in favor of those with more

QALYs likely? Would it mean that some people would be allowed to die sooner than otherwise?

h. What, exactly, are the practical ramifications of these concepts? What dimensions of a person's life seem to be omitted from such calculations?

i. Would this presuppose that all quality-of-life factors can be factored into a formula to enable assignment of a numerical value on a single continuum (for example between zero and one)? This is an instance of what is sometimes termed an *incommensurability* or meshing problem—typically described with the "apples and oranges" metaphor.

j. The preceding questions have suggested a number of unclarities and problems about DALYs. Nevertheless, is it wrong to expect some correlation between the rank-orderings of the diseases listed in the "DALYs Funding Facts" table in terms of funding dollars and their Disability Rankings?

DALYs Funding Facts

	1999 NIH Funding in Millions of Dollars	Disability Ranking [Using DALYs]
AIDS	1793	15
Breast Cancer	475	14
Diabetes	458	8
Heart Disease	269	1
Schizophrenia	201	10
Stroke	186	4
Prostate Cancer	178	19
Lung Cancer	163	6
Asthma	140	17
Parkinson's	132	21
Multiple Sclerosis	97	25

SOURCE: Claudia Kalb, "Stars, Money and Medical Crusades," in *Newsweek*, May 22, 2000, p. 60. Kalb cites The New England Journal of Medicine and NIH as her sources.

15.21   CREATING FRAUDULENT DIAGNOSES TO ENABLE TREATMENT

Dr. U writes a diagnosis other than the actual one on an insurance claim form to enable his patient, Miss L, to receive the needed care. He knows that, *legally,* he is committing fraud but believes that, *morally,* he is doing the right thing.

a. Is this physician doing something morally wrong? How much regret is appropriate for what he does? Might it be something that is "suberogatory"—that is, wrong although not morally forbidden?

b. How strictly should the laws about insurance fraud be monitored and enforced?

c. Is fraud done solely to protect someone else from significant harm morally comparable to fraud committed to benefit oneself? If not, might allowing fraud based on patients' needs open the door to many sorts of abuse? Or is need just the right sort of standard to distinguish between justified and unjustified instances?

d. Are there alternatives in this case to allowing the patient to go untreated or committing fraud to enable the patient to receive medical attention? Suppose no known alternatives exist. What then?

e. Should Dr. U factor into his decision also the extent and degree of probability of harm to himself and to Miss L if a review process catches the fraud?

CHAPTER 16

Other Issues

HEALTH RISKS AND RESPONSIBILITY

Some of the most serious ethical questions have to do with prevalent health risks, such as tobacco use, obesity, and alcohol use, and the appropriate, proportionate responses to these from heath professionals, government, and individuals.

The most obvious example is tobacco. Tobacco use, mostly in the form of cigarette smoking, represents a major public health problem. Some people have made a forceful case that it is *the* most serious public health problem. Tobacco is habit forming, addictive, and, by virtually unanimous scientific consensus, very harmful to many people's health. Tobacco accounts for more than 400,000 deaths each year in the United States, and still more in other countries. People have, however, less than rational ways of assessing and managing this risk.

A different ethical question arises when the public becomes alarmed about what appears to be a mysterious new epidemic. What is an appropriate response by media and health workers to these fears?

SHORT-TERM GOALS; AESTHETIC GOALS

Sometimes skills acquired for healing and helping people may be directed toward short-term goals, such as temporarily enabling an athlete to complete a game or a season. In what circumstances, if any, might this use of skills be acceptable? Sometimes medicine can be used for cosmetic purposes. Is there anything wrong with this? If so, what? (See also case 7.8., page 56.)

PUZZLES ABOUT IDENTITY

Questions about identity hover around many of the most difficult, profound, and interesting ethical problems in bioethics. While there are challenges to specifying identity conditions for normal, fully functioning adults, it can become even more vexing when we attempt to gain clarity about other classes of instances. These conceptual and metaphysical puzzles turn out to have major practical implications for our attempts to understand ourselves and for health care decision making. To think about these problems, it would help to establish what people understand, in different cases, by *identity*. Is it ascribed by others or experienced as a subjective self-consciousness? What are the roles of memory, perception, and complex cognitive function in identity?

We can view these difficult cases as belonging to several classes:

+ beginnings and ends of individuals (Examples: stem cells, embryos, fetuses, newborns, and dying people),
+ beginnings of our species (early humans and pre-humans, such as Australopithecines),
+ manufactured and planned individuals (genetically modified and engineered humans, cyborgs, and intelligent machines),
+ malfunctioning individuals (brain-damaged people, anencephalic babies, people with certain severe mental illnesses or mental retardation, people in comas or vegetative states), or
+ individuals who may lack some of the usual or paradigm features of human persons (clones, members of other sentient species), members of other intelligent species (primates and dolphins), beings from other worlds (assuming they exist).

What we have here are not mere curiosities and anomalies. Although lumping all these together may strike us as weird and unsettling, they test our concepts and theories, and can force us to think and re-think our basic beliefs about ourselves. What does it mean to be human, to be a person, to be the same person? Who deserves moral status and who/what does not? What is there about people that justifies ascription of their moral status, such as basic human rights? The beings on these lists may at times seem alien and other, yet they could be considered part of our extended families and, in some cases, ourselves.

Study of these topics prepares us not only for foreseeable decisions we are likely to confront, such as those at the end of life, but also for thinking about new issues that emerge every year from the advance of science and medicine.

16.1   ALCOHOL USE ISSUES

Mr. A, thirty-three years old, drinks more than is good for him ("maybe eight or nine beers") a few times a week. This fact emerges when his family doctor, Dr. G, is updating his patient's history during an office visit for a serious ankle sprain. A general/family practitioner, Dr. G tries to inquire further and attempts to advise Mr. A about factors related to health and well-being. Mr. A, however, seems unconcerned about his drinking.

a. If Mr. A does not meet all the criteria of alcoholism, should Dr. G refrain from further commenting about his patient's drinking?

b. Suppose Mr. A becomes defensive when asked more about his drinking. Should Dr. G let the subject drop?

c. If the drinking seems to be affecting the patient's home life, even though his physiology remains unaffected, should that be the concern of the physician?

d. Suppose Mr. A acknowledges that he abuses alcohol but appears unconcerned about the adverse effects of his behavior. When pressed by Dr. G, he states, "Everyone has to die sometime." How aggressively should Dr. G encourage Mr. A to change his perspective?

16.2   OBESITY ISSUES

Miss B, forty years old, is moderately obese. She worries about how it affects her social and work situations. Yet she seems unable to lose weight. The health workers at her clinic have read that between a third and two-thirds of adults in their nation are obese, yet they assume either that Miss B lacks the willpower to lose weight or that the problem is essentially cosmetic and so not very serious.

a. At what point does a factor or condition that causes unhappiness become medically significant?

b. At what point does something that is statistically associated with illness(es) become medically significant?

c. Should treatment of obesity be thought of more as indulgence of vanity or correction of a source of (actual or potential) harm?

d. Suppose a physical or psychological condition causes harm, such as job discrimination. Should this possible harm affect the justification for having the condition addressed medically?

16.3   TOBACCO: RISKS, RESPONSIBILITIES, AND PUBLIC HEALTH

Mrs. F, thirty-five, smokes, although she has often tried to stop. She has frequent sore throats and has had bronchitis several times. She has been told that smoking exacerbates her borderline high blood pressure. She smokes as she looks after her three children, ages thirteen, five, and one. The thirteen-year-old son, G, has classmates who "dip" chewing tobacco, as they have seen athletes do. He is tempted to try it.

a. *About perception:* People often seem to understand, but not necessarily appreciate, the risks of smoking. Many people who see the statistics that smoking accounts for more death and disease than AIDS, homicide, and alcohol-related causes combined nevertheless tend to have less aversion to smoking. Why is this? How might it be changed?

b. *About public policy:* If indeed smoking results in so much death and illness (especially from cancers and heart disease), then what sorts of public policies are justified? Harm caused has to be balanced against the fact that some element of choice is involved in smoking.

  i. What are reasons—other than its present legality—for treating it differently than other substances that are equally addictive?

  ii. If regulations other than prohibition seem justified, what sorts of regulations? For example, how much tax should be imposed to discourage consumption and to help pay for health costs of smoking?

  iii. What sort of education campaign might substantially reduce cigarette consumption?

  iv. In what ways does the addictiveness of something, such as heroin, decrease people's ability to make autonomous decisions about its use?

c. *About individual responsibility toward others and toward oneself:* To what extent do people have moral responsibilities toward maintaining or improving their own health, and toward placing themselves in circumstances conducive to improved health? If Mrs. F smoked during her pregnancy and around her children even when they were babies, can she be held responsible if they suffer health problems known to be statistically related to the smoking?

d. *About corporate responsibilities:* To what extent do advertising, denials of adequate evidence of smoking's harm, and lack of enforcement of bans on sales to minors contribute to the harm? Do the warnings printed on the packages and advertisements absolve them of responsibility for any harm their products cause?

e. *About tobacco profits and suppliers:* People labeled as "drug kingpins" are perceived as evil because they supply addictive, destructive substances and profit from them. What similarities and what differences are there between those who sell and distribute cocaine and those who grow, manufacture, distribute, and sell tobacco products?

16.4   A REASONABLE HEALTH CONCERN, ANXIETY, OR PHOBIA?

News media regularly inform the public of what seem to be serious health risks. These risks range from epidemics, such as AIDS, to clusters of cases, such as necrotizing fasciitis (a rare but usually treatable condition that appeared to be a mysterious new epidemic in 1995), to less urgent health problems. The broadcast and print media usually try to base their reports on expert opinion, but sometimes they create or reinforce fears bordering on hysteria. "Mad cow disease," or BSE (bovine spongiform encephalopathy), created an alarm throughout Europe in 1996 after several dozen people died from a neurological condition hypothesized to be caused by a disease previously believed confined to livestock. The mere possibility of a connection to eating beef sent shock waves through the world's beef markets, and caused a crisis of confidence in the British government.

A tabloid writer labels a new, as yet unexplained condition "S-syndrome," since it first appeared in Suriname. Epidemiologists and public health officers have not determined its mode of transmission. They have found no causal connection to any known pathogen or environmental factor. With daily front-page news coverage, the public becomes increasingly concerned, even though the condition has not spread beyond Suriname. Some people in other countries have called for a banning of all people and products from Suriname until more is known about S-syndrome.

a. How should the media report puzzling new health problems so that they both inform the public and refrain from fostering irrational fears?

b. A dramatic situation of which people are aware often disproportionately affects their judgments of risks. Thus, publicity of airplane crashes causes many people to fear flying even though it is safer than driving. How should public health authorities and news media present information so that people keep health risks in perspective?

c. As a result of misunderstandings, many people fear AIDS more than they need to. Does this result from irresponsible publicity of AIDS or from people's preexisting prejudices? People should fear the bad effects of smoking more than AIDS. Is it the obligation of the medical profession—individually or collectively—to draw the statistics and information to the attention of the public?

16.5   PUZZLES ABOUT REFERRALS

In medicine and nursing, people learn that if, for some reason, one cannot or will not provide care, then one should make a referral to someone who can and will. This policy applies not only to areas in which one has insufficient expertise but also to situations in which one refuses to do something because of conscience. This latter sort of case, however, generates some puzzles.

Miss Q, who is twenty years old, approaches her physician with the request for an abortion. She explains that she is unwilling to go through pregnancy and raising a child at this stage of her life. The pregnancy is in its sixteenth week, and Miss Q is in good health. Dr. Z is opposed to almost all abortions, and he believes that Miss Q's reasons are not weighty enough to justify performing the abortion in this case. He tells her this. Meanwhile, he feels torn about whether to refer her to someone who will do the abortion.

a. On one side of this issue is the following question: If a person believes a sort of action to be seriously morally wrong, then how can he or she feel bound by a moral obligation to ensure that someone else do the action?

b. On the other side of the issue, one can ask: If a form of professional service is legal *and* accepted as such by one's profession, *and* if there is reasonable controversy about the morality of the activity, *and* if one will not provide that service, then why should one not provide a client or patient access to the service?

c. Suppose convention or an existing code of ethics within a profession states that an action is morally obligatory (or forbidden). Apart from the legal or quasi-legal enforcement consequences for a person, how strong a *moral* obligation does that place on a practitioner within that profession? In this instance, both medical convention and nursing codes of ethics prescribe that one refusing to provide a treatment because of conscience do a referral to someone who will. Does that settle the issue?

16.6   LACK OF HEALTH SCREENING

Ms. L learns she has a lump that is 40 percent of the time associated with breast cancer. As is true of most people, including most women, she has not had sufficiently regular screening tests for cervical, colon, breast, and other sorts of cancer, as well as for other significant health problems. Ms. L now lives in dread and regret.

a. To what extent does Ms. L deserve blame (although destructive guilt feelings may not be too helpful at this point) for negligence in monitoring her own health? Are such tests too inconvenient? Too frightening? Too expensive? Too often not covered by insurance?

b. To what extent should responsibility be shouldered by Ms. L's physician, who may have failed to educate, or perhaps require, regular screening tests? By insurance companies who refuse to cover it?

c. To what extent should medical societies, and perhaps governmental agencies, more aggressively promote universal screening for the appropriate populations?

d. Should health insurers and managed care plans build such screening requirements into their programs? Would such requirements constitute an unacceptable violation of the patients' autonomy?

16.7   PATCHING UP AN ATHLETE

As part of his practice, Dr. E is the physician for a very competitive soccer team. Occasionally, he makes what he believes to be a compromise: he will patch up an injured player to enable him to complete that game. Sometimes, he views it as part of his job to enable a player to finish a season, or a sports career, even when he recognizes that doing so might jeopardize the athlete's health and ability to function afterward.

a. Would the morality of Dr. E's practices depend, at least in part, on whether the team members were children or adults, whether they were playing for a school or professionally?

b. Suppose a player, rather than the coach, pressures Dr. E to keep him competitive. Would this alter the morality of the situation?

c. How well informed and educated are the players about the likely consequences of these medical practices? How well informed are the coaches who should have some knowledge of these practices? What effect would the existence of more knowledge or less knowledge by players or coaches affect the morality of the procedures?

d. To what extent does Dr. E have a loyalty to each of the following?

  i. The team's high performance level.

  ii. The team's players—their expressed wishes and their interests, medical or otherwise.

  iii. The coach or coaches.

  iv. The team's owner or supervisor.

  v. Others.

16.8   ENHANCEMENT OR THERAPY?

+ Mr. M is seventy-five years old, and finds that, given his inconsistent sexual abilities, Viagra helps him.
+ Mr. N, fifty-five years old, finds that, although he has less inconsistent sexual functioning, Viagra helps him also.
+ Mr. O, twenty-five, and of normal sexual function, also takes Viagra to improve his sexual abilities.

Each of these three men has a prescription and insurance coverage that authorizes five pills per month.

a. How should the insurance company decide about the appropriate number of pills to authorize per month?

   i. Should they allow more for younger men, since younger men tend to be more sexually active?

   ii. Should they allow more for older men, since older men tend to be more in need of such assistance?

   iii. Should they allow the same number for each group of men, since it would treat people of all ages equally?

b. Should they provide unlimited coverage—assuming a copayment—since sexuality is an important part of most people's lives?

c. Should insurers not provide pills for any of the men, since the pills can be thought of as "lifestyle enhancers," rather than as therapy for an illness?

d. Does the maximum of five pills per month covered by insurance involve a judgment about what number of instances of sexual activity represent "normal" function? Would coverage allowing eight or twelve per month mean that the line between the recreational and the therapeutic had changed?

e. Can a distinction between enhancement and therapy be drawn clearly for this drug? Would drawing such a distinction require specifying whether it is in the context of insurance coverage, accurate clinical labeling, or a moral judgment?

f. Can the same symptoms be a disorder or not depending solely on someone's age? For example, adult endocrine functions in young children are generally considered disorders.

16.9   PLACEBOS

During most of the second half of the twentieth century, the placebo effect had been taken for granted as an important part of the practice of medicine. This included the universally accepted belief that, for many conditions, up to 35 percent of instances could be effectively treated by means of nothing more than placebo. Some Danish researchers decided that this needed to be tested. Their method compared the rates of improvement of patients receiving placebo with those receiving no treatment. When they compared the results from one hundred fourteen such studies, they found that, except for relief of pain, placebos were not associated in a statistically significant way with a therapeutic effect. It had been assumed that, somehow, the power of suggestion triggered chemicals (such as endorphins, a class of brain chemicals) produced naturally by the body—and thereby brought about healing. (Based on The New England Journal of Medicine articles from May 24, 2001)

Patient S has depression. Dr. G considers prescribing a placebo to enable S to feel better. Dr. G reasons that, assuming the placebo works, it will be preferable to other medications since it is significantly less likely to have side effects or to interact with other medications.

a. Is it deceptive to prescribe placebos, given that their effectiveness depends on the false belief of the patient that it is an active drug? If it is deceptive, then is it also dishonest?

b. If a placebo turned out to be effective, then would it not have been given deceptively after all, since it was prescribed with the understanding that it would be effective? What exactly would have been the deception?

c. Which of the following would make use of a placebo ethically questionable?

   i. Belief/intent: That the patient was misled about whether the drug was a placebo;

   ii. Outcome—if the placebo is not effective: That the patient was misled about whether the drug would make her or him feel better;

   iii. Evidence: That the patient was misled about whether the drug would make her or him feel better because it was pharmaceutically active;

   iv. Other: That it involved a violation of role-responsibilities of health care professionals; or

   v. That placebos are not demonstrably effective.

d. Is it fraudulent for the pharmaceutical companies or pharmacists to produce pills that are not identified as placebos, that is, if the pills are labeled or sold as pharmacologically effective?

16.10   A PLACE FOR A PLACEBO?

Nurse M's patient, Ms. E, has been suspected of drug-seeking behavior because Ms. E complains of pain without having a clearly diagnosable cause of the pain. A colleague of Nurse M suggests that she should give the patient a placebo pill, to help test for the truthfulness of the pain reports. A physician agrees, and writes an order for the placebo "p r n," that is, as needed.

a. Why might this use of a placebo be a good or bad decision?

b. Should giving the placebo be considered a diagnostic test? If not, is it sufficiently analogous to a diagnostic test? Why or why not?

c. Suppose, after taking the placebo, Ms. E says she feels better. What should the nurse say to her patient? Should she consider getting the placebo prescribed on a long-term basis?

d. Suppose Ms. E says that the "medicine" did not help. Should it be explained to her? If so, then how?

e. Would the complications of the deceptions required for explaining (or avoiding explaining) use of the placebo be the main reason against it? Is it mainly wrong—if it is—because it is deceptive? Or does any wrongness arise from the fact that it violates a basic role-responsibility of honesty incumbent upon health care providers?

16.11   A WHOLE NEW KIND OF PERSON

It is the year 2015. Mr. A has suffered a devastating injury that deprived him of the use of most of his body, but his mind is still sharp. He suffers from the condition referred to as being "locked in." This is the nightmarish state of being aware of the world, yet paralyzed and unable to interact with it. Scientists connect Mr. A to a computer that detects his brain waves, and—working with his "neurotherapists," who are part physical therapist, part behavior therapist, part neurologist, and part electrician—he then learns to use those waves to communicate via a computer screen. Mr. A becomes able to express himself in this way. Next, he is fitted with prosthetic arms and legs he can maneuver by means of the brain waves. In this way, he has become a chimera of sorts: a *cyborg*, something previously encountered only in science fiction.

a. If Mr. A could do all of this with a "new, improved" body, would that be morally questionable? If so, why? Would he have undergone a *body transplant?*

b. Telekinesis—moving things at a distance just by the power of thought—is generally viewed as a superstition. Would Mr. A's movement of the computer cursor or the prosthesis be either analogous to or actually a form of technologically supported telekinesis?

c. If he now consists *mostly* of inorganic materials, such as metals, has he lost something central to being human? If he isn't human, though, then what *is* he?

d. Is he still the same person? The same human? How?

e. Would such technologies involve an impermissibly excessive expenditure for that society, if many people do not even receive adequate health care? Or would such objections to technologies, based on concerns of justice, prevent acceptance of anything costly that would otherwise benefit someone?

16.12   HE DOESN'T THINK; THEREFORE, WHAT?

Mr. C suffered increasingly severe brain damage following a series of strokes (cerebrovascular accidents, or CVAs). His problems unfolded as follows:

♦ First, he lost his sense of self—of *who* he was—but he could still communicate with people.

+ After another episode, he became unable to communicate sufficiently well to enable people to assess whether he understood his situation or recognized anyone.
+ A third episode caused him to become stuporous, so that he was minimally responsive to stimuli.
+ Then, he fell into a persistent vegetative state (PVS), and irretrievably lost all higher brain function—as confirmed by reliable diagnostic tests. His brainstem-governed breathing and heartbeat, however, still functioned.
+ Finally, he experienced shutdown of the remaining part of his brain.

Some people would say that Mr. C was gone as of the first stage, while others would assert that he ceased to exist as of the second. Still others would defend the third stage as the point at which his existence ended; likewise the fourth and fifth stages. Although legally, he could only be pronounced dead after undergoing total brain death, a number of conceptual and ethical questions remain unanswered.

a. Is it possible for someone to cease to exist as a person, and yet still be biologically alive as a human being? If so, how? In answering this question, how do you understand what it is to be a *person* and *human being?*

b. What are the best reasons for saying that Mr. C ceased to exist at each of the stages? What are the problems with considering each stage as the point of his end?

c. Some of the stages are only sustainable given recent technologies. How should these new technological powers be used in optimal ways? These questions would not have arisen in earlier eras; but we now need to decide how best to proceed in thinking about these matters.

Ethical Theory Glossary

(See also the appendix, "Approaching Ethical Problems: A Guide to Analysis.")

Altruism: Concern for others as the basis for action. Contrasted with selfish action. Action can be more or less altruistic.

Applied ethics: An area of ethics that attempts to determine what is morally justified or unjustified in specific areas of activity, whether global (such as famine relief), societal (for example, the death penalty), occupational (for instance, clinical ethics), or personal (such as truth telling to friends). The global, the societal, the occupational, and the personal overlap in many ways.

Autonomy: Self-determination. Sometimes interpreted as the derivation of one's moral judgment from one's reason, sometimes as an ability to structure one's own life goals. One of the most important values or principles in many ethical theories.

Beneficence: Action intended to bring about goodness.

Beneficence, principle of: The moral obligation to bring about (or to try to bring about) the good of others. Sometimes formulated to include the obligations to prevent and remove harm and to avoid causing harm. See **nonmaleficence.**

Benevolence: Action based on good intentions or a good will.

Casuistry: A methodology for doing ethics that begins with cases, then develops moral perspectives based on insights gained by generalizing from clusters of cases. These generalizations are then applied to other, similar cases.

Categorical: A factor that determines the moral nature of something (such as its rightness or wrongness) regardless of what other factors also exist in that situation. To say that an obligation is categorical, then, is to say that it applies absolutely, inflexibly, exceptionlessly—and regardless of any other factors that may also apply. If deception were categorically impermissible, then even if deceiving someone momentarily would save many lives, it would still be impermissible. See **prima facie.**

Categorical imperative: A method for judging people's actions' principles based on whether those principles are acceptable rationally—that is, whether the principles would apply to anyone in relevantly similar circumstances.

Conflict of moral considerations: In ethically difficult or complex situations, an action might be right for one reason and yet wrong for another reason. Moral judgment, then, requires the weighing of the respective moral claims. A health worker might, for example, have responsibilities to family members and also to clients or patients, or she might have obligations both to her profession and also to individuals.

Consequentialism: A theory that judges moral rightness and wrongness as a function of good or bad consequences of actions. See **deontology.**

Cost-benefit (risk-benefit) analysis: A method for assessing justifiability of decisions based exclusively on weighing the benefits against the risks or costs. This is sometimes calculated in economic terms, in which case it is not, as such, about moral justifiability.

Cultural relativism: A minimally controversial descriptive claim that cultures, groups, or societies sometimes have different moral beliefs or opinions. An observation of the existence of diversity of moral opinions among cultures. See **ethical relativism.**

Deontology: A type of ethical theory that determines actions' rightness or wrongness by considering factors other than (or in addition to) the actions' consequences. Deontologists maintain that actions or rules in themselves can have basic moral force. See **consequentialism.**

Dilemma, ethical: A situation in which there are equally strong moral considerations pulling in opposite directions. Colloquially, people often label as a "dilemma" any moral problem or conflict, such as one between temptation and moral obligation.

Egoism: A theory about pursuit of self-interest. The two main forms are ethical egoism and psychological egoism.

1. **Egoism, ethical:** The normative theory that the only justified motive of any behavior is the pursuit of one's own actual or perceived self-interest. See **psychological egoism; nonegoism.**

2. **Egoism, psychological:** The descriptive theory that the only source of motivation is the pursuit of one's own self-interest. See **ethical egoism; nonegoism.**

Ethical hedonism: A theory that identifies pleasure (or happiness) as the only sort of intrinsic value. Thus, the only goal worth pursuing for its own sake is pleasure/happiness (usually also accepting long-term happiness and others' happiness rather than merely one's own short-term happiness). Contrast **psychological hedonism.**

Ethical nihilism: A theory that denies the validity of any moral judgments. No moral judgments are justified, according to this view. This view is usually defended by claiming that some necessary condition (for example, measurability, God's existence, unanimity about morality) for justified moral judgments is lacking. See **ethical relativism; ethical objectivism.**

Ethical objectivism: The assertion that *some* moral judgments are justified and that some are not—independent of the acceptance of the judgments. It rejects both ethical relativism, which accepts all moral judgments as correct, and ethical nihilism, which denies the correctness of any moral judgments.

Ethical relativism: The view that all moral opinions of all people (or of all societies) are correct and justified. It rejects both ethical nihilism and ethical objectivism. It is often defended by the same sorts of reasons as ethical nihilism.

1. **Individual ethical relativism:** The form of ethical relativism that asserts that each moral judgment of each person is justified. Thus, each person would be morally infallible.

2. **Group ethical relativism:** The form of ethical relativism that asserts that each moral judgment of (a majority of) each society is justified. Thus, each society would be morally infallible.

Ethics: The discipline that attempts to think critically and systematically about morality and to provide criteria enabling people to make justified moral judgments.

Extrinsic/instrumental value: The sort of value that is found in efficiency or worth as a means to something. See also **intrinsic value.**

Intrinsic value: The sort of value that is worthwhile in itself, independent of the consequences associated with it. Such values constitute ultimate goals for living. All other goals would be means to these. See also **extrinsic value.**

Just distribution: A situation in which benefits and/or burdens meet the standards of justice. Applied to questions of fairness in allocation of resources, such as scarce health care resources. The scope of justice can be thought of globally, societally, or as more restricted.

Libertarianism: The belief that liberty is the preeminent value and thus that paternalism toward adults is difficult or impossible to justify.

Liberty-limiting principles: Four principles concerning proposed reasons for limiting people's freedom of action. The harm principle is the most generally accepted. The principles are as follows:

1. The **harm principle:** A person's liberty may justifiably be limited to prevent that person from harming others.

2. The **principle of paternalism:** A person's liberty may justifiably be limited to prevent that person from harming him- or herself.

3. The **offense principle:** A person's liberty may justifiably be limited to prevent that person from offending others.

4. The **principle of legal moralism:** A person's liberty may justifiably be limited to prevent that person from doing something wrong (whether or not anyone is harmed).

Monism: A theory that asserts the existence of one most basic sort of moral rule, intrinsic value, or virtue. See also **pluralism.**

Natural law: A theory that asserts the existence of a universally valid moral law knowable by use of reason.

Nonegoism: A view that denies that egoism is correct. It does not deny that people often act for their own good; it asserts rather that self-interest is not the only motive (the claim of psychological egoism) or the only determinant of moral rightness (the claim of ethical egoism).

Nonmaleficence: The moral duty to refrain from causing harm. Often considered to override the duty to bring about good.

Nonnormative judgments: Descriptive judgments about what is claimed to be the case. For example, "This pen is blue"; "His illness was caused by *E. coli.*"

Normative judgments: Judgments about what is ought or ought not to be the case. For example, "For her to have an abortion would (or would not) be morally wrong"; "This instance of euthanasia was (or was not) morally permissible."

Optimal: Something that is best.

Override: To have greater moral force or stringency. When two conflicting moral rules or principles apply in a situation, one sometimes overrides the other and thus prevails, such as when a mentally impaired patient's good is judged to override her or his autonomy (or, alternatively, when respect for a patient's autonomy overrides what one believes to be in that person's best interest).

Pluralism: A theory that asserts a multiplicity of basics, such as intrinsic values, virtues, or basic rules. Contrasted with monistic theories.

Prima facie: If an action is prima facie morally right, then it is right unless other, overriding circumstances make it morally wrong. Similar to the notion of a presumption in the law.

Principle of utility: The principle that the only sort of moral obligation is to produce the greatest good for the greatest number or, at least, greater good for more of those affected.

Principlism: Principle ethics; a type of understanding of ethics that invokes basic moral rules to address problems in ethics, especially in clinical ethics. Central principles often mentioned include beneficence, nonmaleficence, justice, autonomy, respect for persons, and truthfulness.

Prudential reasons: Considerations that appeal to one's self-interest; distinguished from moral reasons, with which they may coincide.

Psychological hedonism: The descriptive theory that the only sort of motivation is the pursuit of pleasure.

Rights, moral: Especially important permitted behaviors or basic needs. Natural rights; universal entitlements that are not dependent on the customs, beliefs, or laws of a particular place.

1. **Rights, negative:** Basic freedoms, such as of political expression, which the rights bearers must be permitted to exercise without interference.
2. **Rights, positive:** Basic goods, such as of the means of subsistence, necessary for a minimally decent existence, to which everyone is entitled.

Supererogatory: An evaluative concept applicable to actions that are morally right but not morally obligatory.

Teleological: Theories according to which goals or consequences are essential elements of moral justification.

Utilitarianism: The normative ethical theory that accepts the principle of utility as the supreme moral standard.

1. **Act utilitarianism:** A method of judging actions individually based on whether the action being judged produces good or bad consequences.

2. **Rule utilitarianism:** A method of judging based on compliance with rules that, in turn, are selected by their tendency to produce good or bad results.

Virtue ethics: An approach for judging morality based primarily on the evaluation of people's characters, their virtues or vices, rather than the individual actions they perform.

Virtues: Morally good traits of character.

Clinical Ethics Glossary

Abortion theories: Theories about the justifiability or unjustifiability of abortions. These are three main sorts of approaches:

1. **Conservative theories:** All or almost all abortions are morally impermissible.
2. **Liberal theories:** All abortions, at all stages of pregnancy, are morally permissible.
3. **Moderate theories:** Abortions are more or less morally permissible, possibly depending on the stage of pregnancy, possibly to prevent harm to the woman or fetus, or possibly for other reasons.

Advance directives: Documents by means of which people provide for health care decision making if they should become unable to make or communicate their decisions. See **durable power of attorney for health care; living will.**

Allocation of resources: See **just distribution; macroallocation; microallocation.**

Assent: Agreement to the provision of treatment. Applicable to children who are unable to legally consent to treatment. In research contexts, usually required for children to participate. See **informed consent.**

Assisted reproduction issues: Controversies about reproductive technologies such as in vitro fertilization (IVF) and artificial insemination (AI). These issues concern whether such methods are beneficial technologies helping infertile people or are wrong, because (for example) they are claimed to be exploitative, dangerous, unpredictable, wasteful, and/or unnatural.

Assisted suicide: See **physician-assisted suicide.**

Baby Doe regulations: Rules promulgated, but almost never enforced, by the federal government; prohibit the withholding of care from infants in almost all situations.

Best interests standard: For surrogate or proxy decision making; a decision is based on what would be in the person's best interest. See also **reasonable person standard; subjective standard.**

Bioethics: See clinical ethics.

Brain death: An irreversible cessation of function of all parts of the brain, including the brain stem and cortex. Clinically diagnosable by absence of various signs. Legally sufficient (but not necessary) for pronouncing death. See also **coma; persistent vegetative state.**

Clinical ethics: An area of applied ethics concerned with questions and problems arising in connection with health care, including biomedical research.

Code of ethics, professional: Documents, usually promulgated by professions, associations, that prescribe conduct for members of the profession, especially emphasizing contexts in which those individuals stand in professional relationships with their clients or patients. These codes often consist of combinations of statements of:

+ ideals and virtues to be strived toward,
+ goals to be attained in the practice of the profession, and
+ types of behaviors identified as obligatory, permissible, or prohibited.

Some professional codes of ethics have enforcement mechanisms to assure compliance and others do not.

Code statuses: Statuses given to patients by attending physicians concerning the extent of aggressiveness of treatment in the event of cessation of heart or breathing function. Protocols vary among health care institutions.

1. **Do not resuscitate:** DNR; "no-code"; an attending physician assigns this code status informing those caring for a patient not to attempt to resuscitate the patient in the event of a cardiac or respiratory arrest.
2. **Full code:** A medical order that, in the event of cardiac or respiratory arrest, all applicable resuscitation efforts should be attempted.
3. **Partial code:** A medical order that, in the event of cardiac or respiratory arrest, only some methods—as specified in the order—should be used in attempts to resuscitate the patient.

Coma: Severe brain damage causing unconsciousness from which one cannot be awakened. Sometimes reversible. See also **brain death; persistent vegetative state.**

Competence, mental: Capacity to make judgments adequately. Might apply differently depending on type of judgment (for example, financial judgments versus medical judgments versus judgments for everyday survival). Usually assumes sufficient rationality.

Confidentiality: The ordinarily assumed informational privacy existing between professionals and their clients/patients. Sometimes, legal or moral factors such as prevention of abuse may conflict with the strong presumption of confidentiality.

Conflict of interests: A type of situation conductive to unethical behavior: a person's professional judgment is actually or potentially compromised by extraneous factors.

Conflict of interests perceived: A situation judged to be unethical because of the appearance of impropriety.

DNR: See code statuses.

Double effect principle: In some Christian ethical thought, a principle allowing one to bring about evil only if certain necessary conditions are met, including not directly intending the foreseen harm.

Durable power of attorney for health care: A type of advance directive by means of which a person designates a trusted person who will make medical decisions for one in case one becomes incapacitated, often termed a health care proxy. See also **living will.**

Emancipated minor: Legally, in many jurisdictions, a minor who can legally consent to treatment since the adolescent lives independently. See **mature minor.**

Euthanasia: Ending someone's life (whether by killing or allowing to die), for the sake of that person.

1. **Active euthanasia:** Euthanasia that involves killing the patient. This practice is currently illegal, although controversy exists about whether to change the law.

2. **Passive euthanasia:** Euthanasia by means of allowing to die.

3. **Voluntary euthanasia:** Euthanasia performed with the person's consent.

4. **Nonvoluntary euthanasia:** Euthanasia done in circumstances (such as with an infant) in which the person is incapable of giving consent.

5. **Involuntary euthanasia:** Euthanasia performed on someone capable of consent against the person's wishes or without consulting the person.

Extraordinary means: Means of treatment that are futile and/or excessively burdensome for the patient. See also **ordinary means.**

Futile treatment: Treatment that will not benefit the person. Sometimes difficult to ascertain, either because of uncertainty or different criteria of benefit. Controversy exists about whether it is an acceptable way to judge whether to withhold life-sustaining treatment.

Informed consent: There are four necessary components for informed consent to be morally and legally valid. They are, in addition to a person's activity of giving permission:

+ disclosure of sufficient relevant information;

+ comprehension by the person being asked to consent;

+ mental competence of the consenter; and

+ sufficient voluntariness, rather than a decision that is coerced, pressured, or manipulated.

Institutional animal care and use committee (IACUC): A committee at an institution performing research on animals, charged with protection of the animals' well-being in the context of such research. This includes balancing the advancement of scientific knowledge with the minimization of discomfort or suffering of the animals.

Institutional ethics committee (IEC): Sometimes called simply "ethics committee"; a committee at a health care institution that attempts to resolve ethical problems brought to them by the institution's employees, patients, or families.

Institutional review board (IRB): A committee, affiliated with an institution performing human subjects research, responsible for protection of those individuals. Such protection includes assuring valid informed consent, confidentiality, and minimization of risk of harm to subjects.

Living will: A type of advance directive by means of which a person specifies in general or specific terms what sort of treatment one wants withheld if one becomes unable to consent to (or to refuse) treatment. See also **durable power of attorney for health care.**

Lottery: A method of allocating scarce resources by means of randomization. Contrasted with utilitarian criteria. Intended to avoid problems about selecting people in a possibly discriminatory way.

Macroallocation criteria: Criteria for allocation of scarce resources on the scale of a societal or an institutional policy decision, rather than individually.

Maternal-fetal conflict: Situations in which the wishes, rights, or interests of pregnant women conflict with the rights or interests of their fetuses.

Mature minor: A legal status, especially in common law (rather than statute); allows minors of at least age fifteen to consent to their own care. See **emancipated minor.**

Microallocation criteria: Criteria for allocation of scarce resources at the level of individual cases.

Moral status of the fetus: Specification of the extent, if any, of moral consideration due to the fetus. Often an important assumption of abortion theories.

Moral workup: Ethics workup; a problem-solving model applied to clinical practice using structures and thought processes common to health care workers' reasoning. Its structured format includes the gathering of factual information, making a tentative moral "diagnosis," and deciding among alternative courses of action based on a number of value factors.

Nontherapeutic research: Research intended only to gain new knowledge, not to benefit the research subjects. See also **therapeutic research.**

Ordinary means: Means of treatment that are neither futile nor excessively burdensome for the patient. See also **extraordinary means.**

Paternalism: Taking action to benefit or protect a person independent of that person's own wishes. In such cases, beneficence (the person's good) is thought to override the person's autonomy (free choice). See also **strong paternalism; weak paternalism.**

Persistent vegetative state (PVS): A condition of severe brain damage in which the person has stages of sleep and wakefulness but otherwise has no cognitive activity or conscious responsiveness. Seldom reversible. See also **brain death; coma.**

Personhood: One of the central contested concepts in ethics. Some identify personhood with membership in the human species. For others, a person is a being possessing all or most of a cluster of characteristics, including consciousness, feelings, sense of self-identity, and rationality.

Physician-assisted suicide (PAS): The action of taking one's own life with a physician having provided the means.

Primum non nocere: Latin phrase for "First, do no harm"; traditionally the most important behavior-guiding principle in medicine.

Proxy consent: Consent provided for someone else.

Quality of life: A concept referring to intrinsic values found in living other than the biological fact of existence. Sometimes mentioned in connection with life and death decision, to challenge the notion that all (human) life, regardless of the person's wishes or level of function, should be sustained.

Shared decision making: Decision making in which both health workers and patients participate in arriving at decisions. Contrasted with paternalistic decision making.

Slippery slope argument: A frequently occurring type of argument in both legal and ethical discourse. Such an argument asserts that a conclusion should be accepted because not to do so would create a snowball effect or because it is impossible to draw the line of justification. For example, "This new technology should be prohibited because it will lead us inevitably down the path to Nazism"; "This new technology should be allowed because one can't outlaw one technology without eventually outlawing them all."

Standard therapy: A norm in which an established treatment is assumed to be most appropriate.

Strong paternalism: Paternalism done to protect a person who is mentally competent. See **paternalism; weak paternalism.**

Substitute judgment standard: A test for judging surrogate decision making; deciding based on what the patient would want. If the person was formerly mentally competent, his or her stated wishes and values provide evidence to guide judgments. For those, such as infants, who never were mentally competent, such judgments become less clear. See also **best interests standard.**

Therapeutic research: Research intended to benefit the research subjects as well as to gather knowledge. See also **nontherapeutic research.**

Truthfulness: The behavior or character trait of veracity; sometimes conflicts with other considerations, such as minimizing harm.

Weak paternalism: Paternalism done to protect someone who is not mentally competent or at least not fully able to understand and think about his or her own treatment. See also **paternalism; strong paternalism.**

Approaching Ethical Problems: A Guide to Analysis

As with any other area of human activity, these are better and worse ways of performing the activity of moral thinking. These following addresses first some don'ts and then some do's of ethical decision making.

This document is intended only as an outline of some important concepts and skills in ethical analysis. For information about terminology, see the Ethical Theory Glossary. For more detailed examinations of the forms and limits of the views presented here, readers should consult other books in ethics.

DON'TS: SOME UNPRODUCTIVE THEORIES AND APPROACHES

This section will briefly explain several commonly held theories and frequently overlooked distinctions, along with one or more criticisms of each. Students and teachers of ethics tend to find these among the most pervasive obstacles to effective ethical thinking. People who have never studied ethics, however, are more often inclined to accept them. An awareness of these notions can help in two interconnected ways: first, to enable people to avoid some commonly held beliefs that lead people to misunderstand the theoretical nature of morality; second, as a result, to help people avoid obstacles to the practice of arriving at justified judgments about morality.

Egoisms

These are theories based on universal assertions about self-interest. They fall into two main sorts:

1. **Ethical egoism** asserts that morality is actually advancement of self-interest. Some of its advocates believe that it follows from the supposed truth of a similar-sounding, yet actually different, view:

2. **Psychological egoism,** which states that all behavior of all people is driven by pursuit of self-interest.

At first glance, it is not difficult to equate these two theories, although they are distinct. Ethical egoism purports to provide a standard for moral rightness—namely, pursuit of self-interest. Psychological egoism, by contrast, presents a perspective about human nature. It maintains that people are, and can only be, motivated by one sort of consideration: the pursuit of what each perceives to be in her or his best interest.

Criticism of Egoisms   As with many widely held theories, it is difficult to find any one objection to either of the two forms of egoism that will prove instantly persuasive to everyone. One who is committed to any theory (such as a form of egoism) will likely find criticisms misguided. Keeping that in mind, however, one might consider the following:

+ About *ethical* egoism, the nature of morality collapses to calculations of self-interest. It would render implausible statements such as, "What he did wasn't moral; it was entirely selfish." Rather, one would have to believe that selfishness is the highest form of morality.

+ About *psychological* egoism, the nature of all motivation amounts to calculation of perceived self-interest maximization. Thus, true intentional sacrifice of one's perceived best interest—as contrasted with merely apparent sacrifice—would become a fiction.

Moral Rules Thought of as Inflexible

Sometimes rules are believed to have the same force no matter what the circumstances. In *one* of the senses of the ambiguous word *absolute,* belief in use of such rules may be said to be a sort of "absolutism."

Criticism of Inflexible Rules   Rules of any degree of generality have exceptions and sometimes conflict with other rules. Rules are often taken to be the most basic justifiers of moral judgments. (For example, "This instance of stealing is wrong *because all* stealing is wrong.") Yet stealing might in some cases conflict with a more important value priority, such as the wrongness of letting people die unnecessarily.

Moral rules are thus more likely of the form "*Most* stealing is wrong," or "Stealing is wrong unless more important considerations prevail." In that case, a question now to be answered is, "How should we decide which instances are the usual ones rather than exceptions?" (See also principle approaches, discussed later.)

Overemphasis on Ethical Dilemmas

Educators may overemphasize ethical dilemmas—that is, situations in which these are equally strong moral reasons on each side. Ethical dilemmas are different from what is termed moral *problems,* problems such as the struggle between the sense of moral obligation and the temptation to give in to an easier path. Another sort of moral *problem* (rather than dilemma) occurs when people do not use the optimal strategies or communication skills to solve problems, and so they create otherwise preventable conflict or unhappiness.

Criticism of Studying Ethics Mainly as Dilemmas   An overemphasis on dilemmas tends to produce frustration and misunderstanding in students, because they may come to think that all real moral situations are dillemmas and thus that the students can never reasonably decide that an action is right or wrong. It seems to preclude closure. Further, students whose teachers present ethics exclusively as the study of dilemmas often—with good reason—get the impression that the study of ethics doesn't correspond to the study of much actual moral thinking.

Algorithmic Models

Cookbook-like methods for ethics make moral decision making seem like the type of activity that can be successfully attained by means of learning a formula and then plugging in the facts. Such a method would then cover all situations satisfactorily.

Criticism of Algorithm Models   To see a problem about this, it helps to compare moral reasoning to the activity of diagnosis. Some conditions can be diagnosed fairly easily and confidently, while others prove very complex and uncertain and cannot be decided by any formula or checklist of diagnostic criteria. Just as diagnosis and treatment can be arts, so too is ethical thinking. Whereas some moral matters can easily be judged right or wrong, others are not readily, mechanically deducible.

Blurring Distinctions

People often equate morality with something that it is *not.*

1. *Taste versus morality:* Morality is *not* merely a matter of individual. whim or taste. Whims, after all, need have no basis or other intellectual constraints such as consistency. Sometimes, disagreements about morality come down to someone asserting, as a discussion stopper, "Well, that's *my* opinion," as though it is thereby immune from further questions or criticism.

2. *The legal versus the moral:* The moral is *not* to be equated with what is legal at that place and time. This puts the cart before the horse, since—to simplify somewhat—what is legal *should* be based on concepts of what is moral, not the converse.

3. *Public opinion versus morality:* What is moral is *not* the same thing as the beliefs of a majority of people—either in one's society or in the world. For the majority can be wrong; people sometimes find themselves disagreeing with what they themselves believe to be the majority's opinion about moral matters. (See also group ethical relativism, discussed later.)

4. *Sincere beliefs versus morality:* Morality is *not* identical with an individual's sincere beliefs at a time. Whereas sincerity is admirable, it is no guarantee of reliability or adequacy. (See also individual ethical relativism, discussed later.)

5. *The nonnormative versus the normative:* Normative (evaluative) moral judgments, such as those about what is right or wrong, morally good or bad, just or unjust, differ in their conceptual functioning from nonnormative, or descriptive, judgments about morality. Beliefs about moral psychology, moral sociology, and moral anthropology are descriptive judgments that can be relevant to evaluative judgments but should not be equated with the evaluative judgments.

Miscellaneous Misleading Sayings

"That's what my tradition says." Reply: Such a statement is more an autobiographical explanation than a moral justification. People might find reasons to critically examine all traditions.

"That's what I was taught." Reply: People have been taught all sorts of things. Only some are justified.

"That's how I was raised." Reply: People have been raised in many different ways. Again, one needs to justify the reason that the way one was raised enabled one to make good judgments.

"We don't know a moral judgment for sure, so we have insufficient reason to believe it." Reply: Certainly is just not necessary, nor is it even attainable, in practical situations.

Ethical Relativisms and Ethical Nihilism

Individual ethical relativism says that each moral judgment of each individual is correct. According to this view, when any person believes that an action is right and any other person believes that the same action is morally wrong, then the action is *both* right and wrong.

Group ethical relativism states that each moral judgment of each group is correct. Thus, if the members of one group believe that a particular action would be morally right and the members of another group believe that the exact same action would be morally wrong, then the action would be *both* right and wrong.

Ethical nihilism asserts that no moral judgments are ever correct. A consequence of this theory would be that if one person believed an action to be morally right and someone else believed it to be morally wrong, then *neither* could ever be correct. The relativistic and nihilistic views are (mistakenly) believed to follow from such reasons as:

1. the goodness of tolerance of others' beliefs,
2. the diversity of basic moral beliefs,
3. the difficulty of proving controversial beliefs,
4. the unobservability of moral rightness and wrongness,
5. the equating of morality with taste, or
6. any of a variety of other grounds.

Interestingly, many of the reasons that are offered as support for *relativism* (the acceptance of *all* moral judgments as equally valid) also frequently appear as arguments for *ethical nihilism* (a belief that *no* moral judgments of anyone are ever valid).

Criticisms of Relativisms and Nihilism Relativisms indiscriminately allow the most outrageous and misguided moral opinions to be considered as on a par with the most profound ones. Nihilists, likewise, would be unable to distinguish among these, since nihilists believe that all moral judgments are equally baseless. Thus, the overly charitable relativist thinks of all individuals (or all societies) as infallible about morality, whereas the excessively cynical nihilist considers all individuals (or all societies) as invariably misguided about morality—that is, as suffering from a false myth, a self-deception, or an illusion.

As it turns out, reasons 1 through 4 are all true statements. None of them, however, provides us with a good reason for accepting either ethical relativism or ethical nihilism.

In between the extremes of all and none exemplified by relativism and nihilism, there exists the more viable option of *some:* that some opinions about morality are correct and some are not. The decision of which judgments are more or less plausible remains to be specified, but that is much of what ethical discourse is intended for. Unless that in-between option is true, then the entire enterprise of ethics, including the attempt to distinguish between better and less supported beliefs, becomes pointless.

POSSIBLE DO'S: SOME MORE PROMISING APPROACHES

Ethical theories are systems of intellectual tools we use to understand and to make moral judgments. We view these as methods of thinking or judging appropriately about morality—that is, as techniques or devices for enabling us to arrive at justified moral beliefs. They consist of theoretical tools, concepts, methods, and processes for arriving at justified moral judgments. These approaches can be used in different ways. The most traditional way to teach these present each approach as an attempt to capture *the* essence of morality and as incompatible with the others. Although that is an effective method in terms of reflecting people's actual thoughts as they had originally formulated these theories, it also, its critics argue, may omit some of the complexity and diversity of sorts of applicable moral considerations.

For purposes of perspective, criticisms, reservations, or questions follow the proposed possible ethical analysis methods described here.

Consequentialist Decision Criteria

These apply to theories such as those of *utilitarianism,* and they determine actions to be morally right or wrong depending on whether those actions—or the rules of which the actions are instances—produce good consequences for those affected. Jeremy Bentham and John Stuart Mill are the best-known proponents of this soft of view. The goodness of the consequences might be viewed as happiness or perhaps as other kinds of things. Consequentialists differ as to the scope of those whose good or harm merits consideration. As two examples, some believe that morality applies to all and only those human beings affected by one's actions, whereas others believe that all sentient, feeling beings should be considered.

Questions about Utilitarian Consequentialism   Do the utilitarian criteria adequately account for all of morality, including justice? Might not most people's good be used to sacrifice the rights or good of a few? Do we owe equally strong obligations to our families and to those far away and in the future?

Deontological Criteria

These methods ascertain morality of actions on the basis of either rules or more concrete factors, such as specific circumstances. For those who emphasize *rules,* the rules can be thought of as exceptionless or of variable weight. The "exceptionless" option has been described earlier in the "Don'ts" section. What makes the factors distinctively deontological is the emphasis on the *intrinsic* rightness or wrongness (of dutifulness, obligatoriness, or moral permissibility) of certain actions, rather than thinking of the rightness or wrongness as springing from the actions' results. For example, a deontologist would say that truth telling is right in and of itself, rather than because it brings about good consequences.

Questions about Deontological Criteria   If these are thought of as rules, then how should the rules be identified and rank-ordered when they conflict? What is the proper role of actions' consequences in moral judgment? Are consequences ever relevant? If so, then to what extent?

Virtue Theories

Such theories focus more on people's traits of character, ways of being, rather than emphasizing the evaluation of the morality of people's actions. Virtue theorists, such as Aristotle, believe that one lives a good life by learning and cultivating good habits of behavior. Moral behavior arises from possession of those good character traits, which are termed virtues.

Questions about Virtue Approaches   Which virtues are most important? How does the virtuous person decide which is the right or wrong thing to do? Does that bring us back to the other sorts of criteria?

Casuistry Methods

These methods attempt to decide about particular cases by converging form easier, more generally agreed-on cases. There is an avoidance of exclusive reliance on individual theories. The term *casuistry* commonly has a negative connotation, but that should not bias people's judgment of the method's appropriateness.

Questions about Casuistry   What is the content of these theories? Do they have substantive criteria for judgment?

Kantian Views

These theories, derived from the thought of Immanuel Kant, tend to emphasize one or more of several considerations. These include the following points:

1. There is a disregard of actions' consequences in favor of the actions' *intentional* considerations. Thus, what the person performing has in mind is important, while the actual outcomes are not. The moral person acts out of a sense of moral obligation, a distinctive feeling of "oughtness," not because she or he wants to act in that way.

2. *Universalizability* is a test of rules. That is, one must act only in ways one reasonably judges would be applicable to anyone in similar circumstances.

3. *Respect for persons* is a central belief. The importance of human dignity is essential to the moral point of view.

4. *Rationality* is the hallmark of moral conduct. Thus, those who are worthy of respect are those who are rational, and one's actions acquire moral worth to the extent that they are performed rationally.

Questions about Kantian Views   In its formality, does it adequately account for flexibility of rules and of goods besides rationality?

Feminist Views

These perspectives often highlight care as an important value, along with other moral emotions. Interconnectedness among people acknowledges actual felt relationships among the people. There is a willingness to think of terms of those one knows and not merely humanity or justice in the abstract, of relationships rather than of blind duty. Feminists attempt to express women's viewpoints and how women are affected by opinions and institutions. The extent to which differences between males' and females' ways of thinking, feeling, and behaving arise from heredity versus from social conditioning remains in dispute.

Question about Feminist Views   Are they to be understood as a more satisfactory alternative understanding of morality or as a complement to traditional views?

Rights-Based Approaches

These stress moral rights as central to much or all moral judgment. The provide for basic freedoms and, possibly, a minimally decent level of existence to which everyone should be entitled.

Questions about Rights-Based Theories   Is all of morality a function of rights? What is the basis of rights, and how should people decide what to do when rights conflict?

Justice-Based Views

These attempt to think of issues based on whether situations fulfill the criteria of justice. Views about the nature of justice range among Marxist, pure libertarian/capitalist, egalitarian, and mixed economic views, and span views including those based on various sorts of outcomes and those allowing for considerations of contribution, luck, effort, and/or fairness of procedure.

Questions about Justice-Based Views

Is justice the most important basis for moral judgment? Is it sufficient to account for all moral judgments? If justice does suffice, then which of the multitude of theories of justice is most adequate?

Combined Approaches or Methods

Such approaches are eclectic. They try to weave together a plurality of approaches, such as a view that accepts as relevant considerations of virtue, justice, consequences, and duties.

Questions about Combined Approaches   These need further clarification about the specific combinations of each particular approach proposed.

Principle Approaches

These have been among the most influential rule-based methods in clinical ethics. They enumerate a few basic moral principles, often including beneficence, nonmaleficence, autonomy, justice, veracity, and perhaps others—and then attempt to apply these to specific circumstances to make moral decisions. These principles may themselves consist of basic justifications, such as deontological rules, or they may arise from further sources, such as by being variations of behavior patterns producing good consequences—in the manner of the theory known as rule utilitarianism.

Questions about Principle Approaches   How should one decide when rules or principles have exceptions, and when they conflict? Is any given proposed list complete? (See also "Moral Rules Thought of as Inflexible.")

Moral Workups

This moral problem-solving model synthesizes the structure of clinical decision making with concepts and concepts of ethics. In medicine, nursing, and other disciplines, information about cases is customarily organized in the form of what is often termed a *workup*. This often has something like the following sequential structure: presenting problem, medical history of the patient, other relevant factual information (such as examination, psychosocial factors, and laboratory findings), consideration of alternative diagnostic and treatment decisions, preliminary treatment plan, and implementation. In the moral workup, one begins instead with the initial moral conflict, then, after considering relevant factual considerations, mobilizes and weights the applicable ethical factors, proceeding to a tentative ethical judgment and its implementation.

Question about Moral Workups   Can all clinical ethics problems be best approached using this particular model? Perhaps different structures or methods work well for different sorts of situations and problems.

Other Relevant Notions

There should be a recognition of priorities and uncertainty: normatively, law and policy *should* be based on morality, not the other way around. But to say that law ought to be based on morality is not to say that *all* morally right actions ought to be legally permissible.

Moral judgments or beliefs should be flexible, informed by relevant factual information, and (as should be true of all beliefs) accepted tentatively, because the judgments are not known with certainty.

To *be* a moral *person* requires more than clear thinking about morality, because behavior is not simply a rational carrying out of lucidly inferred judgments by beings who lack emotions, conflicting feelings, biases, and loyalties. To be moral involves a sense of empathy for others and a willingness to do what one believes to be the right thing. It also includes willingness to continue to examine one's beliefs and to grow.

Codes of Ethics

THE HIPPOCRATIC OATH

Reprinted with permission of Johns Hopkins University Press.

I swear by Apollo Physician and Asclepius and Hygieia and Panaceia and all the goddesses, making them my witness, that I will fulfill according to my ability and judgment this oath and this covenant:

> To hold him who has taught me this art as equal to my parents and to live my life in partnership with him, and if he is in need of money to give him a share of mine, and to regard his offspring as equal to my brothers in male lineage and to teach them this art—if they desire to learn it—without fee and covenant; to give a share of precepts and oral instruction and all other learning to my sons and to the sons of him who has instructed me and to pupils who have signed the covenant and have taken an oath according to the medical law, but to no one else.

I will apply dietetic measures for the benefit of the sick according to my ability and judgment; I will keep them from harm and injustice.

I will neither give a deadly drug to anybody if asked for it, nor will I make a suggestion to this effect. Similarly I will not give to a woman an abortive remedy. In purity and holiness I will guard my life and my art.

I will not use the knife, not even on sufferers from stone, but will withdraw in favor of such men as are engaged in this work.

Whatever houses I may visit, I will come for the benefit of the sick, remaining free of all intentional injustice, of all mischief and in particular of sexual relations with both female and male persons, be they free or slaves.

What I may see or hear in the course of the treatment or even outside of the treatment in regard to the life of men, which on no account one must spread abroad, I will keep to myself holding such things shameful to be spoken about.

If I fulfil this oath and do not violate it, may it be granted to me to enjoy life and art, being honored with fame among all men for all time to come; if I transgress it and swear falsely, may the opposite of all this be my lot.

THE NUREMBERG CODE

1. The voluntary consent of the human subject is *absolutely* essential. This means that the person involved should have legal capacity to give consent; should be so situated as to be able to exercise free power of choice, without the intervention of any element of force, fraud, deceit, duress, overreaching, or other ulterior form of constraint or coercion; and should have sufficient knowledge and comprehension of the elements of the subject matter involved as to enable him to make an understanding and enlightened decision. This latter element requires that before the acceptance of an affirmative decision by the experimental subject there should be made know to him the nature, duration, and purpose of the experiment; the method and means by which it is to be conducted; all inconveniences and hazards reasonably to be expected; and the effects upon his health or person which may possibly come from his participation in the experiment.

The duty and responsibility for ascertaining the quality of the consent rest upon each individual who initiates, directs, or engages in the experiment. It is a personal duty and responsibility which may not be delegated to another with impunity.

2. The experiment should be such as to yield fruitful results for the good of society, unprocurable by other methods or means of study, and not random and unnecessary in nature.

3. The experiment should be so designed and based on the results of animal experimentation and a knowledge of the natural history of the disease or other problem under study that the anticipated results will justify the performance of the experiment.

4. The experiment should be so conducted as to avoid all unnecessary physical and mental suffering and injury.

5. No experiment should be conducted where there is an *a priori* reason to believe that death or disabling injury will occur; except, perhaps, in those experiments where the experimental physicians also serve as subjects.

6. The degree of risk to be taken should never exceed that determined by the humanitarian importance of the problem to be solved by the experiment.

7. Proper preparations should be made and adequate facilities provided to protect the experimental subject against even remote possibilities of injury, disability, or death.

8. The experiment should be conducted only by scientifically qualified persons. The highest degree of skill and care should be required through all stages of the experiment of those who conduct or engage in the experiment.

9. During the course of the experiment the human subject should be at liberty to bring the experiment to an end if he has reached the physical or mental state where continuation of the experiment seems to him to be impossible.

10. During the course of the experiment the scientist in charge must be prepared to terminate the experiment at any stage, if he has probable cause to believe, in the exercise of the good faith, superior skill, and careful judgment required of him that a continuation of the experiment is likely to result in injury, disability, or death to the experimental subject.

WORLD MEDICAL ASSOCIATION DECLARATION OF HELSINKI

Reprinted with the permission of the World Medical Association.

Ethical Principles for Medical Research Involving Human Subjects

Adopted by the 18th WMA General Assembly Helsinki, Finland, June 1964 and amended by the:

+ *29th WMA General Assembly, Tokyo, Japan, October 1975*
+ *35th WMA General Assembly, Venice, Italy, October 1983*
+ *41st WMA General Assembly, Hong Kong, September 1989*
+ *48th WMA General Assembly, Somerset West, Republic of South Africa, October 1996, and the*
+ *52nd WMA General Assembly, Edinburgh, Scotland, October 2000*

A. Introduction

1. The World Medical Association has developed the Declaration of Helsinki as a statement of ethical principles to provide guidance to physicians and other participants in medical research involving human subjects. Medical research involving human subjects includes research on identifiable human material or identifiable data.

2. It is the duty of the physician to promote and safeguard the health of the people. The physician's knowledge and conscience are dedicated to the fulfillment of this duty.

3. The Declaration of Geneva of the World Medical Association binds the physician with the words, "The health of my patient will be my first consideration," and the International Code of Medical Ethics declares that, "A physician shall act only in the patient's interest when providing medical care which might have the effect of weakening the physical and mental condition of the patient."

4. Medical progress is based on research which ultimately must rest in part on experimentation involving human subjects.

5. In medical research on human subjects, considerations related to the well-being of the human subject should take precedence over the interests of science and society.

6. The primary purpose of medical research involving human subjects is to improve prophylactic, diagnostic and therapeutic procedures and the understanding of the aetiology and pathogenesis of disease. Even the best proven prophylactic,

diagnostic, and therapeutic methods must continuously be challenged through research for their effectiveness, efficiency, accessibility and quality.

7. In current medical practice and in medical research, most prophylactic, diagnostic and therapeutic procedures involve risks and burdens.

8. Medical research is subject to ethical standards that promote respect for all human beings and protect their health and rights. Some research populations are vulnerable and need special protection. The particular needs of the economically and medically disadvantaged must be recognized. Special attention is also required for those who cannot give or refuse consent for themselves, for those who may be subject to giving consent under duress, for those who will not benefit personally from the research and for those for whom the research is combined with care.

9. Research Investigators should be aware of the ethical, legal and regulatory requirements for research on human subjects in their own countries as well as applicable international requirements. No national ethical, legal or regulatory requirement should be allowed to reduce or eliminate any of the protections for human subjects set forth in this Declaration.

B. *Basic Principles for all Medical Research*

10. It is the duty of the physician in medical research to protect the life, health, privacy, and dignity of the human subject.

11. Medical research involving human subjects must conform to generally accepted scientific principles, be based on a thorough knowledge of the scientific literature, other relevant sources of information, and on adequate laboratory and, where appropriate, animal experimentation.

12. Appropriate caution must be exercised in the conduct of research which may affect the environment, and the welfare of animals used for research must be respected.

13. The design and performance of each experimental procedure involving human subjects should be clearly formulated in an experimental protocol. This protocol should be submitted for consideration, comment, guidance, and where appropriate, approval to a specially appointed ethical review committee, which must be independent of the investigator, the sponsor or any other kind of undue influence. This independent committee should be in conformity with the laws and regulations of the country in which the research experiment is performed. The committee has the right to monitor ongoing trials. The researcher has the obligation to provide monitoring information to the committee, especially any serious adverse events. The researcher should also submit to the committee, for review, information regarding funding, sponsors, institutional affiliations, other potential conflicts of interest and incentives for subjects.

14. The research protocol should always contain a statement of the ethical considerations involved and should indicate that there is compliance with the principles enunciated in this Declaration.

15. Medical research involving human subjects should be conducted only by scientifically qualified persons and under the supervision of a clinically competent medical person. The responsibility for the human subject must always

rest with a medically qualified person and never rest on the subject of the research, even though the subject has given consent.

16. Every medical research project involving human subjects should be preceded by careful assessment of predictable risks and burdens in comparison with foreseeable benefits to the subject or to others. This does not preclude the participation of healthy volunteers in medical research. The design of all studies should be publicly available.

17. Physicians should abstain from engaging in research projects involving human subjects unless they are confident that the risks involved have been adequately assessed and can be satisfactorily managed. Physicians should cease any investigation if the risks are found to outweigh the potential benefits or if there is conclusive proof of positive and beneficial results.

18. Medical research involving human subjects should only be conducted if the importance of the objective outweighs the inherent risks and burdens to the subject. This is especially important when the human subjects are healthy volunteers.

19. Medical research is only justified if there is a reasonable likelihood that the populations in which the research is carried out stand to benefit from the results of the research.

20. The subjects must be volunteers and informed participants in the research project.

21. The right of research subjects to safeguard their integrity must always be respected. Every precaution should be taken to respect the privacy of the subject, the confidentiality of the patient's information and to minimize the impact of the study on the subject's physical and mental integrity and on the personality of the subject.

22. In any research on human beings, each potential subject must be adequately informed of the aims, methods, sources of funding, any possible conflicts of interest, institutional affiliations of the researcher, the anticipated benefits and potential risks of the study and the discomfort it may entail. The subject should be informed of the right to abstain from participation in the study or to withdraw consent to participate at any time without reprisal. After ensuring that the subject has understood the information, the physician should then obtain the subject's freely-given informed consent, preferably in writing. If the consent cannot be obtained in writing, the non-written consent must be formally documented and witnessed.

23. When obtaining informed consent for the research project the physician should be particularly cautious if the subject is in a dependent relationship with the physician or may consent under duress. In that case the informed consent should be obtained by a well-informed physician who is not engaged in the investigation and who is completely independent of this relationship.

24. For a research subject who is legally incompetent, physically or mentally incapable of giving consent or is a legally incompetent minor, the investigator must obtain informed consent from the legally authorized representative in accordance with applicable law. These groups should not be included in research unless the research is necessary to promote the health of the population represented and this research cannot instead be performed on legally competent persons.

25. When a subject deemed legally incompetent, such as a minor child, is able to give assent to decisions about participation in research, the investigator must obtain that assent in addition to the consent of the legally authorized representative.

26. Research on individuals from whom it is not possible to obtain consent, including proxy or advance consent, should be done only if the physical/mental condition that prevents obtaining informed consent is a necessary characteristic of the research population. The specific reasons for involving research subjects with a condition that renders them unable to give informed consent should be stated in the experimental protocol for consideration and approval of the review committee. The protocol should state that consent to remain in the research should be obtained as soon as possible from the individual or a legally authorized surrogate.

27. Both authors and publishers have ethical obligations. In publication of the results of research, the investigators are obliged to preserve the accuracy of the results. Negative as well as positive results should be published or otherwise publicly available. Sources of funding, institutional affiliations and any possible conflicts of interest should be declared in the publication. Reports of experimentation not in accordance with the principles laid down in this Declaration should not be accepted for publication.

C. Additional Principles for Medical Research Combined with Medical Care

28. The physician may combine medical research with medical care, only to the extent that the research is justified by its potential prophylactic, diagnostic or therapeutic value. When medical research is combined with medical care, additional standards apply to protect the patients who are research subjects.

29. The benefits, risks, burdens and effectiveness of a new method should be tested against those of the best current prophylactic, diagnostic, and therapeutic methods. This does not exclude the use of placebo, or no treatment, in studies where no proven prophylactic, diagnostic or therapeutic method exists.

30. At the conclusion of the study, every patient entered into the study should be assured of access to the best proven prophylactic, diagnostic and therapeutic methods identified by the study.

31. The physician should fully inform the patient which aspects of the care are related to the research. The refusal of a patient to participate in a study must never interfere with the patient-physician relationship.

32. In the treatment of a patient, where proven prophylactic, diagnostic and therapeutic methods do not exist or have been ineffective, the physician, with informed consent from the patient, must be free to use unproven or new prophylactic, diagnostic and therapeutic measures, if in the physician's judgement it offers hope of saving life, re-establishing health or alleviating suffering. Where possible, these measures should be made the object of research, designed to evaluate their safety and efficacy. In all cases, new information should be recorded and, where appropriate, published. The other relevant guidelines of this Declaration should be followed.

INTERNATIONAL CODE OF MEDICAL ETHICS

Adopted by the 3rd General Assembly of the World Medical Association, London, England, October 1949 and amended by the 22nd World Medical Assembly, Sydney, Australia, August 1968 and the 35th World Medical Assembly, Venice, Italy, October 1983.

Duties of Physicians in General

A PHYSICIAN SHALL always maintain the highest standards of professional conduct.

A PHYSICIAN SHALL not permit motives of profit to influence the free and independent exercise of professional judgement on behalf of patients.

A PHYSICIAN SHALL, in all types of medical practice, be dedicated to providing competent medical service in full technical and moral independence, with compassion and respect for human dignity.

A PHYSICIAN SHALL deal honestly with patients and colleagues, and strive to expose those physicians deficient in character or competence, or who engage in fraud or deception.

The following practices are deemed to be unethical conduct: (a) Self advertising by physicians, unless permitted by the laws of the country and the Code of Ethics of the National Medical Association. (b) Paying or receiving any fee or any other consideration solely to procure the referral of a patient or for prescribing or referring a patient to any source.

A PHYSICIAN SHALL respect the rights of patients, of colleagues, and of other health professionals and shall safeguard patient confidences.

A PHYSICIAN SHALL act only in the patient's interest when providing medical care which might have the effect of weakening the physical and mental condition of the patient.

A PHYSICIAN SHALL use great caution in divulging discoveries or new techniques or treatment through non-professional channels.

A PHYSICIAN SHALL certify only that which he has personally verified.

Duties of Physicians to the Sick

A PHYSICIAN SHALL always bear in mind the obligation of preserving human life.

A PHYSICIAN SHALL owe his patients complete loyalty and all the resources of his science. Whenever an examination or treatment is beyond the physician's capacity he should summon another physician who has the necessary ability.

A PHYSICIAN SHALL preserve absolute confidentiality on all he knows about his patient even after the patient has died.

A PHYSICIAN SHALL give emergency care as a humanitarian duty unless he is assured that others are willing and able to give such care.

Duties of Physicians to Each Other

A PHYSICIAN SHALL behave towards his colleagues as he would have them behave towards him.

A PHYSICIAN SHALL NOT entice patients from his colleagues.

A PHYSICIAN SHALL observe the principles of the "Declaration of Geneva" approved by the World Medical Association.

DECLARATION OF GENEVA

Adopted by the 2nd General Assembly of the World Medical Association, Geneva, Switzerland, September 1948 and amended by the:

+ *22nd World Medical Assembly, Sydney, Australia, August 1968*
+ *35th World Medical Assembly, Venice, Italy, October 1983*
+ *46th WMA General Assembly, Stockholm, Sweden, September 1994*

At the time of being admitted as a member of the medical profession:

I SOLEMNLY PLEDGE myself to consecrate my life to the service of humanity;

I WILL GIVE to my teachers the respect and gratitude which is their due;

I WILL PRACTICE my profession with conscience and dignity;

THE HEALTH OF MY PATIENT will be my first consideration;

I WILL RESPECT the secrets which are confided in me, even after the patient has died;

I WILL MAINTAIN by all the means in my power, the honor and the noble traditions of the medical profession;

MY COLLEAGUES will be my sisters and brothers;

I WILL NOT PERMIT considerations of age, disease or disability, creed, ethnic origin, gender, nationality, political affiliation, race, sexual orientation, or social standing to intervene between my duty and my patient.

I WILL MAINTAIN the utmost respect for human life from its beginning even under threat and I will not use my medical knowledge contrary to the laws of humanity;

I MAKE THESE PROMISES solemnly, freely and upon my honor.

A PATIENT'S BILL OF RIGHTS

Reprinted with the permission of the American Hospital Association, copyright 1992.

Introduction

Effective health care requires collaboration between patients and physicians and other health care professionals. Open and honest communication, respect for personal and professional values, and sensitivity to differences are integral to optimal patient care. As the setting for the provision of health services, hospitals must provide a foundation for understanding and respecting the rights and responsibilities of patients, their families, physicians, and other caregivers. Hospitals must ensure a health care ethic that respects the role of patients in decision making about treatment choices and other aspects of their care. Hospitals must be sensitive to cultural, racial, linguistic, religious, age, gender, and other differences as well as the needs of persons with disabilities.

The American Hospital Association presents A Patient's Bill of Rights with the expectation that it will contribute to more effective patient care and be supported by the hospital on behalf of the institution, its medical staff, employees, and patients.

The American Hospital Association encourages health care institutions to tailor this bill of rights to their patient community by translating and/or simplifying the language of this bill of rights as may be necessary to ensure that patients and their families understand their rights and responsibilities.

Bill of Rights

These rights can be exercised on the patient's behalf by a designated surrogate or proxy decision maker if the patient lacks decision-making capacity, is legally incompetent, or is a minor.

1. The patient has the right to considerate and respectful care.

2. The patient has the right to and is encouraged to obtain from physicians and other direct caregivers relevant, current, and understandable information concerning diagnosis, treatment, and prognosis.

Except in emergencies when the patient lacks decision-making capacity and the need for treatment is urgent, the patient is entitled to the opportunity to discuss and request information related to the specific procedures and/or treatments, the risks involved, the possible length of recuperation, and the medically reasonable alternatives and their accompanying risks and benefits.

Patients have the right to know the identity of physicians, nurses, and others involved in their care, as well as when those involved are students, residents, or other trainees. The patient also has the right to know the immediate and long-term financial implications of treatment choices, insofar as they are known.

3. The patient has the right to make decisions about the plan of care prior to and during the course of treatment and to refuse a recommended treatment or plan of care to the extent permitted by law and hospital policy and to be informed of the medical consequences of this action. In case of such refusal, the patient is entitled to other appropriate care and services that the hospital provides or transfer to another hospital.

The hospital should notify patients of any policy that might affect patient choice within the institution.

4. The patient has the right to have an advance directive (such as a living will, health care proxy, or durable power of attorney for health care) concerning treatment or designating a surrogate decision maker with the expectation that the hospital will honor the intent of that directive to the extent permitted by law and hospital policy.

Health care institutions must advise patients of their rights under state law and hospital policy to make informed medical choices, ask if the patient has an advance directive, and include that information in patient records. The patient has the right to timely information about hospital policy that may limit its ability to implement fully a legally valid advance directive.

5. The patient has the right to every consideration of privacy. Case discussion, consultation, examination, and treatment should be conducted so as to protect each patient's privacy.

6. The patient has the right to expect that all communications and records pertaining to his/her care will be treated as confidential by the hospital, except in cases such as suspected abuse and public health hazards when reporting is permitted or required by law. The patient has the right to expect that the hospital will emphasize the confidentiality of this information when it releases it to any other parties entitled to review information in these records.

7. The patient has the right to review the records pertaining to his/her medical care and to have the information explained or interpreted as necessary, except when restricted by law.

8. The patient has the right to expect that, within its capacity and policies, a hospital will make reasonable response to the request of a patient for appropriate and medically indicated care and services. The hospital must provide evaluation, service, and/or referral as indicated by the urgency of the case. When medically appropriate and legally permissible, or when a patient has so requested, a patient may be transferred to another facility. The institution to which the patient is to be transferred must first have accepted the patient for transfer. The patient must also have the benefit of complete information and explanation concerning the need for, risks, benefits, and alternatives to such a transfer.

9. The patient has the right to ask and be informed of the existence of business relationships among the hospital, educational institutions, other health care providers, or payers that may influence the patient's treatment and care.

10. The patient has the right to consent to or decline to participate in proposed research studies or human experimentation affecting care and treatment or requiring direct patient involvement, and to have those studies fully explained prior to consent. A patient who declines to participate in research or experimentation is entitled to the most effective care that the hospital can otherwise provide.

11. The patient has the right to expect reasonable continuity of care when appropriate and to be informed by physicians and other caregivers of available and realistic patient care options when hospital care is no longer appropriate.

12. The patient has the right to be informed of hospital policies and practices that relate to patient care, treatment, and responsibilities. The patient has the right to be informed of available resources for resolving disputes, grievances, and conflicts, such as ethics committees, patient representatives, or other mechanisms available in the institution. The patient has the right to be informed of the hospital's charges for services and available payment methods.

The collaborative nature of health care requires that patients, or their families/surrogates, participate in their care. The effectiveness of care and patient satisfaction with the course of treatment depend, in part, on the patient fulfilling certain responsibilities. Patients are responsible for providing information about past illnesses, hospitalizations, medications, and other matters related to health status. To participate effectively in decision making, patients must be encouraged to take responsibility for requesting additional information or clarification about their health status or treatment when they do not fully understand information and instructions. Patients are also responsible for ensuring that the health care institution has a copy of their written advance directive if they have one. Patients are responsible for informing their physicians and other caregivers if they anticipate problems in following prescribed treatment.

Patients should also be aware of the hospitals obligation to be reasonably efficient and equitable in providing care to other patients and the community. The hospital's rules and regulations are designed to help the hospital meet this obligation. Patients and their families are responsible for making reasonable accommodations to the needs of the hospital, other patients, medical staff, and hospital employees. Patients are responsible for providing necessary information for insurance claims and for working with the hospital to make payment arrangements, when necessary.

A person's health depends on much more than health care services. Patients are responsible for recognizing the impact of their life-style on their personal health.

Conclusion

Hospitals have many functions to perform, including the enhancement of health status, health promotion, and the prevention and treatment of injury and disease; the immediate and ongoing care and rehabilitation of patients; the education of health professionals, patients, and the community; and research. All these activities must be conducted with an overriding concern for the values and dignity of patients.

AMERICAN MEDICAL ASSOCIATION PRINCIPLES OF MEDICAL ETHICS

Reprinted with the permission of the American Medical Association, copyright 2000.

The medical profession has long subscribed to a body of ethical statements developed primarily for the benefit of the patient. As a member of this profession, a physician must recognize responsibility to patients first and foremost, as well as to society, to other health professionals, and to self. The following Principles adopted by the American Medical Association are not laws, but standards of conduct which define the essentials of honorable behavior for the physician.

I. A physician shall be dedicated to providing competent medical care with compassion and respect for human dignity and rights.

II. A physician shall uphold the standards of professionalism, be honest in all professional interactions, and strive to report physicians deficient in character or competence, or engaging in fraud or deception, to appropriate entities.

III. A physician shall respect the law and also recognize a responsibility to seek changes in those requirements which are contrary to the best interests of the patient.

IV. A physician shall respect the rights of patients, colleagues, and other health professionals, and shall safeguard patient confidences and privacy within the constraints of the law.

V. A physician shall continue to study, apply, and advance scientific knowledge, maintain a commitment to medical education, make relevant information available to patients, colleagues, and the public, obtain consultation, and use the talents of other health professionals when indicated.

VI. A physician shall, in the provision of appropriate patient care, except in emergencies, be free to choose whom to serve, with whom to associate, and the environment in which to provide medical care.

VII. A physician shall recognize a responsibility to participate in activities contributing to the improvement of the community and the betterment of public health.

VIII. A physician shall, while caring for a patient, regard responsibility to the patient as paramount.

IX. A physician shall support access to medical care for all people.

Fundamental Elements of the Patient-Physician Relationship

From ancient times, physicians have recognized that the health and well-being of patients depends upon a collaborative effort between physician and patient. Patients share with physicians the responsibility for their own health care. The patient-physician relationship is of greatest benefit to patients when they bring medical problems to the attention of their physicians in a timely fashion, provide information about their medical condition to the best of their ability, and work with their physicians in a mutually respectful alliance. Physicians can best contribute to this alliance by serving as their patients' advocates and by fostering these rights:

1. The patient has the right to receive information from physicians and to discuss the benefits, risks, and costs of appropriate treatment alternatives. Patients should receive guidance from their physicians as to the optimal course of action. Patients are also entitled to obtain copies or summaries of their medical records, to have their questions answered, to be advised of potential conflicts of interest that their physicians might have, and to receive independent professional opinions.

2. The patient has the right to make decisions regarding the health care that is recommended by his or her physician. Accordingly, patients may accept or refuse any recommended medical treatment.

3. The patient has the right to courtesy, respect, dignity, responsiveness, and timely attention to his or her needs.

4. The patient has the right to confidentiality. The physician should not reveal confidential communications or information without the consent of the patient, unless provided for by law or by the need to protect the welfare of the individual or the public interest.

5. The patient has the right to continuity of health care. The physician has an obligation to cooperate in the coordination of medically indicated care with other health care providers treating the patient. The physician may not discontinue treatment of a patient as long as further treatment is medically indicated, without giving the patient reasonable assistance and sufficient opportunity to make alternative arrangements for care.

6. The patient has a basic right to have available adequate health care. Physicians, along with the rest of society, should continue to work toward this goal. Fulfillment of this right is dependent on society providing resources so that no patient is deprived of necessary care because of an inability to pay for the care. Physicians should continue their traditional assumption of a part of the responsibility for the medical care of those who cannot afford essential health care. Physicians should advocate for patients in dealing with third parties when appropriate.

CODE OF ETHICS FOR NURSES—PROVISIONS

The ANA House of Delegates approved these nine provisions of the new Code of Ethics for Nurses at its June 30, 2001 meeting in Washington, DC. Reprinted with the permission of the American Nurses Association.

1. The nurse, in all professional relationships, practices with compassion and respect for the inherent dignity, worth and uniqueness of every individual, unre-

stricted by considerations of social or economic status, personal attributes, or the nature of health problems.

2. The nurse's primary commitment is to the patient, whether an individual, family, group, or community.

3. The nurse promotes, advocates for, and strives to protect the health, safety, and rights of the patient.

4. The nurse is responsible and accountable for individual nursing practice and determines the appropriate delegation of tasks consistent with the nurse's obligation to provide optimum patient care.

5. The nurse owes the same duties to self as to others, including the responsibility to preserve integrity and safety, to maintain competence, and to continue personal and professional growth.

6. The nurse participates in establishing, maintaining, and improving healthcare environments and conditions of employment conducive to the provision of quality health care and consistent with the values of the profession through individual and collective action.

7. The nurse participates in the advancement of the profession through contributions to practice, education, administration, and knowledge development.

8. The nurse collaborates with other health professionals and the public in promoting community, national, and international efforts to meet health needs.

9. The profession of nursing, as represented by associations and their members, is responsible for articulating nursing values, for maintaining the integrity of the profession and its practice, and for shaping social policy.

THE ICN CODE OF ETHICS FOR NURSES

An international code of ethics for nurses was first adopted by the International Council of Nurses (ICN) in 1953. It has been revised and reaffirmed at various times since, most recently with this review and revision completed in 2000.

Preamble

Nurses have four fundamental responsibilities: to promote health, to prevent illness, to restore health and to alleviate suffering. The need for nursing is universal.

Inherent in nursing is respect for human rights, including the right to life, to dignity and to be treated with respect. Nursing care is unrestricted by considerations of age, colour, creed, culture, disability or illness, gender, nationality, politics, race or social status.

Nurses render health services to the individual, the family and the community and co-ordinate their services with those of related groups.

The Code

The *ICN Code of Ethics for Nurses* has four principal elements that outline the standards of ethical conduct.

Elements of the Code

1. Nurses and People

The nurse's primary professional responsibility is to people requiring nursing care.

In providing care, the nurse promotes an environment in which the human rights, values, customs and spiritual beliefs of the individual, family and community are respected.

The nurse ensures that the individual receives sufficient information on which to base consent for care and related treatment.

The nurse holds in confidence personal information and uses judgement in sharing this information.

The nurse shares with society the responsibility for initiating and supporting action to meet the health and social needs of the public, in particular those of vulnerable populations.

The nurse also shares responsibility to sustain and protect the natural environment from depletion, pollution, degradation and destruction.

2. Nurses and Practice

The nurse carries personal responsibility and accountability for nursing practice, and for maintaining competence by continual learning.

The nurse maintains a standard of personal health such that the ability to provide care is not compromised.

The nurse uses judgement regarding individual competence when accepting and delegating responsibility.

The nurse at all times maintains standards of personal conduct which reflect well on the profession and enhance public confidence.

The nurse, in providing care, ensures that use of technology and scientific advances are compatible with the safety, dignity and rights of people.

3. Nurses and the Profession

The nurse assumes the major role in determining and implementing acceptable standards of clinical nursing practice, management, research and education.

The nurse is active in developing a core of research-based professional knowledge.

The nurse, acting through the professional organisation, participates in creating and maintaining equitable social and economic working conditions in nursing.

4. Nurses and Co-Workers

The nurse sustains a co-operative relationship with co-workers in nursing and other fields.

The nurse takes appropriate action to safeguard individuals when their care is endangered by a co-worker or any other person.